SING ME BACK HOME

# SING ME BACK HOME

## Love, Death,
## and Country Music

## Dana Jennings

FABER AND FABER, INC.

*An affiliate of Farrar, Straus and Giroux*

*New York*

FABER AND FABER, INC.
*An affiliate of Farrar, Straus and Giroux*
*18 West 18th Street, New York 10011*

Library of Congress Cataloging-in-Publication Data
Jennings, Dana Andrew.
    Sing Me Back Home : love, death, and country music /
Dana Jennings.— 1st ed.
        p.    cm.
    Includes bibliographical references (p.    ), discography (p.    ),
and index.
    ISBN-13: 978-0-86547-960-9 (hardcover : alk. paper)
    ISBN-10: 0-86547-960-7 (hardcover : alk. paper)
    1. Country music—History and criticism.    I. Title.

ML3524 .J45 2008
781.64209'045—dc22

                                            2007047955

*Designed by Cassandra J. Pappas*

www.fsgbooks.com

1   3   5   7   9   10   8   6   4   2

*For my sons, Drew and Owen.*
*Country music belonged to their great-great-grandparents,*
*their great-grandparents, their grandparents, and then me, their father.*
*And now it belongs to them.*

For we need more barnyard poets.

—THEODORE ROETHKE


You got to have smelt a lot of mule manure
before you can sing like a hillbilly.

—HANK WILLIAMS

# Contents

SING ME BACK HOME

# Prologue

*Johnny Cash with His Hot and Blue Guitar (1957)*

These are the liner notes to my childhood:

When my parents, all of a scared and trembling seventeen, tumbled into marriage in the fall of 1957 (my old man owed Ma eighteen bucks, which she never let him forget), the first thing they bought of any consequence was a gray and white Sylvania record player at Custeau's Supermarket in Hampstead, New Hampshire. Besides a squat glistering stack of 45 rpm records, they owned two long-players, *Rock and Rollin' with Fats Domino* and *Johnny Cash with His Hot and Blue Guitar.*

I was born just eight days after my parents got married, and those two record albums (I am convinced) became my nursery rhymes, comforted me as much as the soothing bass of my mother's girlish heart: funky New Orleans (Domino) and redneck Memphis (Cash) stirring my fledgling soul. The behind-the-beat rhythm and blues of Fats Domino and his Crescent City brethren still thrill me, but it was Johnny Cash who marked me for life. My Gothic hick childhood began with that record; Cash's music steeled me for a dirt-poor world of tar-paper shacks, backwoods Grendels (my relations), and freight-train seduction.

Now, you might wonder how a Yankee born and raised in New Hampshire can so brazenly lay claim to country music, given its apparent Southern provenance. All I can say is that I came of age in some rogue northeastern extension of Appalachia. My daddy raced stock cars when I was a boy, we gratefully ate fried Spam and hornpout, and sometimes, of a summer's night, we'd set out to the porch and listen to music: Hank Williams, Patsy Cline, Johnny Horton, and, of course, Mr. Cash. In the late 1950s and early '60s, country had only just started its long journey out of the ghetto of *twang* and toward uptown popularity. Country music—as it was for rural and working people from Portland, Oregon, to Portland, Maine—was our music.

*Johnny Cash with His Hot and Blue Guitar* (Sun Records 1220, by the way) still sounds as fresh as it did in 1957—Cash's voice (and wisdom) as deep, Cash's voice as clear, as a good well.

It's a record ripe with country darkness: starless nights on snake-black roads; stark songs of God, trains, prisons, and love (that other prison); hot, rocking hick-boy guitar licks by Luther Perkins and Marshall Grant's railroad bass—boom-chicka . . . boom-chicka . . . boom-chicka. Porch music, beer-drinking music, raw corn-liquor music before Johnny was a *big* star, still on Sam Phillips's shit-kicker Sun label at Seven-Oh-Six Union Avenue in Memphis, Tennessee, that past and future home of deities like the Howlin' Wolf and Ike Turner, Carl Perkins and Jerry Lee Lewis. And, *oh yeah*, that Elvis fella, whose musical moan my teenage mother couldn't get enough of. And Johnny Cash—just a poor sharecropper's son from Dyess, Arkansas—before he became a *Columbia Recording Artist*, before he became that flawed latter-day prophet known as the Man in Black.

Johnny Cash, just as country as us. In "Wreck of the Old 97," when he sings, "He was found in the wreck with his hand on the throttle, scalded to death by the steam," that summed it up, *that* was life as we knew it. Most the men we knew didn't concede in bed in satisfied twilight. Old age was a middle-class luxury.

In twelve songs, Cash delivers on many of the music's timeless (and relentless) themes, themes that haunted not just good country people at mid-century but Americans who lived in town, too: trains ("Rock Island Line," "Wreck of the Old 97"); prison ("[I Heard That] Lonesome Whistle," "Folsom Prison Blues," "Doin' My Time"); the ache for the past ("Country Boy"); love ("If the Good Lord's Willing," "I Walk the Line," "Remember Me [I'm the One Who Loves You]"); cheating ("Cry, Cry, Cry"); melancholy ("So Doggone Lonesome"); and God ("I Was There When It Happened").

I have carried these songs with me my whole life, and they have helped shape the man I've become. There are songs on *Hot and Blue* that I still respond to as simply as I did as a boy: "Rock Island Line," "Country Boy," "Wreck of the Old 97." But the wild vines of "I Walk the Line" grow in complexity and density as the years pass. It's the most haunting and troublesome song on the album, maybe of Cash's entire career.

"I Walk the Line" can be taken at face value as a courtly pledge of love and devotion, or as a renewed vow, or as an act born of guilt— or, even, as an outright lie. However you want to hear it, the song— Cash's first huge hit—struck a nerve in 1956, idling for forty-three weeks on the country chart (six at No. 1) and even going to No. 17 Pop.

Cash wrote the song for his first wife, Vivian Liberto, and he swears to her, "Because you're mine, I walk the line." If only wishing, or singing, could make it so. The song's crucial line is its first: "I keep a close watch on this heart of mine." As any country sage will tell you, you only keep a close watch on a thing you can't trust, like a brushfire on a windy day, or a shifty-eyed mutt near the chicken coop, or a foreman. And the reason his woman is on his mind both day and night is because you can't escape the damning vision of the one you're cheating on.

The hymnlike hum throughout feels like mourning, makes "I Walk the Line" sound as if it was written in penance, late in the morning after a night of faithlessness. Luther Perkins's propulsive guitar gives the sense that Cash is walking the line, all right—straight into the arms of another woman, even as he sings his hollow vow of love. This is the same man, after all, who steered his life toward hell, even as he, like Jacob, wrestled with God.

Poor ol' John still believes in this love—says he finds it very easy to be true—but he's too weak to resist the sirens of the road. He sings the right words, but his voice and the music are tense, knotted. (In country, it often makes sense to trust the music and not the words.) It's as if he wants to confess his sins of the flesh to his wife, but the strength just isn't in him. As Tammy Wynette knew, a man, after all, is just a man.

"I Walk the Line" is the fine lie that Johnny Cash wrote, sang, and walked before the true song of his confession—a song that he never did write.


Across the road from my folks' house on the Old Danville Road in Kingston, a broke-down barbwire fence lurks, shrouded in puckabrush. Vines and tendrils, creepers and claspers, have riven the posts, ravished the guts. It's impossible to tell where that fence ends . . . and where the bushes begin. And for me, it's impossible to tell where my family ends . . . and where country music begins. And vice versa.

Johnny Cash takes me back to Kingston, 1957, where the night freights *wail* country high and country lonesome, their whistles sorrowing like railroad rain-crows ahead of a storm. Where the painted turtles, sunning on a log, Alka-Seltzer into the muck. Where the ax speaks in its blunt dialect, and a soul wind whispers through the cracks of the house, curtains waltzing to the tune. Poverty-gray sheets bark and billow on knock-kneed clotheslines; well buckets smirking with rust dangle from porch nails; children, barefoot and bareass, screech, stalk each other with stickaburrs and rubbery rhubarb whips as drooling mutts with piss-yellow eyes yowl and size up the squealing brats as if they're porkchops. Patsy Cline pines away on "Crazy" above the everyday reek of apple pie and squirrel carcass, burning motor oil and sizzling Pow-Wow River pickerel.

Yes, this is where I and several million other Americans grew up, a famished kingdom of swaybacked shacks, sheds, and out-houses. A place where Johnny Cash could've pulled up a three-legged chair on an out-of-true floor, cracked open a Pabst Blue Ribbon beer, and felt right at home.

# Hillbilly Fever

*Country Music, 1950–70*

*Listen!*

Country music is the backfire of a rattletrap pickup truck creaking down a dirt road and the lowing of a lone cow. It's music for scouring junkyards, setting out to the porch, and shooting horseshoes. It's tar-paper shacks, shoveling chicken shit for a living, and chugging cheap whiskey. It's TB music, orphan music, and outhouse music. It's potato-sack dresses, loyal three-legged dogs, and water lugged from the well.

*Listen now!*

Country is the incandescent *keening* of Hank Williams and the preternatural harmonies of brothers like the Monroes, the Delmores, the Stanleys, the Louvins, and the Everlys. It's the hick jazz of Bob Wills, Spade Cooley, Moon Mullican, and the Light Crust Doughboys. It's Jimmie Rodgers and the Carter Family, the foremothers and forefathers of commercial country music, being discovered in Bristol, Tennessee, in 1927. It's the bleak chasms of

Johnny Cash and the deep pop of Patsy Cline, and the feisty example Patsy set for her musical heirs like Loretta Lynn and Tammy Wynette. It's Hollywood's singing cowboys—those primal "Hat Acts"—like Gene Autry and Roy Rogers, and unexpected yet essential black men like DeFord Bailey and Charley Pride, and Ray Charles and Chuck Berry; if you don't think Chuck Berry is country, give a hard listen to "Maybellene" and "Johnny B. Goode." It's the fierce 1950s honky-tonk of Webb Pierce, Lefty Frizzell, and Faron Young, and the fine Cajun pining of Harry Choates and the Kershaw brothers, Doug and Rusty. It's Waylon, Willie, and the boys. It's the blackface minstrelsy of Emmett Miller and the pill-fueled brilliance of Roger Miller. It's consummate git-tar pickers like Merle Travis, Chet Atkins, Hank "Sugarfoot" Garland, and Grady Martin, and that Bakersfield, California, riot sparked by Buck Owens, Merle Haggard, and Wynn Stewart. And, yeah, country music is that greasy punk from Memphis-by-way-of-Tupelo, Elvis Aron Presley, breaking the sound barrier.

*I said, "Listen!"*

It's two-stepping rats, poverty-stricken existentialists, and gravel roads that wash out each and every spring. It's patches on the knees of your britches, voices coarse as rasps, and a Depression that lasted thirty or forty years—now *that's* a Great Depression. It's music heard from the back of flatbed trucks at Laundromats, drive-in movie theaters, and quarter-mile stock car tracks. It's living for overtime up the mill, and living for your weekend case of Schlitz down home. It's tremoring at the kitchen table at four in the morning, in the grip of a George Jones moaner, as you wonder where the years of your life have flown.

*Are you listening?*

It's crazy arms and cold, cold hearts, heartaches by the number and setting the woods on fire . . . It's the wreck of the Old 97, a wreck on the highway, and that honky-tonk angel who made a wreck out of you . . . It's waltzing across Texas in thrall to the "Tennessee Waltz" and the "Kentucky Waltz" . . . Seeing the light, preachin', prayin', singin', and hearing Mother pray . . . The great speckled bird and the bird of paradise that flies up your nose . . . Pistol-packin' mamas, daddies that walk the line, and being your own grandpaw . . . Mountain dew, white lightnin', and whiskey rivers . . . Slippin' around, backstreet affairs and dim lights, thick smoke and loud, loud music . . . Six days on the road, sixteen tons, and being busted . . . Waiting for a (mystery) train, the Fireball Mail and the Golden Rocket, the Wabash Cannonball and the Orange Blossom Special . . . Being king of the road on that Lost Highway where there's a tombstone every mile . . . Wildwood flowers, tumbling tumbleweeds, and flowers on the wall . . . Rough and rowdy ways and walking on the sunny side . . . Hungry eyes watching the ring of fire on which you keep your skillet good 'n' greasy . . . Drivin' nails in your coffin and slapping down cash on the barrelhead . . . Bloody Mary mornings and blue suede shoes, heartbreak hotels and jail-house rock . . . Being so lonesome you could cry, cry, cry.

*Listen!*

With the deepest country music, there are no casual listeners because the music is curse and redemption, the journey and the homeplace, current events and ancient tales. The very best country music is prayer and litany, epiphany and salvation. That's why it's still with us.

Country music made between about 1950 and 1970 is a secret history of rural, working-class Americans in the twentieth century—a secret history in plain sight. But, too, much of it is music that has endured, music full of wit and wisdom that has made the cultural migration from being "just" country music made by a bunch of hillbillies to being, simply, American music.

———

Commercial country music was whelped, came of age, and eventually thrived in the twentieth century. The traditional take on that century—the American Century—canonizes the United States as it soars in an unrivaled arc, with the occasional glitch like the Depression, the world wars, and institutional racism. Even so, convention has it, Americans gladly climbed aboard the Capitalist Express, a glorious train that only made stops at gleaming stations like Prosperity, Happiness, and Satisfaction.

Country music has a different story to tell.

Country music knows broader and deeper truths about the twentieth-century American Dream, universal truths that resonate well beyond the music's original audience. Country music knows that the Great Depression didn't conveniently end the day the Japanese bombed Pearl Harbor, but instead lingered like an economic malaria in some regions deep into the 1960s . . . and later. Poverty never goes out of style, as Hurricane Katrina and the destruction of New Orleans painfully reminded us.

Country music knows that the dark heart of the American Century beat in oil-field roadhouses in Texas and in dim-lit Detroit bars where country boys in exile gathered after another shift at Ford or GM. Bobby Bare might've pleaded in "Detroit City" that he wanted to go home. But we all knew he wouldn't, that he couldn't. Country profoundly understands what it's like to be trapped in a culture of alienation: by poverty, by a shit job, by lust, by booze, by class. Country music knows that even in your hometown you can be a rank stranger.

If you truly want to understand the whole United States of America in the twentieth century, you need to understand country music and the working people who lived their lives by it.

Country music is a key to unlocking the lives of the rural white working poor from 1950 to 1970. People who, when the paycheck shriveled up and blew away in the middle of the week, had to beg a half gallon of milk and a loaf of bread on the cuff at the neighborhood grocery store. People for whom country music was holier than church. Because if there's a song that kills you, that brings tears to your eyes most every time you hear it—Loretta Lynn's "Coal Miner's Daughter," let's say—you always carry a vital remnant of that song within you. And to own a record that killed you where I grew up was to reclaim a part of yourself that daily circumstance had erased; for a couple minutes you could forget that you were two months behind on the rent and that the light company was threatening to shut the electric.

That song is a divine spark in your starved soul, a healing presence. I find it impossible to conjure my dead without conjuring remnants of country songs. Hearing an old country tune is always a return to the homeplace, and listening to a classic country singer is like catching up with an old friend.

Decades before celebrity journalism turned its cynical eye on country musicians, "knowing" your favorite singer was an act of creation. In the days before the mass media tried to mediate our very lives away from us, you could decide for yourself what kind of person Ray Price or Loretta Lynn was. My aunts and uncles and grammies cobbled together imagined lives for "their" singers, quilting together record-jacket photos and bios, snatches of radio conversation gleaned from the *Grand Ole Opry* or the *Wheeling Jamboree*, and lucky glimpses caught on hick TV shows like Porter Wagoner's or, up in New Hampshire, Clyde Joy's.

Most important, my relations knew their favorites by their distinctive voices and styles. That's why artists worked so hard to fashion an idiosyncratic sound in the 1950s and 1960s. It didn't pay to be a musical chameleon. You *were* your sound:

Ernest Tubb was his gravel honesty, while Patsy Cline was her exquisite ache. Little Jimmy Dickens was a hillbilly cut-up, while Kitty Wells played the demure small-town housewife. A new single by your favorite singer was a fresh love letter from Nashville or Bakersfield or Memphis, another two-and-a-half-minute scrap of vinyl DNA from which you could conjure an entire human being.

Cultural historians like to obsess over the Jazz Age 1920s, ease into the romantic era of the big bands in the 1930s and '40s, then elaborate on the birth of youth culture and rock 'n' roll—*oh, Elvis!!!*—with a pit stop for Kerouac, Ginsberg, bebop, and the Beats. By the time we roar into the 1960s, our chrome-heavy '57 Chevy burning rubber, the Beatles and Dylan are demigods and we're nearly in the fevered grip of psychedelic hippie hegemony. (Hey, man, could you please pass the LSD? Owsley, if you don't mind.)

A tidy notion, but country music's tale is different, earthier.

The years 1950 to 1970 were a golden age of *twang* as the postwar giants of country walked the earth: Hank Williams and Johnny Cash, George Jones and Merle Haggard, Webb Pierce and Faron Young. Women found their voices, too, with singers like Kitty Wells and Patsy Cline, Loretta Lynn and Tammy Wynette. Many of the standards that still define the music were recorded then: "Folsom Prison Blues" and "Ring of Fire" by Cash, "Your Cheatin' Heart" by Williams, "Mama Tried" by Haggard, "Crazy" by Cline, and "Stand by Your Man" by Wynette, to name just a few. In the popular imagination—then and now—country music, the *deepest* country music, is still Hank and Cash and Cline and their postwar peers. And some of these were songs that made a dent in the broader culture. You didn't need to be a farmer or raised in a holler to feel the cheatin' heat in "Ring of Fire" or the pain in "Stand by Your Man."

Still, in those years, country music belonged mostly to country people. The music told us that we were *something* after all—just as postwar rhythm and blues and, later, soul told blacks that they mattered—even as America made its transition from rural nation to urban nation, from local culture to a national television culture. (In 1920, just before the dawn of commercially recorded country music, the U.S. Census characterized 48.8 percent of the population as rural, 43.5 percent in 1940, and 30.1 percent in 1960. Meanwhile, there had been just ten thousand television sets in America in 1947; by 1957, there were forty million.)

Performers like Red Foley, the Delmore Brothers, and Merle Travis were still stars in the early 1950s, but country music, like the entire nation, was in transition, and those singers sounded old-fashioned to the young men and young women who were still trying to sort out their lives in postwar America. In the voices of the best country singers of the 1950s—Hank Williams, Lefty Frizzell, Webb Pierce, Johnny Cash, and Elvis—there is struggle, yearning, and confusion. In a world of vanishing farms, the lure of the city and its jobs, and an unknowable Cold War shadowed by the threat of nuclear annihilation, these singers didn't have the luxury of wallowing in traditional music's centuries-old tropes of God, mother, and home.

Many country people still could not manage to snatch their small piece of postwar prosperity, but Hank Williams was their sad-eyed Alabam prophet and Patsy Cline the smoldering high priestess of Nashville. My relations and I had more in common with the country singers we loved than we did with the snobs who lived in the colonial-dotted center of town. We had been peasants in the Old World, and we were peasants in America, too.

Though I was born in 1957, I grew up during the Great Depression. In my particular chicken-scratched swatch of New Hampshire, postwar prosperity was a rumor. The Depression had not ended for my people, who lived from odd job to odd job, for whom supper was never a given. I was born into a ramshackle husk of a house that had no indoor plumbing except for cold running water that froze in the pipes come winter—and the occasional hot running rat. Everyone learned to chop wood and lug water. Flush toilets were another rumor, the outhouse the reality.

Back then, country music wasn't an accessory; it was a way of being. Through the power of radio and recordings, music became central to most Americans' lives in the twentieth century. Whether jazz and the blues, rock and pop, Cajun and Celtic, or country and soul, certain kinds of music became *our* music, certain songs became *our* songs, at our beck and call with the drop of a needle or the push of a button. Freed of concert hall and back porch, of schoolhouse and church, music became a cultural badge, seized us with its intimate intensity, granted us solace and meaning.

Yet, much writing on music spurns the listener's half of the equation. It succumbs to musicological mumbo-jumbo or mere dirt-and-dreams biography, or to that obsessive-compulsive disorder of music writing, infatuation with discography and recording-session lineups. It leaves no room for the listener.

Well, for me, my family, and all those like us, sometimes you couldn't distinguish the listener from the country song.

In 1970, country music began to change—it more doggedly chased the broader culture, sought crossover hits—even as our lives began to change. The interstates brought in wealthier people from Massachusetts to southern New Hampshire, and my old man's jobs started to pay a bit better. Times were still tough, but my folks were able to buy a modest saltbox with the help of the federal Farmers Home Administration.

The singer-songwriter Iris DeMent understands those hard old days. The first time I heard her "Mama's Opry," I cried. The next six times I heard "Mama's Opry," I cried. And though I first heard it in 1992, the year it came out on DeMent's debut album, *Infamous Angel*, the song can still ambush me.

The song is simple. DeMent, the youngest of fourteen children born into an Arkansas farm family, tells how her parents and grandparents loved country music, and how her mother dreamed of singing on the *Grand Ole Opry*. Simple. But when DeMent starts in with her wistful Arkansas keening—"She grew up plain and simple in a farming town"—I lose it most every time.

Suddenly it's 1960 again, Ma's hanging wash out to the cedar-post clothesline, I'm handing her the wooden clothespins . . . and I'm once again undone by those floodwaters from the past.

"Mama's Opry" won't let me forget that even though I live in a prosperous New Jersey suburb, though I work in midtown Manhattan in an exquisite new building designed by the renowned architect Renzo Piano, I'm a son of the boondocks. I know more about old Ford pickup trucks than I do the New York City subway system. And just because I like Coltrane and cabernet doesn't mean, at heart, that I'm not a beer and Hank guy.

The journey from the outhouse to Renzo Piano's dream house has been long and full of mystery. But since 1992, anyway, the good tears that my hick sister Iris DeMent makes me cry have suffused that journey.

Like Kingston, New Hampshire, country music was still a tiny town in 1950. The singer and songwriter Tom T. Hall once compared it to an ethnic business that had realistic expectations; there was only a small segment of the American public buying country records back then. This was before Glen Campbell and Johnny Cash had network TV shows in the late 1960s, before the Urban Cowboy fad/debacle of the 1980s, before Garth Brooks sold CDs as if they were Big Macs, before Shania Twain's navel became the talk of Nashville. Hall, in his fine autobiography, recalls a time when the *Grand Ole Opry* could still make you or break you, when sales of 100,000 singles meant you had a No. 1 hit, when most country stars were still grateful to travel the Cornpone and Kerosene circuits of schoolhouses, town halls, and outdoor country music parks, when there were only 81 full-time country music stations in the land (1961)—by 1969 there were 606. The music executives in Nashville were determined to break country out of its ghetto holler; but the folks who loved the music didn't even know they were in one.

In its first fifty years or so, commercial country was music meant for those who'd been bypassed by the American Dream. For people who lived in shacks and cabins and farms off the Lost Highway, or who'd been grudgingly harried to the big city to try to make a living. It was outsider music for farm folk, for people who worked in small local factories that made barrels and boxboards and shoes. For broad-backed, eight-fingered men who limped and worked the woods or trudged along at the brickyard. For men and women who knew what work was. And who also knew that work wasn't meant for satisfaction, but merely as a means to tread water. Satisfaction had to wait. It might come from a six-pack . . . or a hymn . . . or a country song on the radio.

When you lived way back in the country, it seemed the radio could be a tool for revelation: news of more heartbreaking nonsense from Washington; a warning of evening thundershowers; or a song that, at least for a couple minutes, could change your life. A song that made you stop washing the dishes, or made you stare into your coffee. And if that song was good enough, strong enough, the next time you were in town you'd scrounge up enough change to buy that record at the Woolworth or the Western Auto.

You could hear the music away from home, too, but you had to pick your spots: On pickup truck radios as we shot rats at the town dump . . . Down to Pines Speedway and at the Plaistow Drive-In picture show . . . At junkyards, and *twanging* on the jukeboxes at the Eagles Club and the VFW Hall . . . In select shack kitchens that reeked of burnt oak and fried doughnuts, and where the radios static-ed like an electric storm . . . From Lucky Strike–killing gittar pickers holding forth on certain summer porches . . . And, if you saved up, you could take a drive over to the Lone Star Ranch country music park in Reeds Ferry, New Hampshire, one weekend afternoon, ride the ponies, pig out on fried dough, then sit on plain wood-plank benches to hear honest-to-goodness Nashville stars like Kitty Wells, Faron Young, Little Jimmy Dickens and, even, Johnny Cash.

What always startled me, though, was how you could hear the music even when it wasn't playing. How watching a tumble of tires burn turned into Cash's "Ring of Fire" . . . How watching a Western got me humming Marty Robbins's "El Paso" or Hank Williams's "Kaw-Liga". . . How when our car broke down one night on the Epping Road, I could hear Bill Monroe soaring away on "It's Mighty Dark to Travel."

But we'd never hear the songs we loved in the places that we'd walk into already cowed, our eyes down, our voices small. Places like Dr. Lee's in Exeter, Simons Department Store in Plaistow, or the loan company, which, with its thieving interest rates, stole from the poor people who could least afford it. In those places, all you ever heard was some sham of music—music that didn't sound much like music at all.

Most my relations could barely read. Some not at all. Being able to sign your name to "a paper" was reason for pride. Nobody read magazines or novels or even the Holy Bible. Country songs were their novels, their Bible:

"Wreck on the Highway" by Roy Acuff, "Back Street Affair" by Webb Pierce, "Wings of a Dove" by Ferlin Husky, "Ode to Billie Joe" by Bobbie Gentry. Songs for working people, songs for country people. My relations knew where whiskey and blood pooled out to the highway—and nobody prayed; knew the ravenous arms of men and women who weren't their husbands and wives; pondered the power of God's love, even as they doubted it; whispered about the suicides, the boys found hanging in barns, the pregnant girls drowned in the lake, the pickups hammered into oaks at ninety miles an hour—*stuck throttle, my ass.*

In Kingston, New Hampshire, in 1957, there were no traffic lights, and cows outnumbered the nine hundred people who lived there. Because we lived in such a backwater, where national and world events were a mere murmur, our most reliable news was whatever was in the air. What mattered back then? Johnny Cash's latest record. Who had won that week's feature race at Pines Speedway. What pictures were playing at the Plaistow Drive-In. Whether the old man got that dime raise. There was little sense of caring about what happened beyond the town line. But that was okay. The best country music was oral history, the kind that never made the textbooks.

We were country people, you know. We had no expectations except that life was hard. All we needed was music that understood that harshness, music that leavened it.

Which brings me to "The Myth."

The myth, perpetuated these days by Nashville music executives who probably believe that Garth Brooks represents "classic country," is that country music is purely a white, rural, and Southern art. It's the same cultural arrogance and/or memory loss that makes Nascar proclaim the roots of stock car racing as a solely Southern phenomenon.

There is no question that the South is vital to country music and its history. But the scholar D. K. Wilgus reminds us that while country music's manifestation was Southern, "its essence was of rural America"—like Kingston, New Hampshire, in the 1950s and '60s. (By the way, my old man also raced stock cars.) Country musicians come from all over: Hank Snow, one of the music's biggest postwar stars, was from Nova Scotia; Merle Haggard and Buck Owens, who owned the charts in the 1960s, defined the Bakersfield, California, sound; Willie Nelson and Waylon Jennings?—Texans through and through; and, heck, Dick ("A Tombstone Every Mile") Curless hailed from Fort Fairfield, Maine.

And the African-American influence runs strong and deep in musicians as diverse as Bill Monroe, Bob Wills, Jimmie Rodgers, Hank Williams, and Elvis Presley, whose first hits came on the country charts. Hank's breakthrough, "Lovesick Blues" (1949), was written by a vaudeville piano player and a Russian-born Jew and popularized in the 1920s by the blackface minstrel Emmett Miller. So much for regional purity.

A good country song lets me become the person who loved it, and even—for a mayfly moment—lets me enter the lives of the dead. When I hear Webb Pierce sing "There Stands the Glass," I can become my late uncle Lloyd, who was devoured by emphysema and cancer after a life happily spent drinking, smoking, and whoring. Musical alchemy.

And all music, not just country, is a kind of architecture in time, a house shared by those who love it, a habitation that can carry us explicitly to the past. Take "No Depression" by the original Carter Family. During the worst of the Great Depression, Nanna George, my great-grandmother, hears that song and, perhaps, gathers a shred of solace, wonders when she'll be granted the right to fly to the land where there's no Depression. I hear it today, and Nanna and I are now—decades apart—living together again, for a couple minutes, in the same sacred house of want. Then I invite my sons inside, and suddenly they are swaddled in the Depression-gray skirts of their great-great-grandmother.

Country lets me, and my sons, listen with our fathers and mothers.

I don't want to give the impression that my love affair with this music has been one long, smooth ramble down lonesome back roads. There has been flight and return, rejection and reconciliation, times when the Moody Blues, Jethro Tull, and Black Sabbath— but never, ever Yes or Emerson, Lake and Palmer (you have to draw the line somewhere)—mattered much more to me than Cash, Cline, and Haggard.

Well, we're all allowed to be young and stupid once upon a time, right?

Now, when I was a kid my folks, my relations, and all their friends called me Andy—my middle name is Andrews—because my Dad's name is Dana, too. (Maybe folks got confused more easily back then.) No one called me Dana till I got to first grade, though I proudly knew I was named after my old man, and Ma had taught me to write my "true" name. While it was Andy who liked to go fishing, hang around when the guys worked on their cars, and listen to the music the old man listened to, it was Dana who fell head-over-heels for books and learning (and pretension, too), who decided in third grade to become a writer, and who knew by fifth grade that he was going to college—no matter what nobody said.

My old buddy Andy probably would've been happy to stay in Kingston, marry some broody, porch-sitting girl, and maybe teach English for fifty years up to the high school. But Dana took one long look around and said, "To hell with this."

I *had* to reject it all, those first eighteen years of my life, before I could become wise enough to start reclaiming what mattered most from childhood: the peepers chorusing in the frog pond . . . stock car racing . . . and country music.

I gradually realized in my twenties that not only did I like *Johnny Cash with His Hot and Blue Guitar*, but that if I was going to understand my life—and the lives of my relations—I needed to understand that album and why it moved me, understand why I'd claimed to have spurned country music even as I sang along to songs by Cash, Jones, and Williams.

I was the quiet child . . . the one who heard everything and forgot just enough. I thrived on stories, craved family tales. I just had to know, *had to know*:

Bristling with questions, I whistle through thistle groves, vast family graves. I'm just five years old, but not a one of 'em trusts me. My mother's mother, Lilla, quails every time I speak, cringes, I know, the way she did when I stole my first blue breaths. It's like I'm pricking needles in her sun-smoked Slim Jim arms.

"When'd you'n Grandpa get married?"

"Why'd you'n Grandpa go and split?"

"Why'd Nanna quit Great-Grandpa, then marry him up again?"

"Why'd Nanna keep Auntie Helen on the tit till she was eight?"

Lilla flinches, balks, ducks each question like a jackknife, her answers a quivering covey of grunts, sighs, clucks, squints. Then, chapped lips peeled, charred stumps bared, Lilla rears up—I sink into the crick-ed creeks of wickedness scored on her cheeks—and snaps: "What're you, writin' a g.d. book?"

Lilla Britton would not like this book. She would scowl, accuse me of "getting too big for my britches"—then take a switch to me. She would want to know how come there's so goddamn much cursing, how come I spilled so many family secrets, and how come I'm so hard on my relations.

But, if I could, I'd take her hard bony hand in mine, look her square in the eye, and tell her that—using the country music that we both love—I needed to stare unflinching into the still-festering wound of my extended family, of my childhood. I would tell her that good stories untold—strong medicine left on the shelf—do no one any good. Would tell her that there's so much cursing because the mouthy bastards I grew up among couldn't stop swearing.

As for being hard on our family, I would tell her that I wrote this book out of love—for the fierce people who raised me up, and for the country music that gave them solace and that they gave to me. I would tell her that this book is a loving letter to our dead.

When I was five years old, the contrary state of New Hampshire tore down my house—a former shoe shop where the rent was six bucks a week—and Great-Grandpa Ora's place, which had stood next door for more than one hundred years, to widen Route 125 through Kingston, to improve the road so that tourists from Massachusetts—Mass-holes, we affectionately called 'em—and Connecticut could get to the White Mountains quicker. Thus was I exiled for the first time. And I'm still not over it.

There aren't many of us left who speak the language of that time, of that place. Like Iris DeMent, all I have left are the memories of the watchful child that I was . . . and the country music that my people loved.

Using country music from 1950 to 1970, I mean to reveal my people's vanished world to you. And using my people's lives, I mean to tell you what country music is really about. I will tell you why it's my music, but also why its emotion-drenched wisdom also belongs to you, belongs to all of us.

# Hungry Eyes

Country music for decades was poor-people music, made by poor people and bought by poor people. It sprang from the heart and the gut, and, like R&B and soul, it was a music of exile, meant to make being banished to the margins, if not a matter of pride, then at least more tolerable. It never surprised no one that the original Carter Family came from Poor Valley. In a sense, that's where we all came from.

Most the singers of country's golden age were shaped (and sometimes scarred) by the Great Depression, "raised rough," as a lot of them liked to say, and their music reflects that. The unspoken truth behind most every *Grand Ole Opry* smile was that pickin' and a-grinnin' sure as hell beat pickin' and a-ginnin'.

Johnny Cash picked cotton as a kid. Hank Williams and George Jones both sang on the streets as boys to help make ends meet. The fourth of twelve children, Dolly Parton was born in a two-room shack on the Little Pigeon River in East Tennessee in 1946; the doctor who delivered her was paid with a sack of cornmeal. Merle Haggard once lived in a boxcar turned into a shack, as did Hank.

People forget, or never knew, the poverty that once suffused country music. There are the songs that are explicitly about being poor, like Haggard's "Hungry Eyes" and Harlan Howard's "Busted," but poverty is also the silent pillar of lots of other country songs. In America, it's poor boys who most often wind up in prison, and it's among the poor that alcoholism is an epidemic. When you're poor, cheatin' isn't just adultery; it's *stealing*. And it's that sense of poverty that made folks in town, people in the upper classes, cringe at that "hillbilly swill." They didn't like being reminded that postwar America wasn't quite as shiny and brand-new as they pretended it was.

Plain as barn cats, my relations and I all lived in "the other America," busted, hurting, silent. It was a salve to the soul to soak up music made by people who really understood our world, our United States of Misery. The history books take postwar prosperity for granted. But as late as 1959, there were an estimated fifty million people living below the poverty line in America, 22 percent of the population. But most people tended to overlook poverty if it was black or Indian or hidden way out in the country.

My grandmother Lilla George and her twin sister, Lelia (we called her Lee), used to wear dresses to school that their mother sewed together from burlap potato sacks. "Oh, they itched like the dickens," Auntie Lee used to say.

After my grandfather Bub abandoned them—vanished like a whiskey-drinking cliché on Christmas Day 1952—my old man, his two little brothers, and Grammy Jennings lived in tar-paper shacks. No running water, no electric, newspaper insulation—shacks, country basilicas of decay. Those rickety husks lit by kerosene lamps were tucked into the puckabrush way off the main road, as if neither my father's family nor the town could bear the weight of that shame.

Like Loretta Lynn and Dolly Parton, we lived in a holler, hemmed in by a snake-infested swamp and a snake-infested gravel pit. Everything was falling apart. The roof, sagging like an old man's gut, leaked. The windows, having shed their caulking, shimmied in the wind. The water froze in the pipes.

Every bit of use was wrung from every little thing. I can't tell you how many pairs of pants I wore whose frayed cuffs skidded to a halt somewhere about six inches above my ankles, whose knees were patched and repatched, and that I fastened with a safety pin because the clasp had worn out. The tonearm of the record player had a penny or a nickel taped to it so it wouldn't jump . . . a match was held to the nib of a nineteen-cent Bic pen to coax a bit more ink from it . . . Ma only doled out half pieces of gum.

So, yeah, I rose up out of the mosquito swamps of backwoods New Hampshire. The snapping-turtle swamps. The hornpout swamps. I came of age on cracked, snake-backed roads, and I still had it better than Ma and the old man ever did. By the time I was a teenager, my knuckles were red, raw, and skun up, my elbows and cheekbones keen as a boning knife—just like the best songs by Merle Haggard.

Of all the great country singers of the 1950s and '60s, Haggard articulated rural blue-collar life best, explaining to his listeners what their lives meant and making them understand that those lives counted. If you subscribed solely to the visions of *Time* and *Newsweek* magazines in the 1960s, we were a nation engulfed in wars: in Vietnam, between the races, and between the generations—all of it leavened by love, Beatlemania, and hallucinogenic drugs. But Haggard, the Depression pulsing in his heart, knew the America where children still went to bed hungry, where Daddy's hands were cracked and bloody from all that backbreaking, bone-grinding work, and where a wild kid wound up in prison, not therapy. And he told those tales in powerful songs like "Hungry Eyes," "Mama Tried," and "Workin' Man Blues."

Haggard didn't write "In the Good Old Days (When Times Were Bad)"; it was written by Dolly Parton, who had a small hit with it in 1968. But the song suits his harrowing take on life as he matter-of-factly tells us about crops failing, about not being able to afford a doctor, and how "anything at all was more than we had."

As he sings, he refuses to cave in to the nostalgia for poverty that some people cultivate after they've shed those chains. Haggard isn't complaining as he sings "Good Old Days," just explaining, which is what he's spent his career doing since he put the poverty of Oildale, California, behind him decades ago. He understands the gift of his music and the gift of the lessons he has learned, and he is able to give back that gift to the listener in the economy of his soul.

That's why I prefer Haggard's take on this song to Parton's. She wrote a fine song and made a good record, but Parton, ultimately, wanted to have a "career," while Haggard just wanted to sing, to tell stories. Like the poor little hick girl she had once been, Parton ached for stardom, craved diva-hood and Hollywood. And she wasn't above trading on her cleavage and Li'l Abner stereotypes to achieve those ends. Finally, she commodified herself into a kind of real-life Beverly Hillbilly. Haggard, for better and for worse, just stayed Haggard, though he learned early on that listeners were fascinated by a man who'd done time in prison.

Parton told the writer Dorothy Horstman that "In the Good Old Days" "is true; every bit of it is true." But its strong truths are better served seined through Haggard's steely soul, and not in Parton's self-conscious little-girl squeak.

Country music was outhouse music, too. Most every singer we loved was once on intimate terms with those forbidding fortresses of necessity, from the days when indoor plumbing was considered a luxury. I swear that I didn't know you could flush a toilet till I was in first grade.

Think of the following as a brief tribute to those outhouses of blessed memory. Let's call it "To the Outhouse," with apologies to that sultry country chanteuse Virginia Woolf . . . Cue up the banjo and twin fiddles, fellas.

I

The outhouse shimmers, simmers, in the summer swoon. It's rank, funky with hordes of blue-black flies and their thick buzz-saw jazz. Those glutton punks—Hells Angels with wings—glisten in the ripe heat: plague viridians, cobalt blues, wild and woolly rakes as big as Cadillacs, but just a warm-up act really for the waltz of the shithouse rats.

The outhouse, marked for Halloween capsizings, some luckless bastard sprawled ass-over-bandbox. The outhouse, made for stashing skunks, possums, and woodchucks . . . every call of nature an adventure.

Just a brusque lumber hole—too limber and you'll be plucking slivers out your cheeks for weeks—complemented by a piss-racked stack of full-bosomed magazines. (Has *something* been gnawing on those pages?) I'm a-scared that my skinny little butt will slick through the hole, knees and elbows not too far behind. (Do Ma and the old man even know I'm out here?)

Then, winter. Unbuckled boots rattle and screak across the snow. The burred door handle is sharp and cold. Stubborn hinges groan. The sky's Arctic script is blizzard blue, but at least the freeze mutes the flies' funk. Snow snakes slinker through chinks and cracks as the wind flays bleak, bold skin.

## II

Our great-grandpa Ora's outhouse—no one else is ordained to ascend that sacred throne—fords dark and holy woods. It has no door. "When I'm doin' my business," says Grandpa, a man who craved rain and ravens, owls, oaks, and snow, "I like to look at nature."

## III

Come mud-kill, Jake Marble, rimed and greased, scours our outhouse, ghosts up from his Cedar Swamp lair through murk and muskeg, sandpit and mist. He feasts on naked Lucky Strikes as he lugs shovels, buckets, quicklime.

Jake haunts a lonely stump-swamp shack. His surly hens are the mangy yellow-white of an old smoker's hair, and in his dooryard a seized-up flat-head eight dangles from a boneyard pine.

And when Jake scrapes together enough "shit money," he takes the long train ride into Boston and pays a woman to make him forget all about all those outhouses.

You've got to be able to laugh when you're poor. Buck Owens understood that. (A guy nicknamed after the family mule had *better* have a sense of humor.) Welfare, though, wasn't one damn bit funny in 1966, when his "Waitin' in Your Welfare Line" stuck at No. 1 for seven weeks. The word "welfare" either conjured Depression memories best left buried in the root cellar of your thoughts or stoked the fury of blue-collar workers who felt that most folks on welfare—"on the state tit," they'd spit—were malignant loafers saving up to buy welfare Cadillacs.

But Owens transforms the idea of welfare into a love song. Well, an unrequited love song. Like the Louvin Brothers, in "Cash on the Barrelhead," in which a guy who's broke and homeless gets arrested for vagrancy, Owens takes a painful situation—his man is out of work, out of luck, and a bit out of his mind—and spins it into a funny tale.

When the song opens, we meet a poor sap who's busted but living on the fumes of love. All he's got is the shirt on his back, and his bedroom is a telephone booth. The only thing that keeps him going is his love for a woman who won't return his calls—maybe that's why he sleeps in the booth—and who now won't even give him a second glance.

When you're out of work, isn't that how it is? The call never comes for that new job, and no one wants to give you a second look—your wife, your kids, your buddies—as you stew in your disgrace.

All our man can do now, scabby hat in hand, is wait in his beloved's welfare line for a handout that the listener knows ain't never going to come.

The poorer you are, the harder you hit your kids.

That's what we get, me and Sis. Hit.

Not just a lickin', but hit, like all the other poor kids. (At school we look at each other, then look away.) Backhanders and rib-kickers, the brute black belt with its brass-buckle bite. Me and Sis, we ain't too bitter about it, this getting hit. If you're *bad*, you're gonna get it, get hit. But no fists. Kids just ain't worth that trouble.

In dusk's shed, my old man's belt snakes, snarls, and rattles out the loops of his rugged dungarees. "Get in here," he says, half father, half hangman, the belt doubled, the belt coiled.

I pull down my pants without being told, shiver, then bend over the altar of my old man's legs.

Me and Sis, we're polite kids.

Written by Harlan Howard, the late Bard of Nashville ("Heartaches by the Number" and "I Fall to Pieces," to name just two), "Busted," by Ray Charles, is, like "Waitin' in Your Welfare Line," laced with humor. But it's humor as dark as an empty wallet.

As Charles overwhelms us with his litany of woes—the bills are all due, the baby needs shoes, the cow's gone dry, the hen won't lay—his workingman's pride turns to pleading, then almost to menace. By the time Charles sings, "Well, I am no thief, but a man can go wrong when he's busted," you know that he's ready to do something irrevocable and rash. The horn section, meanwhile, cries behind him the whole way.

Brother Ray's version of "Busted" made it to No. 4 Pop and No. 3 R&B in 1963 but didn't sniff the country charts, though a lesser version by Johnny Cash did. Charles was a poor, talented country boy born in Albany, Georgia, in 1930 who begged to listen to the *Opry* as a kid, who started his career playing the honky-tonks, and who had even recorded an album called *Modern Sounds in Country and Western Music* in 1962, but the country music establishment wouldn't let him in even through the back door. Ray Charles was too black for country music in 1963.

Just a few years later, country fans and the Nashville *twang*-erati tripped over each other to congratulate themselves over Charley Pride, their preferred Negro. Now, here was a black man they could get behind, a guy who joked about his "permanent tan," who *probably* had nothing to do with the Watts riots—wherever the hell Watts was—and who sounded, get this, Homer, *white*. Hell, they eventually made him country music's Entertainer of the Year—and he deserved it—though at first RCA declined to offend the delicate sensibilities of its customers by putting his handsome black face on any record sleeves. For the time being, only the vinyl itself could be black.

Charley Pride was the flip side to Elvis. Where Sam Phillips and Sun Records had discovered a poor white boy who sounded kind of black, Pride, one of eleven children born to a Sledge, Mississippi, sharecropper, was a poor black boy who sounded kind of white.

All three of them—Charles, Pride, and Elvis—knew what it was to be busted, though. That's the one thing that poor blacks and poor whites had in common: poverty. And when he sings "Busted," Ray Charles knows that being broke transcends the color of your skin.

The Bible says that after all is said and done, we're purified back to the dust we once were before we were suffused by the holy breath that sustains the universe. That dust part never shocked my people, who spent most their lives as dirt. Trampled on. Unseen. *Dirt*.

And when you're dirt, you lug water from the well and chop wood.

When you're dirt, you trip on floors so out of true that chairs won't sit flat.

When you're dirt, you slaughter rats at the town dump for sport . . . then shop there.

Don't have no phone.

Go snow-sledding on the black hood of a dead Ford.

Whittle the switch for your own lickin'.

Nail shut the front door—because ain't nothin' good ever come through it.

The men guzzle diesel.

When the baby cries, you stick a Karo syrup sugar tit in its little pink trap.

Play race car in a stove-up Ford Fairlane fermenting in the dooryard.

Eat Spam, that thick tongue of meat product.

Folks cluck and say you ain't going to amount to a piss-hole in
    the snow.
When you get caught stealing, you whine, "But weren't nobody
    using it."
Get more than your share of the short end of the stick.
Are always hungry . . .
. . . always hungry.

And when you're dirt, you don't insist. When you cling to the
vine-strangled margins, you're polite . . . quiet . . . shy but sly. You
scrape by on roads that are barely roads. But you cannot insist.
*Cannot.*

And when you're dirt, you shiver at the gritty sweetness of a
    sugar sandwich.
Relish the stink of cow shit.
Work throbs in your knotted fingers, even the ones that're
    missing.
You wash your hair with vinegar . . . and brush your teeth with
    baking soda.
Scuffle paycheck to paycheck.
Have a cousin named Junior junior.
Your roof leaks.
Bless April snow, spring's wet kiss, because it's the poor man's
    fertilizer.
Eat snapping turtle, gray squirrel, and woodchuck . . .
. . . and are thankful for it.
Great-Grandpa Ora stockpiles bicycle skeletons plucked from
    the town dump as he seeks Schwinn salvation.
So many uncles cannot hold a woman . . .
. . . cannot hold a dollar . . .
. . . cannot hold their liquor.

The knobbier the back road, the better you like it.

Know that rusty water is better than none at all.

You're thankful you don't live over to Tippy-Toe Lane where all
those inbred cripples live.

And when you're dirt, your mother's mother, that gristly vulture
called Lilla, scowls at you like she's starved, scissor lips snicking,
and keeps snarling: "Us kids never had nothin'. Us kids never had
nothin'."

If you have ever spent any time in the land of want (and maybe even
if you haven't), Merle Haggard's "Hungry Eyes" is sure to make you
cry, no matter how many times you hear it.

When you listen to "Hungry Eyes," which came out in 1969, it
doesn't matter that Hag had dozens of No. 1 hits, doesn't matter that
he spent nearly three years in San Quentin for burglary, doesn't
matter that as a kid he lived in an abandoned refrigerator car-
turned-shack snug against the Southern Pacific train tracks.

All that matters is his mama's hungry eyes. My childhood, too, is
haunted by the hungry eyes of women:

Grammy Jennings, who tried to feed her hunger through booze
and sex . . . Grammy Britton, who, for a while, ran off and deserted
my mother . . . Auntie Fat Dot, who cleaned houses and who, her
sisters-in-law insisted, traded her pride for trinkets.

I'll never forget Estelle, married, in her teens, just a couple
years older than me, visiting our house, the first and only house my
parents have ever owned. The old man was still working in factories, but through sweat equity and a government program he'd been
able to buy a little cracker box of a place for us.

And Estelle, who'd always had less than nothing, stared at our tiny house with her ravenous crow's eyes and said: "It must be nice to have money."

"With two hard working hands," Haggard sings, his father "tried to feed my mama's hungry eyes."

But once that hunger fastens on you, the way a hound muckles ahold of a rabbit around the neck, it never lets go, no matter how rich you get. It can't be satisfied by sex, by drugs, or by whiskey, either: just ask Waylon, Hank, Cash, and all their dead buddies.

Haggard sings on the verge of tears here, urged on by the sobs of the steel guitar. He tells us: "Mama never had the luxuries she wanted, but it wasn't 'cause my Daddy didn't try."

Hard work ain't enough sometimes. If you subscribe to the American Myth of Hard Work, all you'll do is work yourself to an early grave. And after you're laid out in your plain pine box, all that you'll leave behind is your widow, who will stare at your dead body with her hungry, hungry eyes.

## Another Day, Another Dollar

Unlike most popular music (and popular culture, too), country knows what work is, knows that its listeners make a living by sweat, hustle, and muscle. Beyond the songs that are specifically about work, there is the understanding in other songs—whether they're about drinking, sex, or God—that it's a down-to-earth working person that those songs are about, that those songs are meant for. Working hard, of course, transcends rural life. Americans still pride themselves on their work ethic, no matter how trying their job might be. It was more than just country fans who made Johnny Paycheck a fleeting cultural icon when he sang "Take This Job and Shove It" in 1977.

Country musicians certainly know what work is. They carried their dreams of picking and singing from the cotton patch, the oil patch, and down-at-the-heels farms. They were welders, coal miners, and bricklayers, and they knew the insides of sawmills, lumber camps, and factories of all stripes. Playing music at the rough and rowdy skull orchards till daybreak looked pretty good compared to flirting with black lung underground, or working from can till can't on the farm. No wonder they wanted to get on the radio so bad, obsessed over the *Grand Ole Opry*, the *Louisiana Hayride*, and the like. It's no surprise, too, that so many of those big strong country boys wanted to play professional baseball. Charley Pride, Jim Reeves, Bill Anderson, Conway Twitty, and Roy Acuff all claimed, at one time or another, that they were *this close* to becoming major leaguers. (And Marty Robbins actually did race stock cars, but only after he was a country music star.)

Their jobs sometimes predicted a kind of musical destiny. Luther Perkins and Marshall Grant were car mechanics in Memphis when they met Johnny Cash in 1954. All three of them were limited musicians, but like the shrewd country boys they were, they cobbled together their distinctive boom-chicka sound with what was at hand—shade-tree mechanics of music. And by the end of 1955, they had their first hit, "Cry, Cry, Cry," with a sound as stripped-down as any hot rod being worked over in the dooryard.

They all sang for men and women who worked two and three jobs and who never turned down overtime. Men and women who felt work stiff and sharp in their fingers at the end of the workweek, who were baked and cured by the sun—working people out in the country always look older than they are. Working up the shop or down the mill or stuck in the factory, wage slave to the line, bristling at the foreman. As the old man used to say: "Never trust a fuckin' foreman. And that goes double for landlords."

Auntie Lee and Grammy Britton, daughters of the Great Depression—hardworking country women who were lured to the city—incinerated a good part of their lives in the textile mills of Haverhill, Massachusetts. During World War II, Auntie Lee put in sixteen-hour days, six days a week, working like two dogs, maybe even three. But she earned enough money to build her own three-room house—a *real* house, with indoor plumbing, not a "friggin' tar-paper shack"—on a knoll off Route 125.

The old man knew factories, too: Spaulding & Frost, a cooperage in Fremont; LaGasse's Furniture in Haverhill; Kingston Steel Drum, which cleaned and reconditioned fifty-five-gallon steel drums; Westville Homes in Plaistow, which built modular homes; and Danville Chenille, a small textile mill.

But there were other jobs, too: killing snakes for Mizz Bake at ten cents per serpent; shoveling chicken shit; baling hay; junking cars; roofing and drywalling; working the woods; digging cellars by hand; driving truck; caring for two draft horses named Babe and Brownie; hauling loam and gravel. Shit work, mostly. Absolute shit work.

So they worked, worked some more, then worked till they couldn't work no more. (Except for those who decided that them and work could never get along.) Some worked themselves to death, just so that they could tread water in this world. Country music gave them solace as they drowned.

Merle Haggard's "Workin' Man Blues" (1969) came out three months before the song for which most non–country fans remember Hag best, "Okie from Muskogee." But where "Okie" is all over-the-top cultural caricature, a kind of shrewd novelty song that has its tongue stuck firmly in your cheek, "Workin' Man" is subtle, restrained. It's like the difference between Erskine Caldwell's *Tobacco Road* and Faulkner's *Light in August*—though, in this case, Haggard wrote both songs.

One of the things that country music has often done, through its stoic realism, is defy the culture of complaint. Here, as in many of his best songs, Haggard doesn't complain. With a trace of Lefty Frizzell gracing his voice, he sings about a limited life of workin' and drinkin'. Maybe after you've been freed from San Quentin, as Haggard was, you understand that you don't have much in this world to bitch about.

He admits that "it's a big job just getting by," and understands that he'll work as "long as my two hands are fit to use." And to find a hint of peace, "I'll drink my beer in a tavern, sing a little bit of these workin' man blues."

Wombed in his bar, the singer can ignore the baby-boomer vanity of Woodstock, the jingoism of the moon landing, and the deadly foolishness of the Vietnam War. All he needs to worry about is the good burn he feels in his throat as he guzzles a couple ice-cold beers after work.

It's a tricky balance, though, beer and work. Alcoholic or workaholic, there's a good chance you'll find your ass dead before the age of fifty.

But tomorrow's another working day, as the song's relentless drive reminds us. And for the workingman and the workingwoman—town or country—all dreams are dreams deferred.

Most of us Americans, for better or worse, don't know what real work is no more. The kind of work where the temperature is 130, 140 degrees and you pour sweat out your workboots. The kind of work where you get slashed, burned, and scarred. Where your hands turn rough with calluses . . . and your soul turns even rougher. Where, no matter how strong you are, your arms and back ache at day's end.

Me and the old man know what work is, though, because we both did time at Kingston Steel Drum.

Kingston Steel Drum skulked in a sandpit off Route 125 and poisoned my hometown for decades. The factory handled paint drums and insecticide drums, peanut butter drums and shampoo drums, acids and solvents, oil and raw alcohol, which some of the men would cut with Sprite or ginger ale, and then drink. There were drums foul with chemicals whose names we couldn't begin to pronounce, but we all understood the skull-and-crossbones stickers plastered on the sides.

We worked with guys named Lurch and Wolf Man, Homer the Cat and G.I. Joe, Dirty Willy and Thistle, Murphy and Double Murphy, and even Billy and Louie. Guys who barely staggered out of eighth grade, who did their jobs drunk and stoned and pissed off—sometimes all three at once.

We all attacked those drums, with fire and steel shot, with scalding water and worse acids. And if you couldn't stack drums three high, you didn't last long.

Kingston Steel Drum: it was like cancer come to life.


Hard work is hard work, paid for each day in muscle, sweat, and blood. Either you're made for it, or you ain't. If you ain't, you don't talk about it. If you are, you don't talk about it, either, because most folks know that you are just by looking at you. But some jobs are more than mere hard work. Some jobs can kill you—will kill you—like logging, like Kingston Steel Drum, like coal mining.

Country music owns a rich vein of powerful coal-mining tunes: "Sixteen Tons" by Tennessee Ernie Ford, "Paradise" by John Prine, "Coal Tattoo" by Hazel Dickens, and "Dark as a Dungeon" by Merle Travis.

Travis, who wrote the song, performs "Dungeon" (1947) spare and acoustic. He sounds as if he's singing from beyond the grave, a dust-blackened ghost looking back at his life in the mines, "where the danger is double and pleasures are few."

Coal helped fuel America's postwar prosperity, but it was a prosperity earned on the backs of dead men, crippled men. If the corrupt and venal mine owners didn't get you, there were always the cave-ins and explosions. And if you somehow dodged those, almost no one escaped the embrace of black lung disease. It was a world that Merle Travis knew well.

Born in 1917, Travis came of age in the black and bleak heart of West Kentucky coal country, in Muhlenberg County. His father and brothers were miners, but music let Travis flee the trap of digging out a living from beneath the hills and hollers. He was one of the stars of country music in the late 1940s, with songs like "Divorce Me C.O.D.," "So Round, So Firm, So Fully Packed," and "Steel Guitar Rag"; he also wrote the No. 1 hits "Sixteen Tons" and "Smoke! Smoke! Smoke! (That Cigarette)." And his finger-picking guitar style, learned from Mose Rager and Ike Everly (father of the Everly Brothers), influenced Chet Atkins, that Segovia of Nashville pickers.

But Travis plays it straight and true in "Dark as a Dungeon," which became a gloomy bluegrass standard, warning all the young men: "Seek not your fortunes in the dark, dreary mines."

Prosperity be damned.

The most dangerous job at Kingston Steel Drum was running the burner, an outdoor blast furnace that scoured and scorched the drums at more than a thousand degrees. One subzero winter morning, when the old man went to light it, the burner lit him up, blew up on him; the shock wave knocked him a good frozen twenty yards over dozens of drums. He shook it off . . . went back to work. It wouldn't be the first time, or the last time, that Dad thought about quitting "that fuckin' pit."

But that wasn't even the worst part about working "the burn," as we called it—it being too much effort to spit out that scrawny second syllable. Out at the burner, you were trapped in an elemental world: on the one hand, you had the fire; on the other, you had drums still slick with paints, solvents, and oils—all created to burn. And us workers—mere red and sweating flesh—stood in between.

We'd grunt and shove the drums out the truck, spill the dregs into a pond-sized pit behind us, then heave the drums onto the track into the burner. A toxic stew scabbed with blobs of paint, that waste pit looked like the set for a horror movie, a mad alchemist's lagoon that seemed ready to give birth to some new Frankenstein's monster. It was one of the countless black secrets of postwar prosperity—the dark side of the twentieth century—right there in my hometown's backyard.

Fire was the constant threat. The watery trough beneath the tracks into the burner was just a glorified fuse always ready to ignite—small rafts of flame floated on it all day. You'd be working, when—*whoosh!!!*—a wall of fire would erupt at the burner's maw. We didn't have no fire extinguisher, though. All we had was a green hose as skinny as hope.

Man, I'll tell you right now, you ain't lived till you've fought a paint fire with a garden hose.

Doug and Rusty Kershaw's "Louisiana Man" (1961) is so ripe with unmediated Cajun paining and pining that it could've been recorded in 1930. In the song, written by Doug, the two brothers tell us how hard their old man has to work just so they can hold their heads up and be poor, and not destitute, *deep* in the Delta bayous.

He's got fishing lines "strung across the Lou'siana River" and traps set in the swamps for muskrat and mink. It's clear that their father is the unbearable difference—"gotta catch a big fish for us to eat"—between whether the family starves or not.

"Gotta make a livin', he's a Lou'siana man," the Kershaws sing over and over, as if their chanting will make it so, "gotta make a livin', he's a Lou'siana man."

Much more than a song, it's an incantation to try to raise the dead. Doug and Rusty's old man shot himself in the head when the boys were just seven and five.

The Kershaws were born in Tiel Ridge, Louisiana, Doug in 1936 and Rusty in 1938. After their father killed himself, Doug writes in his autobiography, the family moved into a "chickenhouse." His mother took in wash and ironing, and Doug took to the streets to shine shoes and squeal away on his fiddle; he ended up playing local honky-tonks as a kid.

The brothers eventually hustled their way out of the bayous and arrived in Nashville, where Doug wrote "Louisiana Man," which became an unlikely No. 10 hit. He told Dorothy Horstman: "I was broke on my ass. I was being kicked out of my apartment, and I was sitting down for the last time, trying to write songs . . . I finally got my head back to when I was a kid, when I was safe. When I wasn't being kicked out, when I had beans on the table."

I spent one summer at Kingston Steel Drum catching drums from the burner. They'd wobble out its ass-end, about thirty yards away, then bobble down the rickety track into the building where I stood. Even after their "cooling" trip the drums were still hot. Their lips glowed orange-red as if they were the lips of apocalyptic hookers, and the cinders singed me. I went through a good two or three pairs of rubber gloves a day, the heat gnawing the rubber thin. Every half dozen drums or so, I'd plunge my hands into a bucket of lukewarm water. My hands peeled like a leper's that summer.

As the drums clanked in, I either stacked them three high or flung them down to the old man, who ran the blaster, which bombarded the drums with steel shot. Dad stood in a gray haze—the dust cloud created when steel ate steel. His face was smeared black by the end of the day. It was as if we were working an aboveground coal mine.

When we got home, we'd strip to our Skivvies in the backyard and soak our clothes in old buckets. We sure as hell weren't going to track the factory's chemical reek into the house. Then Dad would sit with a Bud at the kitchen table as Ma caressed his nose and ears with a magnet, gathering the steel shot that'd clotted in those places.

After the old man was hospitalized with a lung infection—at first, we thought he had TB—he didn't have to run the blaster no more.

One of the goofy fantasies of postwar America was that, like a lightning strike, you could get discovered by Hollywood. You could be pumping gas, bucking lumber, or working as a waitress, and suddenly some Hollywood talent scout speaking faster than the speed of sound would materialize before you—like an angel sent by Louis B. Mayer—and say: "Son, I like the cut of your jaw. Let's get you a screen test."

Be in the movies? Well, it sure as hell beat working.

Buck Owens fools with that myth in "Act Naturally" (1963), and it must've resonated with his listeners because the song spent a solid month at No. 1—the first of his fifteen-straight No. 1 Country hits from 1963 to 1967.

"They're going to put me in the movies," Buck *twangs*, "they're going to make a big star out of me." And the most important thing is, "all I gotta do is act naturally."

Which didn't seem too far-fetched to country kids who'd been watching Elvis up on drive-in movie screens for a few years in films like *Love Me Tender* and *Jailhouse Rock*. Hell, ol' Elvis weren't no real actor; he was a hick just like them. All he had to do was act naturally.

Buck was the avatar of the hard-driving Bakersfield, California, music scene that said "Fuck you" to Nashville, its conceits, and its snobs. With songs like "Together Again," "I've Got a Tiger by the Tail," and "Buckaroo," he helped define West Coast honky-tonk in the 1960s. Buck, who was born in Sherman, Texas, in 1929 and whose family was part of the great Dust Bowl migration west, always felt that if you sanded the raw edges off country music, then you ain't got no country music left. You just got to act naturally, you know.

And when you do, good things happen. Just ask Johnny Russell and Voni Morrison, who wrote "Act Naturally." It was enough that Buck shot the song to No. 1 Country, but how about what happened in 1965 when the Beatles recorded it with Ringo Starr (now, there's a name for a country singer) on lead vocal? The four lads from Liverpool, who knew a thing or two about growing up poor and acting naturally, parked the song at No. 47 Pop.

We worked from six till three at KSD come summer—unless there was overtime to be sucked up—and got paid for our lunch hour because we only took half of it. At about a quarter till three the old man'd shut the blaster, the burner track would grind and snick to a halt, and the factory would settle into intermittent hiss and sizzle from its usual boom, bellow, and roar. We'd head to the paint room, which was wallpapered with photographs from *Playboy*, *Penthouse*, and *Hustler*, and wash our hands and arms in MEK solvent. It stung like hell, but it got us clean.

We'd wait there for the buzzer, staring at the paint-room pussy, too tired to get much of a rise out of it. A lot of the guys hovered at the time clock in the lunchroom, watching it as if it were the best show on TV. And when that buzzer blatted, signaling the end of the workday, most the men ran out to their cars and trucks, bumping and jostling each other through the door—ragged and filthy cattle on stampede. Once in their cars, they'd tear out of there, spitting rocks and gravel, fishtailing up the hill to Route 125, then peeling, squealing (and pealing) onto the highway. To watch 'em leave, it's a wonder any of 'em ever came back.

The Justice Department and the Environmental Protection Agency shut the place down in the early 1980s, and it was named one of the one hundred most dangerous Superfund waste sites in the country. I covered the closing as a local newspaper reporter. When I worked at Kingston Steel Drum, I used to wear dungarees and a T-shirt, rubber gloves, and steel-toed boots. Before the EPA let me on the site, I had to put on a hard hat, goggles, a respirator, and an impermeable Tyvek suit.

Wynn Stewart was a cornerstone of the California country music scene, one of the men who helped create the West Coast sound that Merle Haggard and Buck Owens refined. He gave Haggard a job playing bass in his band, then wrote Hag's first hit, "Sing a Sad Song." Stewart, born in Morrisville, Missouri, in 1934, even (inadvertently) helped out Buck. He recorded Harlan Howard's "Above and Beyond (the Call of Love)" in 1959—which went nowhere—but his good buddy Buck heard it, then had a hit with it in 1960.

Stewart's "Another Day, Another Dollar" (1962) can be heard as a kind of prequel to Haggard's "Workin' Man Blues." The song echoes with the same sledgehammer striking a spike that you hear on "Workin' Man," but Stewart's song is less optimistic than Haggard's, maybe more realistic. As the phrase "another day, another dollar" gets repeated over and over—almost in an assembly-line rhythm—it's as if the narrator ages as we listen. We see his hands crab in pain, his back begin to bow before his spine splinters.

Though he gets paid "weakly," he keeps on working hard for the sake of his family, whom he calls his "thanksgiving." But as the song fades, Stewart, as if in a trance, keeps repeating, "Workin' my whole life away, workin' my whole life away . . ."

And I see the man sitting in his pickup one day after work, parking lot desolate, staring at the factory. He doesn't know no more whether to go home, drown himself in whiskey—or reach for the gun that he keeps loaded in the glove box.

# Dixie Fried

*or, My Old Man Was a
Beer-Drinking, Stock-Car-Driving,
Rockabilly Daddy*

When rockabilly broke post-Elvis, it sounded like raucous apocalypse to most fans of country music, seemed as if some psychotic and peroxided fox had sneaked into Roy Acuff's henhouse and killed all his banjo-plucking chickens. But with more than fifty years of hindsight, we understand now that rockabilly was just country souped up the way you'd soup up an ordinary '55 Ford, then take it to the local drag strip—or some lonesome back road. It was a brief flowering, really, from Elvis's first recordings on Sun Records in July 1954 to Buddy Holly's death in February 1959.

But what is rockabilly?

*Weeelll*, it's thirty-two cobbled-together stock cars in the bomber division bellering out of Turn 4 to take the green flag at some quarter-mile bullring in the sticks.

It's pounding the piss out of each other for no good reason other than being seventeen and feral.

It's you and your girl lurching up the fire-tower washboard road to park where no one can see.

It's guzzling more Schlitzes on a sizzling Saturday night than your illiterate old man can count.

It's fuck-you-buddy, white-trash music—wicked enough to make the cheap tin walls of Grammy Jennings's house trailer shimmy.

It's taking your girl to the drive-in picture show, then winging cherry bombs and Black Cat firecrackers at your pals two rows back.

It's when the rooster, instead of crowing at sunrise, straps on his Les Paul solid-body electric git-tar and rocks.

What's rockabilly? It's music that firmed up the *rock* in rock 'n' roll, just as rhythm and blues secured the *roll*. And it wasn't just music for country kids. City girls swooned over Elvis right along with the hick chicks. Middle-class high school kids wanted to boogie in a pair of "blue suede shoes" and "not fade away." And, for the most part, their parents, who'd lost their rhythm ages ago, were horrified—and terrified that their kids were getting, in Carl Perkins's phrase, Dixie fried.

Still, in the mid-1950s, working-class men in their late teens and early twenties—hard workers, hellions, and fuckups alike— understood rockabilly through and through for what it truly was: music to raise hell to after working all week. It was music that delivered down-home *twang*, but also thundered like a big-block mill. Music by guys like Perkins, Jerry Lee Lewis, Buddy Holly, Elvis Presley (at first), and Chuck Berry.

The opening guitar riff on Chuck Berry's "Maybellene" (1955) is like the brazen *honk!* of a Mack truck barrel-assing down a superhighway: "Get out the way, man! I'm coming through!" That ringing riff calls for a new kind of freedom, insists on sex and the open road—and Jack Kerouac and the other Beat boys, too busy dabbling in heroin, bebop, and Buddhism, are nowhere in the rearview. Then Berry's half-grinning moan, "*Oh, Maybellene*, why can't you be true?" as his V-8 Ford scats after Maybellene in her Cadillac Coupe DeVille for a little automotive foreplay in a perfect populist metaphor.

His electric ax slung low like a tail-dragging '49 Merc, the St. Louis–born Berry and his fierce and wicked guitar playing are one of the building blocks of rock 'n' roll. But, surprisingly, there's a lot of country in the former hairdresser, who, early in his career, was sometimes billed as "the black Hank Snow." "Maybellene," the hard-charging child of car songs like "Rocket 88" by Jackie Brenston and His Delta Cats on the R&B side and "Hot Rod Race" by Arkie Shibley and His Mountain Dew Boys on the country side, went No. 5 Pop and No. 1 R&B, but never even got close to the country charts.

"Maybellene" came out of Berry noodling around with "Ida Red," an old western swing favorite, and parts of the song are total honky-tonk, with no juke joint in sight. His guitar break is pure late-1940s hillbilly boogie, and the indispensable Johnnie Johnson steals in for some saloon piano to buttress that 'tonk feel.

But country music couldn't countenance a black man back in 1955, especially a strong, proud black man like Chuck Berry, who refused to play the Good Negro. But country boys recognized hopped-up hick music when they heard it, and they claimed songs like "Maybellene" as their own because "my, that little colored boy could play," as Berry, who was born in 1926, wrote three years later in the original lyrics to his defining hit, "Johnny B. Goode."

Rockabilly culture, early rock 'n' roll culture, was also car culture—from the palmy suburbs of California to the lonesome back roads of southern New Hampshire, and all points in between.

Mercs and Caddies, Fords and Chevys—real American steel, pal—chromed and flamed, chopped and channeled, Dutched and decked, Frenched and fuel-injected. Cars that seemed to *run* on rockabilly, where that rumble under the hood sounded just as good as any song by Perkins or Lewis or Holly. Cars that laid defiant ribbons of rubber on Route 125, tires *smoking*, tires *squealing*, cars *peeling* out—then they were gone, daddy, *gone*. Whitewalls, wide ovals, and mag wheels, blown, raked, and slicked. And, *man*, check out those suicide doors.

Cars not quite as cool as those in *Hot Rod* magazine or *Rod & Custom*, but cool enough. Cars transfigured by muscle, sweat, and junkyard know-how into 140-mile-an-hour pride. Yeah, rockabilly was junkyard music, too, music for scouring Detroit boneyards run by guys named Kenny Hoyt, Brandy Brow, and Old Man Battles. Some Saturday afternoons our broad gravel dooryard looked like the pits at a racetrack: four or five cars jacked up, their greasy owners wormed under their cars, grunting, drinking, cursing.

Once your ride was purring like a satisfied lion, there were the drag races on Route 125 at three in the morning, daring the hummocks and ruts of the power-line road, bombing along the logging trails in Cedar Swamp. Even Ma would bundle up me and Sis, slide us into the backseat of her old, bent-frame Ford, and go slewing through the sandpit down back the house.

When the guys weren't swapping paint with each other, you'd find them come Saturday at the local stock car tracks watching country boys just like themselves raising some fine, fast Cain on a hot summer's night.

———

One of the crucial rules in racing is to stay cool. Whether you're racketing around a homemade dirt track in East Kingston, spitting rocks and clods at the drunken and ducking spectators, or rocketing through the high banks at Daytona, you've got to be cool, riveted, becoming, you know, one with the horsepower. And imagine how cool you'd have to be to race with the Devil. Well, Gene Vincent and His Blue Caps answer emphatically on "Race with the Devil" (1956): pretty goddamn cool.

The Blue Caps' influential (but nearly forgotten) lead guitarist, Cliff Gallup, dispenses all the horses needed in "Devil," giving a quick, smooth ride to Vincent's vocals, which sound like Elvis lapsed into a Chet Baker coma: "I said move, hot rod, move man! Move, hot rod, move man!" Sorry, ladies, but Elvis—that too-pretty mama's boy from Tupelo—was never this cool.

Vincent's biggest hit was "Be-Bop-a-Lula," but "Race with the Devil," which only hit No. 96 Pop, captures youth culture's obsession with speed, hot rods, and stock cars. My old man and his buddies, like Vincent, who was born in Norfolk, Virginia, in 1935, asked: "Why not race the Devil? Aren't we all racing ol' Scratch, anyway?" Gallup's guitar keeps pushing the pace, the drums bang like pistons, and there's utter faith and confidence in speed. If you go fast enough, ain't nothing going to catch you, not even the Devil. When you're slamming along at more'n a hundred miles an hour, speed feels like temptation, seduction, and resurrection all rolled into one. Problem is, you can't stay in your car forever.

But so what? The Devil and Dan Webster never had this much fun.

Racing, always racing, as if they thought they could somehow outrace their hard lives, their unexpected marriages, their even more unexpected children. No wonder some of them ended up at Pines Speedway in Groveland, Massachusetts, and Hudson Speedway in Hudson, New Hampshire, when the workweek ended.

One spring, the old man, Dick Faxon, and Orrie George (Ma's first cousin) bought a crow-black 1937 Pontiac coupe for twenty bucks, splashed bold red 75s on the doors, sealed off the gas tank, welded in a roll cage, and went racing. They couldn't afford the right tires, so instead bought odd-sized truck tires to race on.

Dick did most the driving, but my old man got in his licks, too, including the time he lost control of No. 75 and almost took out the shit-houses over to Hudson Speedway: "You never saw people run so fast in your life," he'd say years later, still laughing about it.

It wasn't Daytona, and they weren't Fireball Roberts or Junior Johnson, but they were racing, man, *they were racing*. What better way to forget the workaday world than to jab, jostle, and jam around a racetrack with thirty other like-minded cars and drivers?

I loved going to the races. Loved how the roar of the stock cars prickled my ears and rippled in my belly. Loved how the cars hissed fire and *whooshed* wind as they dervished around the track, the swervy cars revving down the backstretch. Loved the smell of burnt rubber, grease, and gasoline as hot steel nicked hot steel, the track grit tasting like a supercharged incarnation of the Host.

Loved it, too, I understand now, because racing let us live beyond ourselves. Dad wasn't just another guy punching the time clock down to the factory, he *owned* a stock car, man. *He raced*. Come Saturday night, at least, he was *something*.

Dad, Dick, and Orrie ran No. 75 for three summers, sacrificing their weekends at the local altars of speed. But it all ended one hot Saturday night at the Pines. A spinout raised a curtain of dust on the backstretch. Ten cars vanished into the cloud . . . none of them came out. All you could hear was steel eating steel. Even before the dust cleared, the flagman, Kenny Small, threw the red to stop the race. There's nothing more quiet than thirty stock cars skidded to a halt on a racetrack . . . their motors shut.

It took two wreckers to ferry No. 75 to the pits. Dick only broke a couple ribs. The men finally got home at four in the morning, stared at the end of their racing careers sitting twisted and gutted on the stock car trailer, shrugged, and got drunk. They always used to say: "If I'm going to hit the wall, I want to hit it hard."

But even without a stock car, there were plenty of other ways to raise hell.

"Whole Lotta Shakin' Going On," Jerry Lee Lewis's barnyard bacchanal ("Baby got the bull by the horn," indeed), on the essential Sun label, was as rabid as it got in 1957. The Ferriday, Louisiana, wild man oozes Pentecostal lust on this slice of vinyl pornography—"All you gotta do, honey, is kinda stand in one spot, wiggle around just a little bit."

Folks didn't know whether to buy it, ban it, or bury it; eventually they bought it, sending "Shakin' " to No. 1 Country, No. 1 R&B, and No. 3 Pop. The song drips with the horny insanity of a guy who's certain that he's getting laid later that night.

Lewis, born in 1935, was the kind of leering, frenzied piano molester who could sing "Mary Had a Little Lamb"—watch out, lambie!—and make it sound dirty. It was songs like "Shakin' " and "Great Balls of Fire" that made it easy for the public to turn on Lewis in 1958 when news of his (third) marriage to his thirteen-year-old cousin, Myra Gale Brown, broke. People couldn't bear the thought of this feral hoodlum bedding his very own Lolita, whether that union was recognized by the state—*well*, a Southern state—or not.

But, to be fair to Lewis, in rural America in 1958, it wasn't unheard of for thirteen-year-old girls to marry. In New Hampshire a few years later, I knew a couple of fourteen-year-olds who married after they got pregnant. So, part of the outcry against Lewis was just classist bullshit. (And didn't Loretta Lynn get married when she was thirteen? But she was just a *country* singer, not a rock star.) But the real problem was that Jerry Lee Lewis, "the Killer" of rock 'n' roll mythology, was unrepentant—or at least felt that he had no explaining to do to nobody—even as his very real chance to overthrow Elvis as the king of rock 'n' roll evaporated in a self-inflicted haze of booze, sex, violence, and misdirected evangelistic fury. (Not unlike what happened decades later to his cousin the TV preacher—excuse me, the television evangelist—Jimmy Lee Swaggart.)

Lewis once bragged to the writer Nick Tosches: "I know what I am. I'm a rompin', stompin', piano-playin' sonofabitch."

Yup.


In popular memory, the 1950s are a sleepwalker of a decade, that long Eisenhower nap in which Middle America curled up in a satisfied fetal ball in the comforting glow of a booming economy (and its new TV sets). Somnolence was a civic virtue. But we sometimes forget those years' roux of anxiety, the underlying fear that led to a kind of cultural chronic fatigue syndrome. In the heartland, people still didn't quite get why the Korean War started—or why, just as suddenly, it ended. There was a Communist in every plot. And the atomic bomb provided the tasty New Testament prospect of nuclear Armageddon.

*"What, me worry?"*

Back in the 1950s, when you came of age in a postage stamp of a place as my old man did, all those national fears were rumors from another country (almost another century), mere murmurs on the fifteen minutes of nightly news. Yeah, there was some kind of war going on in Korea, and in the big, faraway cities Communists—

whatever those were—seemed to be raising some kind of ruckus.

And the hydrogen bomb? "You know what, man? The H-bomb can just go fuck itself."

What mattered to guys in the small towns and hamlets of America was making their cars go faster (or at least *look* faster), that the music they liked was getting louder and fiercer by the week, and chasing, to be a gentleman, women.

When you're seventeen and hungry and crazy, rockabilly sticks to you when you're working, when you're chopping cordwood and fetching water from the well. It's the reason you wired the house, shed, and barn with little car speakers, so you could always have the music with you. Because it was yours, lifted you up, an electric current sustaining your days and nights.

Those hard-muscled boys in their clean white tees, stiff dungarees, and shit-kickers who'd been raised on brawling were ready for Carl Perkins, Jerry Lee Lewis, and Chuck Berry.

Then again, nobody was ready for Billy Lee Riley.

Riley's "Flyin' Saucers Rock 'n' Roll" (1957) is where the socio-political-cultural freight trains of rockabilly and Cold War paranoia crash head-on—with no one tapping the brakes.

In a textbook case of cultural sublimation, Hollywood in the 1950s intuitively alchemized the nation's free-floating anxiety—about the bomb, about the Soviets, about juvenile delinquents—into a clutch of science fiction and monster movies, with films about flying saucers and invading aliens a thriving subset of the genre: *The Day the Earth Stood Still* (1951), *Earth vs. the Flying Saucers* (1956), *Invasion of the Body Snatchers* (1956), *It Came from Outer Space* (1953), *20 Million Miles to Earth* (1957).

It seemed that every small town in America—mine included—harbored some lunatic who claimed to have been abducted by aliens, been forced to knock back their intergalactic whiskey, and then had sex with 'em. (Well, it *might've* been sex. But it *might've* just been their take on a home perm.)

Enter Mr. Riley and his, um, Little Green Men.

More than any other rockabilly inferno, this insane, unparalleled song *brings it*, like an unblocked middle linebacker blindsiding the quarterback. Riley, his voice as raw as a fly-festering wound, bleats in tongues; the guitarist Roland Janes's whammy bar catapults the song to the Twilight Zone; J. M. Van Eaton batters the drums as if he's tattooing the skull of a guy who tried to run off with his girl; and you can be sure that Jerry Lee Lewis, not yet a star when this song was recorded, gleefully brought the matches, kerosene, and grain alcohol necessary to complement his piano pounding. (And, *oh*, those blood-clotting shrieks that detonate throughout the song.) This is proto-metal.

Riley and the band aren't only trying to bust out of their skins. They want out of Memphis, out of the South, out of America . . . out of this world. And they want whoever listens to this song to feel that same elemental ache.

Men like Riley (who was born in 1933 and grew up in Arkansas and Mississippi, the son of sharecroppers) spent their lives intimate with the bitter taste of failure, lived in what the writer Greil Marcus calls "desolate America." They came of age among weather-beaten people who lived weather-beaten lives in weather-beaten country shacks or city tenements.

But Riley and company, with their jagged edges that could never be sanded smooth and their high, hard cheekbones, understood that maybe music could save them if they played it fierce enough, loud enough, fast enough. Riley *had* to be sold on this song when he recorded it because it represented an escape from his cotton-patch past in Pocahontas, Arkansas. For Riley, this song was the getaway car idling outside the prison of his life.

When he rasps, "They brought rock 'n' roll all the way from Mars," he means it. And when he admits, "I couldn't understand a thing they said, but that crazy beat it just stopped me dead," there's a *yearning* in his voice. You sense that he wishes those little green bastards were real, because maybe Martians could understand him a whole lot better than any earthbound folk ever could.

And back in '57, only Sun Records would've had the guts to put Riley's record out.

If this chapter had a sponsor, like some old-time radio show, it'd be Sun Records, 706 Union Avenue, Memphis, Tennessee.

Sun was run on a frayed shoestring by Sam Phillips, a good ol' boy born in Florence, Alabama, in 1923, who had the good ears and the good heart to make the first recordings by, among many others, Howlin' Wolf, B. B. King, Johnny Cash, Jerry Lee Lewis, Carl Perkins, Roy Orbison, Charlie Rich, and Elvis. Phillips, in his quest for a different sound, instinctively peered into the raw musical souls of poor blacks and poor whites and tried to coax from them what he saw there. Along the way, he became one of the accidental shapers of American culture in the second half of the twentieth century.

As in any creation myth, there is at its heart a great mystery: Just what did Sam Phillips see and hear in Presley, a nineteen-year-old truck driver with a dirt ring around his neck who mumbled and couldn't look him in the eye?

There are some clues on Elvis's first record, "That's All Right," which was recorded on July 5, 1954, and released on July 19 as Sun 209. (For rock 'n' roll geeks, that number is as magical as Babe Ruth's sixty home runs in 1927, or Ted Williams's .406 batting average in 1941.)

With Scotty Moore on guitar and Bill Black on the big bull fiddle,

"That's All Right," originally a blues written and recorded by Big Boy Crudup, sounds pretty darn country, a pleasant hillbilly trifle. But there's something more to it—it simply doesn't sound like anything else, creates its own reality. First, it sounds as if it's coming out of some tinny drive-in movie speaker. Second, the guy singing sounds like some country kid *playing* at being a bluesman, but he's having fun—in the same way that the Beatles and the Stones had bluesy fun early in their careers. He sounds a little sexy, and already has the hint of an attitude in his voice.

"That's All Right" didn't chart nationally—Elvis, Scotty, and Bill hijacked Bill Monroe's "Blue Moon of Kentucky" for the flip side—but it was a local hit. No one, though, would have predicted that Elvis was less than two years away from being an RCA Recording Artist with a No. 1 Pop hit, "Heartbreak Hotel."

Then, the conventional wisdom goes, Elvis and his slick-haired, leather-jacketed buddies—those Brandos who *twanged*—proceeded to ruin country music and everything it stood for. The way people acted, you would have thought that Elvis and the boys had raided the Old Homeplace, ripped off Mother's gingham apron, flipped the Good Lord the bird, and taken a leak in the corn and tomatoes. Elvis, *by Gawd*, was the Antichrist of country music.

But, really, what Elvis and singers like Lewis and the Everly Brothers ultimately did was bring country music to a wider audience, pave the way for what was, in the 1950s, still a handshake-and-a-smile industry to experience unprecedented growth that began in the 1960s and continues today. Not to say that there weren't growing pains. Country fans raised on Jimmie Rodgers and the Carters, on Ernest Tubb and Red Foley, spit on the ground and sneered right back at Elvis and his rock 'n' goddamn roll. But even with its R&B beat, the music *twanged* hard, was suffused with hick attitude, and trained the ears of a generation to accept the music of unrepentant country boys.

What everyone forgets is that before everything else—before the Sullivan show, before the torrent of mediocre movies, before Vegas—Elvis Presley had become a country music star. He appeared early on the *Grand Ole Opry* and was a regular on the *Louisiana Hayride* in Shreveport, just like Hank Williams. He had four hits on the country charts before "Heartbreak Hotel" transformed American music in 1956, including "I Forgot to Remember to Forget," which spent five weeks at No. 1. Between 1955 and 1977, when he died, Elvis hit the country charts sixty-seven times, including No. 1 ten times.

And Elvis did fling wide the rockabilly floodgates, for Perkins, for Lewis, and for Holly, but also for one-hit, near-hit, and no-hit wonders, for singers who are only remembered and revered today by completists, cultists, and fetishists: Sonny Burgess and Ruckus Tyler, Tooter Boatman and Buck Griffin, Huelyn Duvall and Werly Fairburn, Sleepy LaBeef and Janis Martin ("the Female Elvis"), Charlie Feathers and the Burnette brothers, Johnny and Dorsey.

I swear that it seems like some of those guys used to get drunk with my old man.

When Dad got off work at noon on Saturdays, the drinking started—and it didn't end till sundown Sunday. It was mostly beer, because beer was cheap. Dad and his friends were guys who had a sweaty brown bottle stuck permanent in their right hands. Most of the first proper nouns I ever learned were brands of beer:

Schlitz, Schaefer, and Schmidt's; Pabst Blue Ribbon and Carling's Black Label; Bud, Ballantine, and Knickerbocker; Narragansett, Michelob, and Miller High Life.

The men judged local stores on how cold they kept their beer—Lindy's by Crawley Falls in Brentwood and Buzzell's by Kingston Lake. The ideal on a ninety-degree day in August was a beer just on the clear side of slush, the bottle so rimed that you could peel the ice with your thumbnail—Jewett's and Bakie's and Rowe's Corner Market. I saw men almost get in fistfights over whose beer was colder, Fecteau's or Custeau's.

One day when I was probably three or four, I walked up and down our dooryard pulling my red wagon. Every time I saw a bottle cap—they had cork in them back then—I dropped it into the wagon. By the end of the day, that wagon overflowed with caps. There were a few from tonic, which is what we called soda in that time and place, but most those caps came from bottles of beer.

The Saturday afternoon drinking, though, was just meant to take the edge off the week as the men worked over their cars or played tackle football, with the radio blasting all the while, and not just country and rockabilly: there was Fats Domino, the Coasters, and—*awopbopaloobopabopbamboom!*—Little Richard.

The real drinking, the *serious* drinking, didn't come till Saturday night.

Carl Perkins's "Blue Suede Shoes" (1956) packs an entire rowdy, country-boy Saturday night onto one 45 rpm single. This is piss-and-vinegar music made by hard-ass country boys for hard-ass country boys. But it also spoke to dissatisfied middle-class teenagers, and "Shoes" went No. 2 Pop and No. 2 R&B, in addition to No. 1 Country for three weeks. A good hook is a good hook, no matter how uncompromising the song, and teenagers nationwide were more than ready to shrug off the suffocating quilt of the 1950s.

Perkins was born in 1932, the son of sharecroppers, on a tenant farm near Tiptonville in northwestern Tennessee. When they got old enough, Perkins and his brothers took a good, long look around and realized that their futures didn't abide in cotton. Prodded by Carl, they formed the Perkins Brothers Band and started honing their hillbilly boogie in the bars and honky-tonks of Jackson, Tennessee.

If not Jackson, then it could've been Bud's Café up in Eppin', New Hampshire, which called itself "the center of the universe." Or the Hotel Maplewood over to Plaistow. Or some mosquito-haunted dance hall set on flood stilts deep in the Louisiana bayous, or a swaybacked beer shack beckoning at some cornfield crossroads in Wisconsin. "Cold Beer" painted on the exterior walls, neon signs promising Jax or Old Style or Lone Star, the screens on the doors bowed and rusted, the women inside even cheaper than the beer. Chapels of dim lights, thick smoke, and loud, loud music—the kind of music the Perkins Brothers played.

As much as "Blue Suede Shoes" is rockabilly, one of the cornerstones of rock 'n' roll that mesmerized the four teenage boys who became the Beatles, it's also pure honky-tonk rant. This is, after all, a song that Perkins wrote on a potato sack at three in the morning, spelling "suede" as "swaed." It also spent twenty-four weeks on the country charts, and for anyone who was moved by it back in 1956 it's still sitting there.

"Lay off my blue suede shoes" is a catchy line, but behind those words is a poor but proud country boy laying down the law. He might be hard up, he might bust his ass seventy hours a week up the mill, but on Saturday night he has enough money for a couple beers and he's got on his blue suede shoes. They are his coat of many colors and, somehow, they redeem him.

So, when this hillbilly cat asks you to lay off his blue suede shoes, what he's really telling you, son, is this: "Don't you dare fuck with me."

I have a black-and-white snapshot of my old man taken in the late 1950s. It's clear that it's early on a Saturday night, and after a long, hard week Dad's ready to head out: crisp white tee, thick hair slicked back, wide garrison belt with a brawler's brass buckle, black dungarees, cradling three 'Gansett "GIQs" (Giant Imperial Quarts), eyes heavy-lidded, the stare blank. His arms are thick with work and he's bowlegged; he looks a little like a muscled James Dean. You know, by just looking at him, that you don't want to fuck with him. He's the only thing in the kitchen that's not out of true: the ceiling is warped, the floor buckled, the windows sit crick-ed, the rug he stands on in front of the sink is curling.

But I keep coming back to his eyes. There's a country darkness there that scares the hell out of me. In that picture, I almost don't recognize my father.

While so much rockabilly celebrates raw youth, bragging rights, and lust, Carl Perkins's "Dixie Fried" (1956) homes in on the dregs of another country-boy Saturday night, the sons of Faulkner's Snopeses waiting for their heads to clear just enough so they can wobble out to their cars and trucks and get on home. It's the metaphorical flip side to "Blue Suede Shoes." No catchy pop-tune hook here, just a Southern Gothic playlet—Flannery O'Connor strapping on a Strat— which probably explains why "Dixie Fried" only skulked to No. 10 Country.

It's almost dawn in this little nightspot outside town, when in lurches Dan, who "reached in his pocket and . . . flashed a quart" and who bellows, "Rave on, children, I'm with ya!" (a line that later inspires Buddy Holly's "Rave On").

You can practically hear the other guys groaning, "Aw shit, it's Dan." You know Dan. He's the rawboned boy who, come Saturday night, is always taking things too far. He's the guy who taunts the night freights, the guy who takes the first swing at the six-foot-eight-inch stranger who has arms like sledgehammers, the guy who never met a man he didn't say "Fuck you" to. (In fact, ol' Dan just might be Jerry Lee Lewis in disguise.)

Over a simple shuffle, Dan urges his buddies, "Let's all get Dixie fried." And when Dan pulls out a razor, "all the cats knew to jump and hop" because "he was borned and raised in a butcher shop." The drums stagger along like Dan's unsure steps, but the electric guitar is as sharp as his razor, and Perkins's voice is full of gravel and rage.

No wonder my old man loved this music. He was wild and didn't give a fuck, and this was the first music he and his buddies had ever heard that was also wild and didn't give a fuck. This was music as tough as they were, made by guys who were as tough as they were. This is country music for hellions, for fistfights and bird-dogging pussy. This is the sound of being young, poor, pissed off, and not knowing why.

Written from the inside out by Perkins—not too far removed from those Tennessee cotton fields—"Dixie Fried" cuts way deeper than most rockabilly ravers. Cuts to the unbearable whiteness of bone.

# Crazy

Well, it's universal, ain't it—from the penthouses of Manhattan to the outhouses of Cedar Swamp—all that *sex* and *love* . . . and *heartache*?

But maybe when you're poor, maybe when you live way out in the country, when you ain't got nothing but the beating of your own wild heart, when life stutters to a halt at the town line, maybe love and sex matter a little bit more, make you a touch crazier. Maybe . . . just maybe.

It's just that the chances for happiness seem fewer and farther between in a small town, sharpening the desperation—a fierce desperation heard in so many country love songs:

The fine Cajun keening of Harry Choates in "Jole Blon"; in Connie Smith—George Jones's favorite female singer—and "Once a Day," in which the heroine only cries "once a day, every day, all day long"; in Hank Williams's "Lovesick Blues" and "Cold, Cold Heart"; in Ray Price's "Heartaches by the Number." Then there's Patsy Cline, with songs like "Crazy" and "She's Got You," who possesses songs of unrequited love even as they possess her. Songs whose pain and honesty let them transcend their country roots and seep into the broader American songbook. It's not too hard, after all these decades, to still find a jukebox where "Crazy" reigns, especially after midnight.

These songs often reflect a blighted world of physical hunger, hope, and pleading fired by the fatalism and selfishness forged by the Great Depression and World War II. At this late date, when we look back at the men and women shaped by those bitter decades, we tend to smear the camera lens with Vaseline and get misty-eyed over the so-called Greatest Generation. I knew plenty of those survivors, though, and where I grew up, there wasn't one of them who wasn't scarred, not one who didn't know the darkest deeps of despair.

Their lives were a mystery to me. I didn't know why Grammy Jennings would stay with a man who mauled her. Didn't know why Auntie Helen sneered whenever she said her husband's name. Didn't understand why Uncle Lloyd had a new girlfriend every other week, the way other guys got a fresh haircut.

I didn't yet know that romantic love is lust's justification.

*Oh*, Uncle Lloyd was a ladies' man. The great love of his life was always the woman whom he was going to meet for the first time that night over to the Eagles Club or up to the Legion Hall, where there'd be some half-assed country band playing or, at the very least, a honky-tonk jukebox.

He was one handsome sonuvabitch, skinnier than a snake slinked around a rake, hair ricked high in a Brylcreem haystack, black Wranglers, black pearl-buttoned shirt with lightning stitches on the breast pockets. He'd half hum, half sing his favorite songs as he got ready for a night out, songs like Faron Young's "If You Ain't Lovin' (You Ain't Livin')" and "Live Fast, Love Hard, Die Young."

There was no shortage of women: Charlotte and Rose, Jenny and

Bea, Shirley and Cindy—and always a little something on the side, just to make life interesting. No shortage of jealous husbands and boyfriends, neither: every once in a while there'd be a black eye to accessorize Uncle Lloyd's black shirt and black slacks.

The only purpose work ever served was to put enough money in his back pocket so that come Saturday night he could sidle on up to some sweet thang and say, "Hey, good lookin'."


The words to Hank Williams's "Hey, Good Lookin' " (1951) sound pretty innocent, what with their references to soda pop and a spot where the dancing's free. But what we forget today, after decades of anything-goes culture, is that in classic country the music itself and the singer's tone of voice often tell us more than mere words. A close listen to "Hey, Good Lookin' " reminds us that it's not 1920, it's 1951 and there ain't too many left who're innocent, not after World War II, not after the Holocaust, not after Hiroshima.

When Hank tears into the song—"Say, hey, good lookin', whatcha got cookin'?"—his voice bursts with a squall of giddy Saturday night adrenaline, and there's a grin in there that's just shy of a leer.

Ol' Hank's feeding this fine, big-boned girl all the lines he thinks she wants to hear—"I'm gonna throw my date book over the fence"—but he's a stone honky-tonk man and this is pure country carpe diem. Hank can make all the giddy promises he wants, but most no one believes a word of 'em—least of all Hank himself.

Some music fans have trouble reconciling Hank's manic highs with their preferred image of him as the doomed troubadour wasting away on songs like "Your Cheatin' Heart" and "Lost Highway"; they'd just as soon forget about the reckless ecstasy of "Jambalaya" and "Settin' the Woods on Fire."

But no matter how gloomy and miserable your workweek—town or country—you're for damn sure going to raise some hell come Saturday night. And if that gal ol' Hank keeps talking to jumps into his hot rod Ford, he'll be fiddling and diddling with her bra strap quicker'n you can say Ernest Tubb.

My parents, Dana Floyd Jennings and Florence May Britton, could've been high school seniors in the fall of 1957. Instead, their eighth-grade educations firmly behind them, they got married on September 27 that season. As I've said, I was born eight days later. (Ma's mother, Lilla, refused to sign the marriage papers till it was clear that I wasn't going away.)

Ma's cousin Orrie got married at seventeen. His wife was fourteen and pregnant. Mom and Dad gave them my big but saggy king-size bed that Grandpa Ora had scavenged from the town dump as a wedding gift. I got demoted to a cot.

Ma used to say that all her friends *had* to get married, that sex always arrived before love, and that, to paraphrase Loretta Lynn, who knew firsthand, they were all babies having babies. Sometimes, to hear my parents tell it, the spring and summer woods were a riot of teenagers lugging along their blankets, their beer, and their lust—if not their condoms.

Then there's my great-aunt Helen, who was seventeen and, yup, pregnant when she married Allen West. She didn't want to marry him, though, thought she could do better—baby or no baby—but Nanna George, her fortress of a mother, told her two things: "That baby's got to have a name," and, "You made your bed. Now lie down in it."

So, Allen and Helen married, then she had a miscarriage. Auntie Lee said her sister never slept with Uncle Allen again, exiling him to his own small bed of shame. Helen spent the next twenty-five years or so nurturing her hate, the only true thing born of their union: she'd kick him out of the house on a whim, just to keep him honest; make him smoke outdoors in the rain; and flaunt her outside men as if they were new dresses.

Uncle Allen died shoveling heart-attack snow. Shoveling with Irving Swett, his best friend and one of his wife's lovers. In his coffin, Uncle Allen got kissed hard on his cold, cold lips—it'd been a long time since he got kissed like that—by Lilla, who did it just to piss off her little sister.

Just one question, though: Why are poor people so goddamn fertile?

The Everly Brothers' "Wake Up, Little Susie" (1957) is another song where the words say one thing and the music another.

Now, Boudleaux and Felice Bryant, the Nashville husband-and-wife team who wrote "Susie," swore until they died that Susie and her boyfriend *certainly did not have sex* at that drive-in picture show; they innocently fell asleep during that double feature.

But the music tells the real story, tells us that it was actually a pretty steamy triple feature.

"Susie" opens with Don Everly's urgent riff on acoustic rhythm guitar—it's the song's most intense moment—and everything after that is release, is postcoital. The movie might not have been so hot, but the scene in the underwear-festooned backseat sure was. They had sex, fell asleep, and didn't wake up till four in the morning. No wonder Don Everly sings, "Wake up, Little Susie, and weep."

Despite the disclaimers from the Bryants and the Everlys, some radio stations banned it, but they couldn't stop "Susie" from shooting to the top of the country, pop, *and* R&B charts. Black or white, hick or city slicker, all the kids knew what the song was really about, and in an eyeblink it entered the canon of early rock 'n' roll.

Though the Everlys' main audience was teenagers, they came straight out of Nashville by way of Brownie, Kentucky, where Don was born in 1937 (Phil was born in 1939 in Chicago). The first songs Don ever sold were to Kitty Wells and Justin Tubb. Their father, Ike, was an accomplished finger-picker (and coal miner), and the boys' close harmonies were directly in the tradition of brother acts like the Monroes, Delmores, and Louvins, who were even their contemporaries on the country charts. But next to Don and Phil, whose singing later influenced the Beach Boys and the Beatles—it's easy to imagine the Everlys singing "Help Me, Rhonda" or "I Want to Hold Your Hand"—the Louvins' hits like "I Don't Believe You've Met My Baby" and "You're Running Wild" sounded as if they were Sand Mountain, Alabama, ghosts whispering from a nineteenth-century well.

What set the Everlys apart from the rest of Nashville, though, and enthralled American teenagers, were their radical R&B rhythms, the Bo Diddley filigree as Don chopped and picked at his guitar as if he were his daddy working a vein of coal.

So, as far as Susie and her disheveled beau in the backseat? Hey, blame it on Bo Diddley.

The marriage(s) of Mary Ella Cosgrove and Ora Porter George, my great-grandparents, was a Northern Gothic love ballad—heavy on the Gothic, light on the love.

Ella, who was half-Indian, had keen cheekbones and eyes as dark and deep as Cedar Swamp. Ora, who played trumpet in a local dance band, stood a rakish six feet four inches. He used to drive the town taxi back and forth from the Newton Junction train station and, apparently, collected women the way he'd later collect old tires.

These are the basic facts: Ella and Ora married on July 17, 1909 (the Honorable F. N. Whiffen presiding), and by 1923, the year they divorced (and the fourteenth year of their domestic war), they had three children. They each remarried right away, but by 1925 had both divorced again—single-handedly creating an epidemic of divorce in Kingston—and come to realize that no one else would put up with either of them. So, they married each other again, on November 25, 1925 (the Honorable Asa M. Bradley presiding), this time for the duration. Seven days before their second marriage, their fourth child was born, Billy George—yet another baby who had to have a name. Ella bore her fifth child in 1929, a change-of-life daughter named Helen and of suspect provenance.

Nanna and Great-Grandpa, as I knew them, were characters from the other side of *Our Town*, from a Grover's Corners siphoned of its sweetness.

Ella, when her children didn't mind her, made them sleep overnight on the hard ground at the foot of the back steps. But when there wasn't enough food, she'd go without so they could eat.

And Ora? Ora never met a problem that he couldn't lick by shrugging and slinking away from it. He'd rather burn his days at the dump, studying the rats—not so different from his neighbors, but a lot more predictable—and listening to the seagulls shriek. He also didn't mind, later, getting lost in a good cowboy show on the snowy television—plucked, of course, from the town dump, where the trickle-down theory of economics had been at work for decades.

Every culture needs its mythologies, and for rural and working-class Americans (and lots of dudes in the cities, too) from the 1930s into the 1960s the Western was one of those powerful myths—sustained through movies, TV, country music, and pulp novels. The music, as it tried to shed its "hillbilly" stigma, was even marketed as country and western for a long while to take advantage of the nation's love affair with Westerns, with singing cowboys and their faithful horses.

You could argue that Marty Robbins's "El Paso" (1959), which hit No. 1 Country and Pop, is about as perfectly archetypal as a Western can get. The director John Ford (*Stagecoach*, *The Searchers*) should've had the good sense to turn that epic ballad into a full-color Hollywood motion picture.

The year 1959 was certainly the age of the Western, especially on TV. There were the big guns like *Bonanza*, *Gunsmoke*, and *Have Gun Will Travel*, the medium guns like *Maverick*, *Rawhide*, and *Cheyenne*, then the off-brands like *Johnny Ringo*, *Riverboat*, and *Hotel de Paree*. And once some of those shows went into reruns in the 1960s, it seemed we'd never get rid of the *ker-ping!* of rifle-happy cowboys.

In those days, there were plenty of Westerns on the radio, too, in the guise of songs: Robbins's follow-up to "El Paso," "Big Iron"; "The Rebel—Johnny Yuma" by Johnny Cash; "(The Man Who Shot) Liberty Valance," sung by Gene Pitney and written by Burt Bacharach and Hal David (and probably one of the few songs by them that Dionne Warwick never sang); the hilarious "Along Came Jones" by the Coasters; and "The Battle of New Orleans," Johnny Horton's hysterical historical that also went No. 1 Pop and Country (not to mention No. 3 R&B) and that nudged Robbins toward writing "El Paso."

But set aside for a moment dastardly masked bandits, six-guns, and horses who love you more than your wife herself, and "El Paso" is one of the greatest love stories ever told in popular music. It's an exquisite four minutes and thirty-nine seconds of cowpoke opera. Our man commits murder, then essentially suicide, for the sake of the woman he loves, the wicked Felina.

As stoic as a cactus, Robbins tells us that "my love is stronger than my fear of death" as he turns his horse around to return to Felina and face the fatal music of the Winchester rifles. The entire journey, into the badlands of New Mexico and back, he is accompanied by the cantina-style guitar of Grady Martin, playing Pancho to his Cisco.

Robbins, born in rural Arizona in 1925, said the song was inspired by the stories his cowboy grandfather used to tell. Grandpa certainly found the right audience in his grandson. Robbins went on to record dozens of cowboy songs, including the *Gunfighter Ballads and Trail Songs* album, and he even wrote a paperback Western.

"El Paso" ends with Felina kissing the bullet-riddled cowboy as he gasps his last breath. That moment sends our man to the Sweet Hereafter with a smile, and sent listeners stampeding to the record shops and department stores.

Lilla and George Britton, my mother's parents, got divorced in 1943. Lilla eventually went off to work in a restaurant owned by her cop boyfriend, Sarkis Bananian, and left my mother to be raised by Nanna George and her aunts. In family history, George Britton was consigned to the dustheap. But decades later, after Sarkis, Lilla's common-law husband, had died and George's second wife had also died, they met again at a bingo game and started dating.

I always wondered what longing they saw in each other's eyes that they hadn't been able to see back in 1943.

Conway Twitty had the kind of voice—imagine a country Barry White—that gave women hot flashes long before they hit menopause. And "Hello Darlin' " (1970) is his pinnacle, the one song of his dozens of No. 1 hits that made female fans' hearts race faster, made their knees weaker than any other.

"Darlin' " tells the oft-told tale of two old lovers running into each other after many years have passed; they had split because he did her wrong. It's clear that the woman, the love of his life, has moved on. But the man is still trapped in a nightmare of his own making. "You made your bed," I can hear Nanna George telling Twitty, "now you can lie in it alone."

When Twitty speaks the song's opening words—"Hello, darlin' "— from deep in the prison where his heart is in exile, the lump starts rising in your throat. By the time he begs, "Let me kiss you just for old times' sake," there's rarely a dry eye to be found. The small talk is killing him, devouring him. And with the pedal steel weeping, he dissolves right before our ears. He tells her that if she can ever forgive him, "Come back, darlin'. I'll be waiting for you." But it's clear that he's going to be waiting for a long, long time.

Twitty, country's love man, was born in Friars Point, Mississippi, in 1933, named Harold Lloyd Jenkins. He told his biographers, Wilbur Cross and Michael Kosser, his secret in attracting female fans: "Women have known me down through the years, through the songs I've written and the music I've recorded. And they sense that here's a man who *does* understand."

Twitty proved back in 1970 that a man who understands could go all the way to No. 1.


All Grammy Jennings ever wanted was to fuck and drink. If you're seeking flour-dappled cheeks and chocolate-chip cookies cooling on the kitchen table, you've got the wrong shack, Jack.

All she ever wanted was an ice-cold beer in one hand and a red-hot man in the other: Frank and Phillippi, Joe and Reggie, Harry and Lou—and others whose names I forget . . . and she did, too.

It's funny, though, for all the men who flowed through her life, when I think of her, I always picture her alone and lonely:

Laura Jennings waits at the crumb-specked kitchen table—a human deadfall—stalled on the train tracks of her life.

She nibbles on cinder toast, sips at gritty and bitter mud coffee. Four in the morning, and sleep has spurned her again. The Boston & Maine wails low, mourning out beyond the Pow-Wow River. November gusts rock her husk of a shack. If she were a praying woman, she'd turn to the Lord. But she hasn't prayed since she ran away from the orphanage when she was a wild and angry girl. She sighs quarry-deep . . . puts on a Patsy Cline record, "She's Got You."

Laura Jennings is thick smoke, dim lights, and loud, loud music. My grandmother is always the *other* woman, loving up Bud-drinking, cigarette-sucking swamp-mucker motherfuckers who spend their lives like firecrackers. *Always the other woman.* And, in the end, she's always alone . . . except for Johnny Cash or Faron Young or Patsy Cline.

Patsy's pure *ache* smolders in Grammy's bones. She savors the crack, pop, and hiss—like bacon sizzling—of the needle-seducing vinyl. The flaws in the record are the flaws in her life. She will tell you that she was "borned and orphaned" way back in the country, and that to her Patsy is practically kin. Cline sings her life better than she can say it herself.

Like Patsy Cline, Laura Jennings knows what it is to go walkin' after midnight searching for her man, to fall to pieces, to be crazy—you don't go chasing your oldest son with a butcher knife if you ain't crazy. But she carries no torches.

She herself is the torch.


In her best songs—"Crazy," "I Fall to Pieces," "Walkin' After Midnight"—Patsy Cline wraps herself in her pain and luxuriates in it as if it's a full-length mink. It's still a man's world, she knows, and in a man's world women will suffer, so you need to learn to savor that hurt. Because, no matter what, you're going to hurt. Cline is always a woman on the verge, caged by desire and despair. In just a handful of songs, Nashville's Belle of Heartbreak encompassed the entire emotional life of a woman—all women.

Cline, who landed thirteen songs on the pop charts during her brief career, knew how to take the unvarnished truths of country and transmute them into a shocking kind of pop sophistication that had nothing to do with cowboy hats and fringed skirts.

Born in 1932 in the Depression-haunted mountains of Virginia, she grew up Virginia Patterson Hensley. It's hard to find a biographical sketch of Cline that doesn't call her brassy and/or sassy, country music code words that mean she liked to screw and carried a pint of whiskey in her purse. Not that the whiskey ever roughed up her voice, the way some of her men roughed her up.

Produced by Owen Bradley, she was always backed by Nashville's best: Pig Robbins and Floyd Cramer on piano; Grady Martin and Hank Garland on electric guitar; the Jordanaires with their silky background vocals.

Though her version of Willie Nelson's "Crazy" is definitive, her finest moment comes in Hank Cochran's "She's Got You" (1962). As Cline stares at photographs of an old love, she knows that all she has left are scraps of paper, scraps of the life they once had together. But what makes this song impossible to forget is the pause in this line:

"I've got your memory . . . or has it got me?"

That pause, and the ever-so-slight erotic moan on the word "or," make for one of the most devastating moments in all American music. It's the pause where every American woman was stuck in 1962, the pause that gave rise to feminists like Betty Friedan and Gloria Steinem. In that pause, Patsy Cline sounds as if she's being entered by that unbearable memory. This is music for adults. Not kids. Not teenagers. Adults.

Patsy Cline died on March 5, 1963, in a plane crash that also killed Cowboy Copas and Hawkshaw Hawkins. She was only thirty years old. President John Fitzgerald Kennedy was assassinated eight months later. To a lot of country people, Cline's death mattered much more. JFK, after all, was just another conniving, slick-talking sonuvabitch politician from Massachusetts, an A1 "Mass-hole."

He never knew our hearts the way Patsy Cline did.

# Ring of Fire

After World War II, during which both men and women had tasted unparalleled freedoms amid a shadow that at times had felt like the end of the world, it was going to be hard to keep couples happily down on the farm, or even in that tiny apartment above Marian's Luncheonette over to Main Street. Country music reflected those postwar tremors, understood that the American family was coming undone. That understanding midwifed some of the strongest country songs of the late 1940s and early '50s: "Slipping Around" by Floyd Tillman, "Back Street Affair" by Webb Pierce, "It Wasn't God Who Made Honky Tonk Angels" by Kitty Wells, "Your Cheatin' Heart" by Hank Williams.

If Americans in those years wanted to hear songs that reflected the shifting ground of their lives, they *had* to turn to earthier musics, like country and R&B. Pop, for the most part, persisted in the postwar fantasy that all was right with the world with the Axis defeated, while jazz, as bebop redefined the music, retreated into insider virtuosity.

I grew up steeped in the working-class culture of faithlessness that Hank sang so well about, knew early that men and women were locked in a cold war in which most negotiations were negotiations by lust. Despite what Johnny Cash proclaimed, there wasn't nobody (except the old man and Ma, it seemed) walking the line.

Most the men I knew drank, hit, and jumped anything that moved—not even a knothole was safe—and some of the women weren't too far behind. And they all loved cheatin' songs.

They couldn't look beyond themselves. The Depression and the war had unmoored them, reduced them to their basest natures. And fucking was free, besides. If it's just waiting there, a-throbbin', why not go ahead and take it? In a clan of thieves and scavengers, what could be better than that?

Despite what most the songs say, though, women got the worse of it. I knew poor, poor women who were cut, burned, and beaten, saw the rich men in town try to pluck vulnerable young women from their rural solitary. In a small town, where the possibilities are less than limited, where the chance of finding that one right person is infinitesimal, cheating on your lover just might be worse than murder. Being cheated on is a living death borne in the midst of everyone who knows you.

Cheating songs (along with their slurring brothers, drinking songs) became a staple of country music in the 1950s and never went out of style. On the surface it would seem that country fans simply liked the vicarious thrill of sinners doing things that they'd only dreamed of, liked songs that reflected the chaos set loose in their hearts and in their towns. But cheating songs can also be heard as a cultural mask, unearthing problems far deeper than those of just two wretched creatures huddled at the dark end of the street.

The best cheating songs are also a music of oppression: all those complaints against faithless lovers are also complaints against society. Just as blacks began to lay claim to their cultural birthright after

World War II, so, too, did poor whites come to understand that they didn't have to be content with inferior educations and working themselves to early graves. Blacks and poor whites always had more in common than either cared to admit—just ask the men and women who accidentally created rock 'n' roll.

The characters in cheating songs are inconsolable not only because their lovers have done them wrong but also because they're struggling to get along in a subculture of despair.

As Kitty Wells pines her way through "It Wasn't God Who Made Honky Tonk Angels" (1952), we already know it isn't God's fault. Honky-tonk angels are made by poverty, ignorance, and a government that couldn't be bothered—and still can't be bothered, brother—with the working poor.

In her nasal Southern gospel voice, Wells, in an answer to Hank Thompson's "Wild Side of Life," laments that "it's a shame that all the blame is on us women," because it's married men thinking they're still single "that has caused many a good girl to go wrong."

The singer sounds like a weary and wise older sister who's seen it all—or what passes for "it all" in her neck of the woods—as she sets out to the rickety steps of some shack in a threadbare cotton dress.

Written by J. D. Miller, "Honky Tonk Angels" was Wells's first hit—selling more than 800,000 copies initially—and showed country music executives that mere "girl singers" could move lots of records and draw lots of jukebox nickels, too, paving the way for later stars like Patsy Cline, Loretta Lynn, and Tammy Wynette.

But even the demure Wells—Muriel Ellen Deason, born in Nashville in 1919—who wore neck-choking gingham and had three children, couldn't avoid controversy with "Honky Tonk Angels." Some radio stations thought it too suggestive—honky-tonk angels? my, my—and she was forbidden to sing it on *Grand Ole Opry* broadcasts.

But it wasn't the hint of sex that bothered the men who banned it: it was the truth the song embodied. Men were always blaming women for the weaknesses in themselves. And Wells lays bare that truth plain and country, with no histrionics. Modern would-be divas could learn a lot from her understatement. The more it hurts, the quieter and more controlled you sing.

In this song, Kitty Wells hurts a lot.

But angels, honky-tonk or otherwise, were pretty rare in my family. Take my great-aunt Helen:

The old man and I are digging a cellar by hand for Auntie Helen. She's paying me a buck an hour. Dad's getting paid in beer, and easily outearning me.

We're being helped by Great-Uncle Allen—who, remember, hasn't slept with Auntie Helen since she miscarried the baby that shotgunned them into marriage in the first place—and Uncle Irving, who isn't my uncle at all but who has lived with Allen and Helen since before I can recall and who is Uncle Allen's best friend and who has slept with Auntie Helen for years. Uncle Allen, who once put his cold bony hand down the back of my sister's pants, is called Zeke. Uncle Irving, who laughs like a cat that's been mauled by a German shepherd one time too many, is called Teddy Bear—or "Tedda Bay-uh," in Helen's thick Yankee accent. Irving calls Helen "Punk," short for "Punkin'."

We're being watched by Albert—he hasn't yet ascended to unclehood—who has recently run away from his wife, Blanche, and who is screwing both Auntie Helen and her sister Lilla, my mother's mother. Sometimes, I think me and Dad are digging this cellar for the sheer entertainment of it all.

(Fortunately, Auntie Lee—Helen and Lilla's other sister—isn't caught up in this catfight. But Lee, all hackles and grudges, did recently tell me everything she thinks I need to know about Luther Graham, her one and only—and dead—husband: "He was a no-good lazy sonuvabitch who drank.")

Back at Auntie Helen's shack, I go in the house to get a drink of water, and she's sitting at the kitchen table: she has pink rollers in her hair; she's slightly cross-eyed; she has a triple chin studded with barbwire whiskers and breasts the size of summer woodchucks. Who wouldn't want to lay a looker like that?

"You know, Andy," she says to me, "I got three men living in this g.d. house. And if you put 'em all together, you ain't got one man."

Cheating is a logistical nightmare. As in real estate, it's all about location, location, *location*.

You need to learn to "wait on the corner" ("Walk On By" by Leroy Van Dyke) or live with your shame on shadowy streets ("Back Street Affair" by Webb Pierce). But, most important, you need to make sure that no one's watching "from the window up above."

The narrator of "Window Up Above" (1960), written and sung by George Jones, is a voyeur to the disintegration of his own marriage. He hears his wife come home late, peers out the window, and sees her in the arms of another man—and he ain't administering CPR. We know it isn't innocent when Jones moans: "For last night he hugged you tightly, and you didn't even shove."

For the moment Jones, that Rolls-Royce of country singers, is paralyzed, haunted by the song's refrain: "I've been watching from the window up above." But his anguish tells us that all the guns are loaded, the ax and the kitchen knives sharpened.

Jones, born in a log cabin in the Big Thicket of East Texas in 1931, was known for his misadventures in whiskey and pills. And it sounds as if his man at the window could use a little fortification, because in a minute he's going to be out that window and tottering on the edge of sanity—and it ain't going to be pretty.

Location *is* everything if you're going to cheat.

The old man and I worked with a couple cavaliers named Al and Chet at Kingston Steel Drum who used to bring women back to the factory after hours and woo them in the trailer trucks, after paying the drunken night watchman to look the other way (if he was still conscious).

Dad and I'd just shake our heads at the stories. Sure, Al and Chet got their weekend pieces, got "something strange." But I always wondered about the women. What kind of a woman lets herself get fucked by a couple of drunks in a dark trailer truck that smells worse than ten dead skunks?

Some songs, through no fault of the singer or the writer, become ciphers. People hear what they want to hear, what they need to hear, the artists' intentions be damned. Merle Haggard's "Okie from Muskogee" is a good example—most folks couldn't hear the sly humor in it.

And Tammy Wynette's "Stand by Your Man" (1968) is another such song. Feminists despised it for what they perceived as its woman-as-doormat sentiment. The Christian Right embraced it for what it perceived as its my-man-right-or-wrong sentiment.

But "Stand by Your Man" is a lot more subtle than all that.

Take the opening line. "Sometimes it's hard to be a woman," sings Wynette, who was married four times, "giving all your love to just one man."

Now, there's a lyric that's as ambiguous as anything Dylan ever wrote. The straightforward reading is that being a working-class chick sucks because you're in love with ol' Nicky Numb-Nuts who only considers paying attention to you when he comes home drunk at four o'clock on Sunday morning.

But the more shaded meaning, the one I think Wynette meant, is that sometimes it's hard to be a woman because you're only allowed to give your love to one man. This reading lets Wynette understand the temptation that her own man can't resist, understand why she'll have bad times, even as he has good times. And it's that under-standing of temptation and sin that allows her to still *love* him, to still *forgive* him—because "after all, he's just a man."

But feminists were in no mood for love and forgiveness in 1968. The taint of their smoldering bras stained the air, and they had their metaphorical straightedge razors out, set on castration. Love was a delusion meant to keep women down, forgiveness was pater-nal Judeo-Christian bull, and consensual sex was a myth because all sex was rape. Tammy Wynette was never going to win over a group of women that wore their politics on their vaginas. But Wynette certainly won over the women of "the silent majority," who made "Stand by Your Man" not only a No. 1 Country hit but a No. 19 Pop hit as well. There were plenty of men in 1968 who needed standing by, and their women knew it.

To be honest, the feminists should've applauded Wynette as a self-made woman.

Virginia Wynette Pugh was born in 1942 in Itawamba County, Mississippi, and weathered the death of her father, abandonment, three horrific marriages (including one to George Jones), poverty, and disillusionment to fulfill her ambition of becoming a country music star. She embodied that myth that sent many a good girl to Nashville, where most of them learned fast that being a good girl wasn't nearly enough. Wynette even co-wrote "Stand by Your Man" with her producer, Billy Sherrill.

I'll even go out on a metaphorical limb here. "Stand by Your

Man" debuted in October 1968, after that summer's violence at the Democratic and Republican national conventions, after the murders of Martin Luther King Jr. and Robert F. Kennedy, as the war in Vietnam tore the United States of America apart. In the fall of 1968, Tammy Wynette wasn't only asking us to love and forgive a mere man. She was asking us to stand by our country . . . to stand by our dear old Uncle Sam.

Shirley Jennings stood by her man, my uncle Lloyd. She was just a kid when they got married, a couple years older than me. But she stood by him.

She stood by him when he drank himself into oblivion.

She stood by him when he chased strange tail.

She stood by him when he hit her—even when her knees buckled.

She stood by him when he wouldn't look for work.

She stood by him when her father, Stubby Gonyer, wanted to beat his sorry ass.

She stood by him until she and three of their children died in a tenement fire in Haverhill, Massachusetts.

And Uncle Lloyd never again, for as long as he lived, found a woman who would stand by him the way Shirley did.

When Hank Williams's fans heard his voice—just on the articulate side of pain, *just*—they knew that the skinny boy born in Mount Olive, Alabama, in 1923, knew feeding the chickens, chopping wood, lugging water (bad back or no bad back), and the sweet reek of cow shit. *Grand Ole Opry* or not, Hank, the son of farmers and loggers, never forgot what it was like to be *poor*. Ol' Hank was a dead man singing. He knew it, and the people who listened to him knew it. But his pure anger, desperation, and loneliness were as bracing as a creek-chilled Bud on a ninety-degree day.

Hank's voice was too country to cross over much when he was alive—though singers like Tony Bennett and Perry Como successfully took his songs pop—but in the decades since his death people from all walks of life have come to appreciate that Hank's was one of those singular American voices that ultimately transcend genre, like the voices of Billie Holiday, Howlin' Wolf, and Elvis.

With "Your Cheatin' Heart," Hank gave his country fans a posthumous gift, a song that let them cry right along with the late Hillbilly Shakespeare. Fueled by booze, pills, and pain, Hank recorded "Your Cheatin' Heart," one of his defining songs, in his last studio session before he was found dead in the backseat of his car on New Year's Day 1953. It was released the month after he died.

"Your Cheatin' Heart" is a good, long cry. Don Helms's steel guitar starts the downpour of tears with three piercing notes that sound like arrows aimed at the heart.

As Hank addresses his faithless lover, he sings out of a profound anguish not only over his woman but over his station in life. Hank's bitter cry is for every shacker who ever had to send his kids to school in bare feet, every man who ever worked himself to death and still died in debt, every woman who ever stood by her man only to end up a honky-tonk angel.

As always, he sings like a man who not only knows that he won't get out of this world alive . . . he won't even get out of this song alive.


All those cheatin' hearts trapped on a trail of tears.

My grandfather Bub Jennings was a trucker who rumbled and rambled as far away as South Carolina—during World War II, he smuggled cigarettes South to North in a chicken truck. When you're on the road like that, there's plenty of opportunity to sample the local produce.

And when you're a trucker's wife, as Laura Jennings was, you can get . . . *restless*, when your husband is away all the time. Grammy Jennings, like Will Rogers, never met a man she didn't like.

Bub and Laura eventually took in a boarder, Frank Nay, who had a steel plate in his skull from the war and lust in his heart that just came natural. Bub and Frank were friends, used to work together at a sawmill over to East Kingston. Wife or no wife, friend or no friend, Frank and Laura carried on when Bub was away. And when Laura gave birth to Uncle Junior—Floyd Earl Jennings Jr., named after Bub—my grandfather took one long look at him and said, "He ain't mine."

After Bub run off, Grammy Jennings set up housekeeping with Frank, tried to raise her three sons, Dana, Lloyd, and Junior. But Frank and Gram's shack bred an epidemic of whiskey and cheating, whose worst symptom was Frank Nay beating up on my grandmother.

But my old man bided his time, grew up, got stronger.

"When Frank was sober, he was so good to me," the old man told me one night as we sat at the kitchen table drinking beer. "I swear he would've given me the shirt off his back if I'd've asked. He treated me like a son. But when he was drinking, he was the most miserable bastard in the world."

So the day came, a few months after my folks got married, that the old man, who was still only seventeen years old, caught Frank slapping his mother.

"I said to him, 'You let go of her, you sonuvabitch.' And he grabbed me and threw me down. And he was just glaring down at me. But his big fucking mistake was letting go of my left arm. I come up and caught him right under the chin, and he just toppled off of me. I got on him and just went to work. Left. Right. His head was snapping back and forth. I just wanted to drive him right into the floor.

"If my buddies hadn't come into the house, I'd a beat him to death. I'd a killed him."

The old man said Frank never touched his mother again. And the morning after Dad pounded the piss out of him, Frank, bruised, limping, and dried out, went up to him and said: "My little boy's come up to be a man."

Johnny Cash was the original burning man, consumed in a conflagration of whiskey, pills, and rage. But it was never clear whether he was trying to kill himself, or just undergo extreme purification.

"Ring of Fire" (1963) was the right song at the right time for Cash, who hadn't had a major hit since 1959. The song was written by Merle Kilgore and June Carter, who was married and struggling to come to terms with her love for another man. That man being Johnny Cash, who was also married, though he'd stopped walking, or even staggering, the line years ago.

Carter was best known as one of the scion-ettes of the Carter Family and a talented comedienne, as they called funny women back then. But there's nothing funny about "Ring of Fire."

This song is about love as a wildfire, about love that may never be reduced to a comfortable smolder. It's the kind of love we all dream about, maybe even crave. But it's also the kind of love that makes us afraid. Even so, "Fire" sizzled its way to No. 1 Country and No. 17 Pop.

Cash sings that he's "bound by a wild desire" that hurls him into a ring of fire. Dante, no doubt, would have approved. This is a love that's going to send him to hell, but angels coo in the background. Or are those moonlighting demons?

By the time Cash shivers out, *"Ohhh, but the fire went wild,"* we know that he's gone over the edge. This better be the love that redeems him. If it isn't, it'll be the love that destroys him. And aren't we all secretly craving that kind of love?

Most folks, in their Hallmark reveries, think of love as heaven, but in "Fire" love is hell. June Carter and Johnny Cash's love for each other incinerated the lives of those around them. It was a love like a fire all shut up in their bones. And like King David's love for Bathsheba, it was a love that was both holy and wrong all at the same time.

# There Stands the Glass

There would be no country music without drinking songs. (Or cheating and prison songs, for that matter. Think of them as the music's Unholy Trinity.)

Seems like someone's always drowning in that Whiskey River, or at least a slough of Schlitz. It was during the 1940s that country established its honky-tonk branch of the family, with the musicians plugging in—talk about *rural electrification*—to be heard over the yawp of the bars and beer halls where they played. It was only natural that they'd start writing and singing songs about a subject that they and their audience perhaps understood better than any other: drinking.

So much to drink, so many songs to lick your lips to while doing it: "Bubbles in My Beer" by Bob Wills, that king of western swing; "Six-Pack to Go" and "The Wild Side of Life" by Hank Thompson and His Brazos Valley Boys; "Swinging Doors" and "The Bottle Let Me Down" by Merle Haggard; and that national anthem of barroom tunes, "There Stands the Glass" by Webb Pierce.

Most country singers and writers knew their way around a fifth of whiskey or two. Suffering from "Hank Williams Syndrome," living lives based on six-strings and six-packs, they'd go roarin' and swarmin' round Nashville stoked on Jack, Bud, and uppers that they called Old Yellers. Guys like Johnny Cash, George Jones, and Roger Miller, and certainly Waylon, Willie, and the boys. In the 1950s and '60s, it seemed Nashville was full of country-boy drunks who knew every honky-tonk, cracker barrel, and broke-down roadhouse in town. And shaving drunk—*ouch!*—was a rite of passage.

The men I grew up among, though, weren't much impressed. They were too busy drinking their own graves—as they nodded knowingly at songs by men doing pretty much the exact same thing they were doing. "I ain't drunk," they'd say, winking at that old blues, "I'm only drinkin'." A lot of them were gone before age fifty.

But that's what working-class men did back then: they *worked*, they *drank*, and they *fucked*. (And I've got a feeling that their lives weren't much different in 1776, or 2006.)

I used to get a ride to work from a guy named Wilfred. At five o'clock of a July morning, he'd ease to the side of the road, tires crackling in the gravel, and there he'd be, a sixteen-ounce can of Bud snugged between his legs—his Ovaltine, he called it—the radio tuned to a country station, WOKQ. On our lunch half hour, Wilfred would lurch and hurry out to his car so he could dismember the six-pack waiting in his Styrofoam cooler. At least he wasn't mixing grapefruit juice and brake fluid the way some desperate drunks did.

So they worked and drank and made their terrified wives and children ride in the pickup truck with them when they were drunk. Some of them laughed—life's a lot funnier when you're drunk—and some of them hit, because life's a lot sadder, too. These were the kinds of men who taught their sons to drive young so the boys could take care of them when they got too blind drunk to even hold the car keys.

That lust for beer and whiskey runs in the blood, runs in the culture. Sometimes it seems that the only thing Prohibition managed to do was spur people to drink even harder. When you're breaking the law, it sure makes your mouth dry.

On Ma's side of the family, Great-Grandpa Ora drank heavy, as did his son Billy. On the old man's side, alcoholism was a DNA inferno, laying waste to too many lives. Dad drank too much when he was young, but managed to pull out of that self-destructive nosedive, and his parents and two brothers were all alcoholics.

Alcoholism is the epidemic I recall best from childhood. All that stood between so many men and women and their cemetery plots was one last bottle—and a good country song.

Just about everyone forgets that Jerry Lee Lewis was one of the best honky-tonk singers of the late 1960s and early '70s, not just a rock'n'roll hellion of the decade before.

They recall his rockabilly conflagrations like "Whole Lotta Shakin' Going On" and "Great Balls of Fire," recall his blond hair, so wavy you could've surfed on it, recall his rampages, indiscretions, and marriage to his cousin. So, yeah, the Ferriday, Louisiana, wild man spent a few years in the wilderness in the 1960s (just like Richard M. Nixon), nearly forgotten but unrepentant—he wasn't kicked out of the Southwestern Bible Institute in Waxahachie, Texas, for splitting hairs over Christian doctrine.

But in 1968, the year he turned thirty-three, he made a comeback with hits like "Another Place, Another Time" and "She Still Comes Around (to Love What's Left of Me)," because country fans forgave him his sins. Most of them understood a feral rural boy like Jerry Lee, men who were constantly seeking forgiveness even as they went right ahead and did the same things over and over that got them into trouble in the first place.

Folks always knew that Lewis could rock, but in 1968 he showed them that he knew how to honky-tonk, too. In "What's Made Milwaukee Famous (Has Made a Loser Out of Me)," Lewis laments that he's lost love and happiness, hearth and home, because he can't quite get himself up off the bar stool. "I know I should go home," he admits, but he can't resist another round.

By the end of the song (written by Glenn Sutton as a nod to the old Schlitz beer slogan), Lewis doesn't sound too broken up, though. In fact, the Killer, still unrepentant, sounds as if he's having a great ol' time pounding on that saloon piano.

Uncle Lloyd, my father's middle brother, always has a cheap beer anchored in his hand: Pabst Blue Ribbon, Schlitz, 'Gansett, Carling's Black Label. And his hair is always just so, dark, slick, ricked country singer high. Maybe it's the hair that gives him his skinny swagger, like a garter snake that thinks it's a timber rattler. He gets beat up all the damn time, pissed-off drunks cutting their fists in his teeth. But he'd rather be busted, hungover, and black-eyed come Sunday morning than not pretend to be a big shot at the Eagles Club on Saturday night.

*"Lloyd, he was loaded."*

Uncle Lloyd, who once tried to fly off the roof of a shed using an umbrella as wings, never escaped sixth grade. He once ate poison ivy (or "ivory," as we said back then), persuaded that doing so could inoculate him against it for good; his throat closed, his eyes swoll shut. And the *itching*? Well, you can imagine. Him and work never see eye to eye—same goes for the truth. No job's good enough for him, and he isn't good enough for no job. He liked everything about being a volunteer fireman—especially the beery weekly meetings—except the fires. He worries an out-of-tune guitar over coffee-brandy breakfasts, and is just good enough at pool and poker to lose money he doesn't have.

*"Lloyd, he was loaded."*

The night that Uncle Lloyd lost his wife, Shirley, and three of their children in a house fire, he'd been drunk and pissed off, had weaseled away from home and to another woman's bed. The front doors never shut tight to their tenement building in Haverhill, that gutted mill town rotting on the Merrimack River in northern Massachusetts. Easy work for the arsonist. That brittle tenement went up like a summer-dry bale of hay. The landlord had spiked the fire exits shut.

I was old enough to wear the white gloves, to help bear my cousins' small coffins. Uncle Lloyd? He was too drunk to walk.

*"Lloyd, he was loaded."*

Seven years after the fire, Uncle Lloyd got a check for $270,000, the lawsuit against the tenement landlord finally settled. The check came on a Wednesday . . . and Lloyd was still drunk on Sunday. "That fire money's going to kill him," my old man said.

*"Lloyd, he was loaded."*

Just one year later, Uncle Lloyd said the fire money was gone. He wouldn't say, "Pissed away," but my old man would. Lloyd was working, grudgingly, at Chick Lumber in Ossipee, New Hampshire.

With that fire money, Uncle Lloyd bought a $600 parrot that then keeled over and died; put $10,000 down on a house, which he then lost; spent $5,000 on a lunch-wagon franchise, then managed to go out of business between Memorial Day and the first of August—the busiest time of the year—not even gasping through till Labor Day; bought thousands of dollars' worth of hard liquor; paid $2,000 for a $100 pickup truck; and threw away $200 on some god-awful painting of the White Mountains, gave it to Grammy Jennings, then told her he wanted it back when she died. Nobody objected.

*"Lloyd, he was loaded."*

Johnny Horton's "Honky Tonk Man" jumps out the speakers like an out-of-control stock car catapulting out of Turn 4 and into the grandstands. It opens with Horton, all bold and brash, bragging, "I'm a honky tonk man, and I can't seem to stop." Within ten seconds, it's clear that he's going to chug your whiskey, steal your woman, and make you like it—then do the same thing to your best pal, too.

Straddling rockabilly and honky-tonk—it could've easily been a hit for Carl Perkins or Jerry Lee Lewis—"Honky Tonk Man" is Horton's crowning moment, his delivery as frisky as Grady Martin's electric guitar and the doghouse bass of Bill Black, moonlighting from Elvis's band.

"Honky Tonk Man," written by Horton, Howard Hausey, and Tillman Franks and recorded in 1956, sizzles with Saturday night anarchy. It's clear from the start that our man has already oiled himself up with a couple whiskeys, and it's also clear that he isn't anywhere near done.

Horton crows that he's living fast and dangerous, paying his respects to Faron Young's hit "Live Fast, Love Hard, Die Young" (1955)—as in: "I wanna live fast, love hard, die young, and leave a bee-yoo-ti-ful memory."

Horton then reminds us that even though it's the Eisenhower years he has plenty of company, and that all it takes is "a purty little gal and a jug of wine" to make for a honky-tonk mind.

Horton was born in Los Angeles in 1925 and died in a car crash in 1960. "Honky Tonk Man" was his first hit and most enduring performance. He's better known for historical sagas like "The Battle of New Orleans" and "Sink the Bismarck," but those songs pale before the frenzy of "Honky Tonk Man."

By the time he begs, screams, and shouts to his mama that he wants to come home, it's as if he's speaking for each and every drunk and broke man in America.

A sweaty Schlitz tucked in his crotch, my old man's buddy Rick casts his convertible down crack-thick back roads. Dad's already attacked his third Bud. All those dead brown soldiers clink and clatter, clack and bicker, rattle and rollick on the back floor.

We're supposed to be ransacking Thomas's Junkyard, scrounging brake shoes for the old man's shitbox. But that was before six-pack seduction, before August's ragtop gust. We ain't going to no junkyard. I'm getting schooled in chucking wives and shucking kids, ducking the devils at home stacked like so much cordwood.

Drinking and driving: Pickpocket Road and Pow-Wow River . . . Tippy-Toe Lane and Rowe's Five Corners.

Driving and drinking: Tricklin' Falls and Bud Cheney's mill . . . Spofford's Point and Uncle Dead's hill.

We ramble toward the rusted-out stop sign at the New Boston Road train tracks (no gates, no lights, no crossbucks), where drunk kids gamble their lives against the night freights.

Rick, all gravel and Camels, rasps: "Hear anything?"

"Nope."

And Rick guns it, runs it, that stop sign, that convertible thudding, shuddering over steel, tie, and spike. The men crow, crocked, drunk on brew, sun, and luck.

I'm the only one *shaking*, shivering on that hot, lost August afternoon.

Country music never shook its roots in the traveling tent and medicine shows of the nineteenth and early twentieth centuries—

vaudeville on wheels for the sticks. A tent show was never complete without a few hick comics and comedy skits, and that comic impulse survived into commercial country music.

Banjo players—Grandpa Jones, Stringbean Akeman, Uncle Dave Macon—were always encouraged to cut up. Then there were the straight-ahead comedians like Minnie Pearl ("How-deeee! I'm jest so proud to be here!"), Whitey Ford—the Duke of Paducah—and the blackface team of Lasses and Honey. Their lineage runs directly to the long-running TV show *Hee Haw*, on to Jeff Foxworthy and the Blue Collar Comedy Tour.

Country fans have always been in the mood for a good, funny tune. Songs like "A Boy Named Sue" by Johnny Cash (setting aside his Man in Black persona for a few laughs and a huge hit), "One's on the Way" by Loretta Lynn (written by the humorist Shel Silverstein, as was "Sue"), and Little Jimmy Dickens's "May the Bird of Paradise Fly Up Your Nose."

You might be broke, the landlord on your ass, and the pickup truck stuck in second gear, but that doesn't mean you can't take time out for a laugh or two—maybe especially in that situation. So, along with its songs of love, God, and murder, country always served up a side order of songs to laugh with.

Not surprisingly, some of them focused on drinking, like George Jones's "White Lightning" (1959) and Roger Miller's "Chug-A-Lug" (1964).

Jones is revered for his deep country soul, but he has a sense of humor, too, as revealed in songs like "Who Shot Sam," "Love Bug," and "White Lightning," which was written by the Big Bopper, J. P. Richardson, who died in the airplane crash in 1959 that also killed Buddy Holly and Ritchie Valens.

"Lightning" starts at a gallop, with Buddy Killen on bass, Floyd Jenkins on 'lectric guitar, and Pig Robbins on barrelhouse piano, and never lets up. The song's so rowdy, it could've been recorded by Jones's rockabilly doppelgänger, Thumper Jones.

The tale takes place in North Carolina, "way back in the hills," and as Jones sings of G-men, T-men, and Revenooers looking for ol' Pappy's still, the music evokes images of some good ol' boy—and future stock car driver—on a 'shine run with the gov'mint on his tail. Meanwhile, back at the farm, faces turn blue and folks moan as they hit the ground after they take a shot of backwoods heat: "Mighty, mighty pleasin', Pappy's corn squeezin'."

"White Lightning" is a tongue-in-cheek romp, but Miller's "Chug-A-Lug" is, like so many of Miller's tunes, a sadder and darker song, but dressed up in novelty drag.

Everyone in Nashville in the 1960s thought Roger Miller was one funny sonuvabitch, especially when he stayed awake for days on end stoked on pills. He got nicknamed the Wild Child, and referred to himself as Jekyll and Hammerstein. Miller became famous for songs like "Dang Me" and "King of the Road," but like the best humorists he's as serious as a scorpion in your morning boots.

"Chug-A-Lug" is a drinking coming-of-age story that makes you laugh till you cry. The tune starts with three boozy whoops as we find out how the kid became father to the drunken man. He discovers "grape wine in a Mason jar," tells how he and his buddies "uncovered a covered-up moonshine still" on a 4-H field trip to a farm, and recalls how he "got snuck in for my first taste of sin" at a jukebox and sawdust honky-tonk.

All the while, he reminds us that he's just a kid by singing the refrain, "Burns your tummy, don't ya know."

It all sounds funny, but it ain't. Not one damn bit. It's the upbeat lament of a drunk remembering how all that sorry drinking started in the first place.

———

Things *are* funnier when you're drunk—unless you're one of those morose drunks no one wants to be around—and funny things happen when you're drunk.

One of my enduring memories is of the old man hissing open a beer or three out to the porch on hot summer nights and telling me and Sis and whoever else might be listening stories about his life. The old man's a great country storyteller—he understands that a poor man can at least own his stories—and he has a Twain-like knack for fashioning life's miseries into comedy.

Like the time he come home pie-eyed, stumbled up the stairs to his room in the dark, and went to flop on his bed. Problem was, Grammy Jennings, in one of her manic drunken fits, had moved all his furniture around. When Dad went to flop, he dropped . . . all the way to the floor. His nose didn't break, but—*Jesus!*—did it bleed.

Or when him and Eddy Mahone—yup, you guessed it, they weren't quite "silver," as they would've said—got ticked off at the local skunk that kept raiding the bags of junk in the shed, and they shot him with a .22. But no one in the neighborhood would speak to them till they carted that skunk down to Cedar Swamp and gave the reeking bastard a proper burial. "I thought that stink was going to peel my skin," Dad used to say.

Then there was the Saturday night him and his buddies stole the chickens. Whenever he told the story in front of Grammy Jennings, she'd just smile and sit there and rock. (She'd calmed down some by then.) I'll let the old man tell this one:

"We're all loaded, and it's like two or three in the morning and we're driving by this farmhouse in Hampstead and we decide to steal some chickens for no good reason. Somehow we got all those bastards into burlap sacks without waking nobody up, and we throw 'em in the trunk of the car.

"Next morning, I'm listening to the radio and the news says the cops're looking for whoever stole a bunch of chickens from Hampstead's chief of police. Well, we sure as hell knew who those stupid assholes were. It was us!

"We got those chickens out the shed and started wringing necks and plucking feathers—you never heard such a racket. And Ma spent all day Sunday cooking up every last one of those fuckers in her skillet.

"We must've ate chicken for a month."

Where I come from, a lot of the kids were whiskey babies, beer babies. You know the scenario: After a big night out raising hell with the guys, hubby lumbers in at two, three in the morning and decides he needs a little pussy nightcap, insists on his marital rights. His breath is rank, his hands heavy, and he's got that malignant smile on his face. And contraception? Yeah, right.

Well, in "Don't Come Home A-Drinkin' (with Lovin' on Your Mind)" (1966), Loretta Lynn draws the line in the bedroom. And if you ever want to get *any* again, pal, you better walk it.

By the time Lynn wrote this song with her sister Peggy Sue, she was fed up. She'd gotten married at thirteen (no, not to Jerry Lee Lewis), had four kids by the time she was eighteen, and was a grandmother at twenty-nine with six children of her own. She knew what it was like to be left home crying and lonely with the kids while her husband went off carousing, knew what it was like to be a glorified sperm depository.

And she's sick and tired of it. "Then you come in a-kissin' on me," she complains, "it happens every time." Pretty radical stuff for 1966, when most women were still expected to assume the position on command.

That's why rural, working-class women loved the Belle of Butcher Holler, Kentucky. In feisty songs like "You Ain't Woman

Enough," "Fist City," and "Your Squaw Is on the Warpath," she articulated their feelings and didn't take any shit. (And Lynn sang a hell of a lot better than Betty Friedan.)

In real life, though, Lynn's husband did beat her. All you need to know about the guy is that he had two nicknames, Moonie—short for Moonshine—and Doolittle, because that's what he did, "do little."

It was Lynn's loyal female fans who sent "Don't Come Home A-Drinkin' " to the top of the country charts, even if the country disc jockeys—mostly male—didn't much like the message.

It was during the mid-1960s that Lynn discovered she could fashion the personal mythology of her life into songs that rang true for her sisters out in the country and to other women, too. The songs were like blue-collar romance novels, hick-chick lit for the masses.

We're talking drinking. But it's really about hunger.

We cannot escape the hard hungers of childhood. At best, they shadow us into adulthood. At worst, they shred our souls: the hunger for love . . . for approval . . . for money.

Sometimes we're just plain hungry, because there was never enough to eat. Even as a grown man, Dad sometimes ate like the starving boy he'd been, sometimes too impatient, even, to cook what he ate: Slim Jims, bologna, and raw hot dogs; frozen Charleston Chews, raw potatoes, and radishes plucked right out the ground.

Hungry, too, for the father he never really had, always calling older men "Pop."

Beer will fill you up for a while, take the edge off your hunger, blunt your anger. It doesn't even matter if the wife pours your beer down the sink (you can always buy more); doesn't matter if the wife locks you out (you can always bust down the three doors into the house); doesn't matter if you find yourself so drunk at two in the morning that you're slugging a cedar-post clothesline.

Doesn't matter, because the bottle—so round, so firm, so fully packed—will always love you.

"There Stands the Glass" (1953) by Webb Pierce opens with a slurred steel guitar played by Jimmy Day that is as warped and fuzzy as being drunk itself. Then Pierce's pained tenor, "There stands the glass that will ease all my pain," sung with a fatalism that actually means "There stands my tombstone." Pierce, a farm boy born in West Monroe, Louisiana, in 1921, had thirteen No. 1 hits in the 1950s, and "There Stands the Glass," written by Audrey Greisham, Russ Hull, and Mary Jean Shurtz, was one of his biggest, sitting atop the country charts for twelve weeks—quite a bender. People in the industry told Pierce not to record it, saying that he'd alienate his core audience. But he reasoned that drinking was something that "80 percent of the people do," and he went ahead and recorded it anyway.

Pierce's instincts were right. The best country songs hold a mirror up to the listener. And when Uncle Lloyd, for example, who favored coffee-brandy breakfasts and Pabst Blue Ribbon suppers, listened to Pierce ache through "There Stands the Glass," it seemed as if his good buddy Webb sang his life. In less than three brutal minutes, Pierce captures a lifetime spent battling the bottle . . . and losing. And as Uncle Lloyd bowed to the song's spell, projected his life into it, the song owned him, and he owned the song. Sure, it belonged to Webb Pierce, but it also belonged to Lloyd Jennings.

The tune got banned by some radio stations—not that Uncle Lloyd cared—but it was destined to become a jukebox staple. Pierce said later that "it doesn't have a lot of moral. I was just singing about what people do."

And what a lot of people do, Pierce knew, is drink.

"There Stands the Glass" is pushed along by a nice little shuffle, a crying fiddle, and Floyd Cramer's saloon-style piano straight out of the Western picture show of your choice. But it's Pierce's singing—a tenor tight as a noose—that makes this song so chilling. When Pierce moans, "It's my first one today," you know it won't be his last, not by a long shot. He plans to spend his day playing Russian roulette with the bottle. He claims that a woman has driven him to drink, but there's an iceberg of woe hidden in Pierce's voice—you can imagine the man licking his lips. Sure, his honey is gone, but there's also the shit job at the local shoe shop and his scars from World War II that are still red and raw. He was good enough to help keep the world safe for democracy, but he wasn't good enough to get a job that'd let him buy that little place down by the river he'd always wanted, find a good woman, and start a family.

The steel keeps slurring, the fiddle keeps crying: "Bartender, set up another one."

# Don't Get Above Your Raisin'

Maybe the greatest—and most coddled—American myth is that we live and thrive in a classless society. The party line, and the indoctrination starts in first grade, is that no matter what station in life you're born to, through pluck, hard work (and maybe just a little luck), you, too, can become president of these United States, or at least of the local Rotary Club. That just because you make a living shoveling out privies doesn't mean you're not just as good as the chairman of your local bank.

Well, *bullshit*—and country music seconds that notion.

Americans love to have red-white-and-blue orgasms over our "classless society." Of course, most those people have never *had* to pick the town dump, never known the shame of using food stamps (and it *does* burn like shame), or never put off going to the doctor because they didn't have the money.

It's no shock that many of the same record companies that specialized in "race" records from the 1920s to the 1940s also specialized in "hillbilly" music. After all, the well-fed record company executives reasoned, the white niggers need their tunes, too.

Until the 1970s, when Nashville gave it totally up in pursuit of that harlot in gingham, the Crossover Hit, country's unspoken sub-text was always class, because it was music meant for poor working hicks and rednecks; the sad, blighted days of the Urban Cowboy were still a ways off. As with blacks and postwar R&B, country hadn't originally been meant to be listened to outside the community of rural, working-class whites.

Still, a good song is a good song, and it wasn't unheard of for country songs to break through to the pop charts. Songs like Tennessee Ernie Ford's "Sixteen Tons," Johnny Cash's "I Walk the Line," and Marty Robbins's "El Paso" reminded white middle-class radio listeners that this was a big nation with a range of voices. Reminded them that a slice of country ham slipped in between the white bread of Pat Boone and Patti Page tasted pretty good. One of the beauties of the old Top 40 radio format at its best was that it served as a cultural melting pot—helped along, of course, by those ingredients that transcend race and class: bribes, booze, and babes.

Amid the doo-woppers and the R&B boppers, the pretty teenage girls and even prettier teenage boys, the rockabillies and the British Invaders, and Elvis, who was a category unto himself, you had the orchestral pop of Lawrence Welk and Ferrante & Teicher; the Rat Pack savoir faire of Sinatra, Dean Martin, and Sammy Davis Jr.; the Latino rock of Malo, Ritchie Valens, and Question Mark and the Mysterians; the raw Southern soul of James Brown, Percy Sledge, and Clarence Carter, complemented by their slicker cousins at Motown; the comedy of Pigmeat Markham and Cheech & Chong; and the occasional country hit by the likes of Jim Reeves and Johnny Horton, Eddy Arnold and Glen Campbell, Tammy Wynette and Skeeter Davis.

Still, country was originally the music of the permanent poor white underclass—both those who had stayed in the country and those who had strayed to the city. It didn't trust hippies, foreign cars, or Philadelphia lawyers. It didn't trust the gov'mint, Gloria Steinem, or New York City. And, let's be honest here, country music never trusted education. When most your relations can barely read and write, it's a reproach to have your nose stuck in a book all the time—the bookworm's version of flipping them the bird.

A lot of the anger in this nation in the 1960s grew out of that tension between people wanting to get ahead and people knowing their place. Teenagers and college students realized that they didn't have to shrug and be programmed for adulthood like good little automatons, decided they could defy a war cooked up by their parents and grandparents. Women began to understand that they didn't need to spend their lives under their man's thumb—no matter what Mick Jagger sang. Blacks cried out and *demanded* their fair share of the American Dream.

That cultural shift was hard on working-class whites. We grew up constantly being told not to "get too big for our britches." Where other groups ached for their children to build better lives, poor whites, all too often, felt that what'd been good enough for them, *by Gawd*, was good enough for their kids. The worst insult that my old lady relatives could levy on some poor soul was, "Oh, that one, he's *real* independent." In their eyes, and in those of so many like them, the worst thing you could ever do was try to get above your raisin'.


Way out in the country, you could drink like a school of fish, rollick and frolic with loose women, and even wind up in the clink, and most folks would still forgive you. But if you tried acting like someone you weren't, that was something else again, as Lester Flatt, Earl Scruggs, and their Foggy Mountain Boys make clear in "Don't Get Above Your Raisin' " (1951).

In his mellow, setting-round-the-cracker-barrel voice, Flatt, who wrote the song with Scruggs, complains about a sweet ol' gal who "ain't what she used to be," who's gotten a little too "high-headed." All that really means is that the poor woman has looked hard into the eyes of her current beau, and all she can see in her future is her mother's past of being tied down to kitchen and bedroom as half-a-dozen brats caper in the dooryard. That flash of insight has made her reconsider the direction of her life.

You see, folks who knew you back when don't like to see you acting as if you're better than they are, see it as some kind of repudiation on your part. So, even if you've worked hard to get ahead, you better still act poor, because they all knew you "when you didn't have nothin' " and were lucky to have a pot to piss in—and they're more than a little happy to remind you of that bitter fact. Some country fans never forgave Eddy Arnold for trading in his "Tennessee Plowboy" persona more than fifty years ago for urbane crooning, tuxedos, and exclusive engagements in Vegas. *Who the hell does that boy think he is?*

Bluegrass is the perfect musical setting for "Raisin'," because it's a style of country where sonic innovation and conservative sentiment rub up against each other and make the sparks fly. (Imagine if, for example, Condoleezza Rice had invented free jazz or, for that matter, if Coltrane were secretary of state.)

Scruggs's seductive banjo urges us to stay down on the farm, sneak into Daddy's barn, and smoke some corn silk, while Chubby Wise's fiddle—no question that it's acting way above its raisin'—struts and wiggles its behind throughout the song.

Flatt sings, "You need not hold your head so high," but the unspoken lyric is that if you do, someone will be glad to take it off for you. That's why so many country people—and whites living in the cities and suburbs, too—despised Muhammad Ali in the 1960s. It *was* racism. But it was also, in their eyes, that Ali thought he was "too good" to join the Army, that he was "too good" to be Cassius Clay anymore. People didn't want Ali to forget what he used to be.

They wanted him to remain "the good boy" from Louisville, Kentucky, who brought his nation glory in 1960 by winning a gold medal at the Rome Olympics.

(Not to soft-pedal here racism of the Northern variety, my great-aunt Helen, who liked to say that her sister Lee kept her cast-iron stove "shinier than a nigger's eyeball," did, after all, vote for that archsegregationist George Wallace in the 1968 presidential election—and she wasn't close to being alone in my hometown.)

As far as knowing your place, you need to know that out in the country the day's second meal is called dinner, and the third is supper. If you start calling dinner lunch, and supper dinner, the home folks (and Flatt and Scruggs) will know right away that you've become a lost cause.

Some people didn't even like it if *your* children got above *your* raisin'. In rural New Hampshire in the 1950s, an eighth-grade education was still something to be proud of. It meant you could read and write, and that you probably had more schooling than your parents had managed to grab ahold of. Both my parents graduated eighth grade, but high school was beyond them.

Me, being the desperate and hungry oldest child, went and overdid things. I was first in Sanborn Regional High School's class of 1975, and the week my picture ran in the local paper, my old man bumped into a guy named Buddy Post whom he'd gone to grammar school with.

"I saw your boy's picture in the paper," Buddy says to the old man. "So, Dana, where'd he get all his brains?"

My father says that Buddy's lucky that he didn't deck him right then and there, in Lafayette's grocery.

"Coat of Many Colors" (1971) is Dolly Parton's supernal hymn to class and poverty. If she had never written or sung another word, we would remember her for this song, in which she shreds the veils and reveals the tears in things.

Backed by a churchy organ and a guitar that's Jesus gentle, Parton tells the story of how her mother sewed her a winter coat stitched together from multicolored rags because it was "way down in the fall" and frost brittled the grass. (When you're poor, it always seems as if it's way down in the fall.) But when the little girl gets to school, the other kids make fun of her and her homemade backwoods coat (and are probably secretly relieved that it's not them who got stuck wearing that *hideous* thing).

With "patches on my britches" and holes in the soles of her shoes, Parton is almost an Appalachian prophetess here. She teaches us how poor families had to cling to each other to suffer the cold outside world, how they had to depend on God and fierce love to fill the holes in their spiritual soles.

And like Joseph in the Holy Bible, who also wore a well-known coat of many colors, Parton pulled her family up out of poverty and hunger, through her heart, talent, and hard work.

"Coat of Many Colors," written in 1969, also speaks to the class divisions in Nashville, both in and out of country music, though Parton probably never meant it that way. Nashville's elite never loved country music until it started behaving like a castrated conglomerate and not like a bunch of drunken shit-kickers come to town to raise hell of a Saturday night. As Colin Escott wrote in his biography of Hank Williams, "The hillbilly music business was poison to the city's image of itself as the self-proclaimed Athens of the South."

The Nashville snobs couldn't tolerate a country star like Webb Pierce, with his silver-dollar-encrusted convertibles and guitar-shaped swimming pools. Couldn't stomach the country boys who found that Nashville was about all the city they could handle.

Then, in the early 1960s, in the wake of the first wave of rock 'n' roll, something strange and unexpected happened—a lot of country music got a *twang*-ectomy. Trying to avoid getting steamrollered by rock 'n' roll, and tired of its own hillbilly stigma, country music started sweeping the true country grit from its plain kitchen. Succumbing to class envy, Nashville record producers like Chet Atkins and Owen Bradley started varnishing songs with strings and pop choruses, giving rise to "the Nashville Sound" and, later, "country-politan." Always defensive about his role in taking country up-town—hell! Eddy Arnold was right after all—Atkins told the writer Michael Streissguth, "I was trying to keep my damn job and sell records."

They did sell records, plenty of them good ones. Patsy Cline's smoky voice, for example, was well served by a plush bed of strings and perfectly pop choruses. Then again, two of the biggest country stars of the 1960s were Buck Owens and Merle Haggard, who looked to their honky-tonk roots in Bakersfield, California, to keep their raw edges intact.

Which brings us back to "Coat of Many Colors," which, even in 1971, sounded pretty damn retro but was a surprise hit. This was when Nashville pined for crossover hits and a record could be dismissed as "too country"—and here's where we get to the cold, hard facts of country music life around 1970:

Dolly Parton, one of twelve children raised in a poverty-stricken holler, writes and records a stunning song about how other poor country kids jeered at her, just another poor country kid, over the coat her mama made her with so much love. Stone country fans responded to the song, but you can be sure that the denizens of

Music Row and Nashville, who'd become sophisticated enough to ruin themselves on cocaine instead of moonshine, snickered at how "country" Parton was—country kids laughing at another country kid again.

No wonder Parton went pop and Hollywood, and never looked back for decades as she left her core country audience behind until she went bluegrass in the late 1990s.

When I was a kid, Sis, the old man, and I would sit out to the front steps and watch the cars swoosh by on Route 125 the same way you'd laze around and watch the Pow-Wow River roll past: poor-people entertainment. When I think back on that road gazing, I realize we weren't just watching cars go by; we were watching prosperity pass us by, too.

When you don't have much, entertainment is where you find it: the wicked waltz of a blizzard or rain sifting on the leaves . . . the Boston & Maine freights groaning and grumbling north . . . a woodpecker's telegraph taps and the mighty gospel chorus of peepers and bullfrogs down back in the marsh. That was all country music, too.

A dead deer could also afford real entertainment. There's a photograph of my mother and she's, oh, seven or eight years old, and she's sitting on a deer that's been propped up on a couple sawhorses. Bambi appears to stare straight ahead at the camera, its stiff front legs splayed. Ma stares at the camera, too, her head wrapped in a country-girl kerchief, and a small smile sweetens her face—it's not every day that you get to ride a deer like a pony at the annual Independence Day carnival on Kingston Plains.

The Christmas wreaths that my great-grandparents used to make and sell hang on the barn behind my mother. So, besides bringing a moment's joy, that deer also means there'll be fresh venison for Christmas.

American popular culture has always had a love-hate relationship with the American Indian. On one end of the spectrum, we have the "noble savages" who helped save the Pilgrims from starving to death—thanks, Squanto, old pal. On the other, we have the "bloodthirsty savages" who raped pioneer women and killed babies, with no gray area—and little truth—in between.

There's not much talk about how the United States of America committed genocide against its Native Americans then herded the survivors to reservations. The cultural cover-up started early with the cowboy-and-Indian penny dreadfuls of the nineteenth century. And for much of the twentieth century, the myth of our triumph over the cunning Indian was a staple of pulp magazines, movies, paperback originals, radio, and TV. We spent a solid hundred years "-izing" the Indian. Demonizing, romanticizing, trivializing.

Country music certainly couldn't resist. Hank Williams's "Kaw-Liga," about a love-smitten wooden Indian, spent thirteen weeks at No. 1 in 1953. Even more unexpected, Johnny Preston's sappy, soppy, but catchy "Running Bear," about another Indian love affair, lingered on the pop charts for twenty-seven weeks in 1959 and 1960, and even hit the top spot.

That's why Johnny Cash's "Ballad of Ira Hayes" was such a bracing antidote back in 1964. In his bottomless pit of a voice, Cash tells the tragic tale of Ira Hayes, a Pima Indian who was among the men who raised Old Glory on Iwo Jima in World War II. The song, written by the folksinger Peter La Farge, opens and closes with taps, reminding us that Ira was indeed a Marine hero, one of just twenty-seven men who survived that brutal battle. But in the end Ira is just a "whiskey-drinkin' Indian" who can't get along after the war, a good man who can't reconcile the medals on his chest with his life on the margins or the hunger in his soul. A man who ended up drowned in two inches of water.

This is a subversive song, given that most of Cash's audience was still made up of country boys in thrall to and thrilled by old-fashioned tales about cowboys and Indians. Sounding as if he's singing from a crypt—there's so much echo—Cash makes his anger and disgust palpable as he spits out the lyrics. "Ira Hayes" dovetails with Cash's own class rage and his mission to make us remember the downtrodden, like the convicts he sang to at Folsom Prison and San Quentin.

Cash tells us that the ghost of the alcoholic Hayes "is lyin' thirsty in the ditch where Ira died."

When it comes to the history of North America, we need to remember that we're the blood-lusting savages. And Ira Hayes? Poor Ira, he was just thirsty.

When school lets out for summer, and it don't get dark till late, us kids get to run barefoot. It's only the kids in town who have to wear shoes all the time. Barefoot, a kind of reckless poor-kid freedom, even though we know that shed deadfalls, the puckabrush, and dusk's thickets are pocked, flush with punk, ant-gutted boards and unlocked nails: head, shank, tip.

Tenpenny nails, rust-red nails, panel-pin nails, and blood-stained nails; finishing nails, lost-head nails, tar-paper nails, and ring-shank nails; double-head nails, crooked nails, drywall nails, and lockjaw nails.

The beer-sweat men flaunt scored, thick-soled workboots and don't give a flying fuck. Sink a nail, pluck it out, and walk on; the women skirt those whetted paths. And who the hell has the time to yank nails out old gray boards, buck all those ghosts to the g.d. dump? Tell me, *who has the time?*

But us kids barrelhouse on, running, *always running*, thorn-scorned, prickaburrs thick in our hair, our knees wicked creeks of blood, in brazen bare feet, or maybe saltine-thin sneakers. And we never look down, will not admit that this world is meant for looking down.

If we get bit by a nail, or worse, there ain't much sympathy, no such thing as rushing to the doctor. You better be bleeding a g.d. river if you think you're going to the doctor's. So we shrug, live with it:

Scabs and scrapes, mashed and bloody knees, bumps and lumps, gashes and slashes, cats' claws and dogs' teeth, jagged glass, ragged steel, knots, knobs, and shiners. Summer-cured skin pricked and pulped, bruised and bit, pebbled and gnawed, burned and nicked. And all the grown-ups can say is, "Oh, you'll live."

Wounds, grim or mild, steeped in hydrogen peroxide, boiled by witch hazel, swathed and swiped in iodine, raw pork clasping the fiercer insults, cigarette smoke blown into aching ears to soothe them: "Oh, you'll live."

Most of it our own damn fault: Frustrated fishhooks seeking eyes, spilling from maples, ladders, and haylofts. Swings in the teeth, swings back the head, bare feet blistered on baking blacktop, barreling into barbwire buried bushes deep: "Oh, you'll live."

But one spring, my right knee bloats, odd, lopsided, like an old, flat football. It's a tumor, the doctors say, we'll cut it out . . . then we'll see. And nobody says nothin'.


Even in Merle Haggard's sure hands, "Son of Hickory Holler's Tramp" (1968) is a strange song. Written by Dallas Frazier, one of Nashville's most successful songwriters ("There Goes My Everything," "Elvira"), it weaves together social commentary, the titillation of implied illicit sex, a whore as heroine, and ends on a triumphal Hallmark moment.

The plot is pure backwoods Movie of the Week: the philandering husband abandons his wife and fourteen (!) children, and when Mama looks at all those hungry, uncomprehending eyes, she just sighs and turns to prostitution; given those fourteen kids, you could argue that she just goes ahead and does what she already knows how to do.

But the real indictment here is aimed at the upstanding neighbors who sneer at the fallen woman, who don't lift one finger to help the destitute family, to help her rise from her fall. Haggard tenderly explores the tension between the looked-down-upon and those who do the looking down, knowing that it's always easier for people to scorn and gossip than to lend a hand.

At song's end, we learn that Mama has died, but that each Sunday her grave is graced by "the fresh bouquet of fourteen roses," and a card that reads, "The greatest mom on earth." You can start sobbing anytime you'd like.

"The Son of Hickory Holler's Tramp" opens with a gospel-like chorus. And that's appropriate, because by the end of the song we understand that Mama wasn't just a mere fallen woman . . . but a fallen angel, too.

I suppose that if you spend too much time at the town dump and in the junkyards, some folks are going to look down on you, stare at you like you're ripe roadkill blood-stuck to the double yellow line out to Route 125. Well, we did, and they did.

I come from a long, proud line of dump-pickers on both sides the family. Great-Grandpa Ora was the king, though, master of the dump. I firmly believe that the happiest day of his life was when he was hired as caretaker of Kingston's town dump. He'd leave early in the morning with his wheezing Ford pickup empty, then come home at the end of the day with it full. It'd be stuffed with warped lumber and copper wire, dinette-set amputees and roofless bird-houses, fractured TV sets and bent and dented washing machines.

He even maintained the old George family dump down back of his place, partly, I suspect, because he didn't want to be too far away from the things that he'd decided to throw out. You never knew when you might change your mind.

The dump was also a good place to hide from the women, hide from the blame and burdens at home. The smoke was bitter and the wheeling seagulls shrill, but the beer was cold and the rats game—"Did you see that fucka jump!"—as the men scuffed through the garbage, the .22-caliber rifles loose in their hands. Wasn't no one going to come looking for us at the dump.

Junkyards, those Detroit boneyards, were another good place to hide, to pretend to be getting something done. Junkyards were a feast of steel, a fairy-tale world where the very earth itself bristled with rust and shattered glass, where oil and gasoline stained the ground. It was mysterious, too, to be where cars went to die. There was no doubting the afterlife at the junkyard.

I'd wander around as Dad and his buddies—drinking again, *always* drinking—explored the canyons of twisted and tortured cars stacked one atop the other, looking for radiators and carburetors, mufflers and starters, hoods, doors, and windshields. Looking mostly, though, for relief from their workaday lives.

Right on the very first page of her autobiography, Jeannie C. Riley describes the night she recorded "Harper Valley PTA," her monster breakthrough hit from 1968:

On this hot, humid July evening in 1968, the entire nation was in turmoil. Men were being killed in Vietnam and no one really knew why.

College students were demonstrating on the campuses.

There had been riots in Detroit and Watts.

My marriage was heading for the rocks.

I was angry and confused.

I was a small-town girl from Anson, Texas, who had been swallowed alive by Music City.

Working as a secretary and demo singer, Riley had crept into Nashville, like hundreds (if not thousands) of other pretty young women, nurturing a dream of becoming a country music star—of owning the stage of the Ryman Auditorium where the *Grand Ole Opry* held sway—cradling that dream the way you would a foundling left on your front doorstep. But for Riley, Nashville had been not Music City but Sin City. She'd spent her time there getting hit on and much worse.

By the time she gets to record "Harper Valley PTA," she's pissed, she's fed up, and she sings the song as if it's a shotgun aimed at the heads of Nashville's movers and shakers.

"Harper Valley" is one of the songwriter Tom T. Hall's masterpieces, a gem of economy and power as he scrutinizes hypocrisy and lust through the prism of one small town. Sherwood Anderson would've smiled and approved.

The PTA has scolded the young widow Johnson for "drinking and running 'round with men and going wild." But the PTA didn't count on Ms. Johnson—let's call her "Ms.," she *is* a proto-feminist after all—to confront them and to detail each member's taste in, if not lust for, booze and sex. Ms. Johnson, a lonely, lovely blue-collar woman, has no patience for their Peyton Place bullshit, no patience for a town ripe with gossips, busybodies, and holier-than-thous. No patience for a town like Nashville.

Neither does Jeannie C. Riley. She rips into the song like a Fury, and Jerry Kennedy's Dobro tears hypocritical flesh the whole way through. There are none of Nashville's artificial sweeteners here. Riley seethes, her voice dripping with venom, sarcasm, and rage. She's addressing not only the PTA but the whole Nashville music establishment and all the good ol' boys (and the bad ol' boys) who have trouble keeping it in their pants.

"Harper Valley" struck an immediate nerve; it was a pop hit on merit, without sucking up to pop styles. In America in the summer of 1968, that riot-smitten Summer of No Love, hypocrisy hung heavy in the air, the way smog smothered Los Angeles. "Harper Valley PTA" sold 1.75 million copies in two weeks (it eventually sold 5 million copies) and went No. 1 Pop, only to be nudged aside by the Beatles' "Hey Jude," as an oblivious Nashville celebrated Riley as its latest country-and-western Cinderella.

Nashville adored its hick Cinderellas in the 1960s, those success stories of the barefoot and poignant variety: Loretta Lynn, Dolly Parton, Tammy Wynette, who, before she became a star, was a divorced beautician with three kids and living in a government housing project.

But Riley was a bit different from her sisters in *twang*: this Cinderella wore miniskirts and go-go boots.

# Sing Me Back Home

The cost of progress is the loss of Eden.

You can take that better-paying factory job in some faraway Emerald City, but you won't be able to pick the wild strawberries down back in the marsh no more and pop them still alive into your mouth. You can get a black-and-white TV (complete with snow and rabbit ears) from Sears, but you stop picking git-tar with your buddies, and don't shoot the shit with your neighbors as much as you used to.

So many country songs go straight to the heart of the American Ache, that lust for the long-lost past, for the homeplace of blessed memory—no matter how harsh and unforgiving it was. Songs like Bill Monroe's "I'm on My Way to the Old Home" and Bobby Bare's "Detroit City," Loretta Lynn's "Coal Miner's Daughter" and Merle Haggard's "Sing Me Back Home." Country music's first commercial hit, Fiddlin' John Carson's "Little Old Log Cabin in the Lane" (1923, Okeh), wrestles with that loss.

That ache informs the lives of country singers from 1950 to 1970, most of them just ordinary country kids who found themselves living in the big city, living in Nashville, traveling the nation, and pining for the good old days . . . when, yes, Ms. Parton, times were bad.

When you spurn the country for the suburbs, for the city, you end up shocked by what you yearn after: the sickle stars and the slightest sliver of moon on a winter's night . . . a grain silo, green paint peeling . . . cobalt-blue darning needles spinning their compulsories on a glassy pond. And dirt roads: Bog roads and dust roads, washboard and ocher clay, mud-up-to-the-hub roads. Ruts and gullies, troughs and trenches, old rugged roads on which you can bear more easily the cross of your life.

I inherited the ache from my old man. Even in his early twenties, Dad hungered after his own good old days. This is a man who came of age in a shack that had no indoor plumbing and that spread its rickety legs to every storm that blew through; whose father whipped him and eventually abandoned the family; who worked in the woods before he was ten years old. Yeah, the good old goddamn days.

But, being a proper country stoic, my old man hardly ever dwelled on the evil done him as a kid. What he missed as an adult was his utter freedom (when Ma and Pa are drinking and whoring, ain't no one paying real close attention to you), his crazy-ass buddies, and how poor people used to look out for each other because it was the right thing to do—and if they didn't look after each other, no one else was going to do it. Then there was racing rust-ravaged Fords and Chevys up and down the power-line road; running bloody boxing matches out to Cedar Swamp; setting the town dump on fire just for the fine hell of it; getting drunk beyond reason.

Those testosterone-suffused good old days, when there weren't even nine hundred people in town, when there was no shortage of woods and fields to light out for, when the chief of police would get into your face so close that you could smell the bacon and eggs he'd had for breakfast. But the chief'd never dream of putting no wild kids in jail. Wild or not, they were just kids after all.

That's what my old man knew was slipping away in 1965, understood in his proud hick heart. He had already started telling me and Sis his stories, as if by planting those stories in us he knew that his good old days would live on.

Those stories are my old man's very own country songs. In his own way, Dad was singing to us, hymning to us. He instinctively knew that the world was made up of stories, and he passed his truths on to me and Sis. He also knew that the world that had shaped him was already vanishing, as were the country singers he loved to listen to.

In the land of country, bluegrass music has become the homeplace. With much of today's country owing more to the Eagles, the Allmans, and Skynyrd than to Rodgers, Wills, and Hank, bluegrass is an acoustic sanctuary for those who long for songs of God, mother, and home, who contend that real country music is made with a fiddle, a banjo, and a mandolin. But even in the early 1960s bluegrass sounded decidedly old-fashioned when compared with honky-tonk fired by whiskey and electric guitars, the pop aspirations of the Nashville Sound, and the rockabilly riot of Elvis and the wolf pack of leering juvenile delinquents he inspired.

But Bill Monroe, the Stanley Brothers, and Flatt and Scruggs persisted, insisting on a kind of musical fundamentalism that required absolute instrumental mastery—the way young preachers were expected to memorize the Holy Bible, chapter and verse—but thematically looked backward to the 1920s and '30s and musicians like the Carter Family, the Blue Sky Boys, Charlie Poole and the North Carolina Ramblers, and Gid Tanner and His Skillet Lickers.

(Strangely, in the late 1950s and early '60s, bluegrass was embraced by effete folkies and latent granola crunchers who would've wrinkled their delicate snouts and winced at Webb Pierce and Faron Young but who—falsely—thought that bluegrass represented some kind of preindustrial musical purity. They didn't understand that Monroe and Flatt and Scruggs, proud sons of the *Grand Ole Opry*, wanted to make a good, honest buck as much as anybody.)

Anyway, in 1950, when Hank Snow was looking ahead and helping to create the future of country music with the freight-train thrust of "I'm Movin' On," Monroe, looking backward, released "I'm on My Way to the Old Home." That was the crossroads America paused at in 1950. Some folks couldn't wait for that big ol' diesel of progress to come thundering through town, while others were still wary of indoor plumbing and getting "the electric" on their place. They didn't quite trust electricity, and they sure as hell didn't trust the government putting it in.

Monroe once told the writer John Rumble that one of his goals was to go back in time with his music. And that's what he attempts in "Old Home," tries to get back to the Rosine, Kentucky, farmhouse where he grew up.

"Old Home" opens with Rudy Lyle's Scruggs-style banjo loping down some back road, in no hurry at all—the total opposite of Hank Snow's explosive locomotive in "I'm Movin' On." In high, lonesome voices filled with longing, Monroe and Jimmy Martin tell us that they're on their way back to the old home and how "the road winds on up the hill," as if that hill were a kind of personal Calvary.

There *is* a gospel urgency in Monroe's voice when he sings, "The light in the window I long to see." With that one line, the old home becomes much more than just the place where he grew up.

It becomes heaven.

---

Home is the blue barren ruin of late autumn . . . Black rain dancing on corn skeletons . . . The vine-strangled hull of a dead Ford.

"I want to go home. I want to go home."

Songs don't get more primal than Bobby Bare's "Detroit City" (1963). The narrator journeyed north, fleeing the small-town South to make some real money out in the real world. And though the "home folks think I'm big in Dee-troit City," our man is miserable: by day he makes the cars, the writers, Danny Dill and Mel Tillis, tell us, and by night he makes the bars . . . when he isn't making up stories for the folks back home.

He yearns for the cotton fields and home, and the girl he left behind. In Dee-troit City, the wash don't snap on the line in the wind . . . and the crickets don't fiddle at night.

Bobby Bare knew a lot about grief and longing when he recorded "Detroit City." He was born into a farming family in 1935 in Lawrence County, Ohio, near Ironton; his mother died when he was five years old, and he spent some time in an orphanage. And, it's apparent, a certain orphan mournfulness informs "Detroit City" and other of his hits like "500 Miles Away from Home" and "Four Strong Winds." What could be sadder coming from the mouth (and heart) of a former orphan than the words "I want to go home"?

But does our narrator really want to go home? Longing is a sweet feast. As each day, each month, each year passes, our hometown becomes a better and brighter place, the very model of Middle America. And that girl we left behind? Why, she just might be the happiest girl in the whole U.S.A., as Donna Fargo sang, not to mention the most beautiful, as Charlie Rich once crooned.

But if you go back—"*Oh, I want to go home*"—everybody you meet might seem to be a rank stranger, as Ralph and Carter Stanley once reminded us.

Home is rhubarb whips and feral brambleberries . . . Fishing for hornpout in Pow-Wow River after midnight . . . Tumbledown stone walls—those chipmunk turnpikes—and unstrung barbwire, that atavistic backcountry DNA.

James Brown *screamed* and *howled* and *rasped* about being black and proud in 1968 and about having "soul pride" in 1969. Still, you didn't hear poor, disenfranchised whites preach much about their humble roots in mainstream country music.

But with "Coal Miner's Daughter," Loretta Lynn essentially says: "I'm a hillbilly, and proud of it." Bold and country, she opens the tune, "Well, I was borned a coal miner's daughter," making no concessions to Nashville or to the prissy conventions of grammar.

Lynn was thirty-five in 1970, when this mini-memoir of her life in Butcher Holler came out, and she tells the tale (she wrote it) with love, compassion, and ease. She knows that she's finally far enough away from those days of backbreaking work, the Bible, and empty pockets that she can't possibly be pulled back now. After all the hurt and hardships, she has the luxury of telling her listeners about which dark side of the American Dream she comes from. Those listeners made "Coal Miner's Daughter" a No. 1 hit and her signature tune, even becoming her first song to sneak into the Hot 100, peaking at No. 83. It eventually led to a bestselling autobiography (beautifully written with George Vecsey) and, finally, the 1980 movie that earned Sissy Spacek an Oscar for best actress.

Lynn was the first female country star to become fully mythologized while she was alive; Patsy Cline passed into myth only after she died. The Culture of Celebrity relished the voyeuristic value of the hick niche that she filled, but it didn't really love her the way her country fans did. The best of her songs still move us, though, decades after the Culture of Celebrity used her up and cast her aside.

In "Coal Miner's Daughter," with the Jordanaires providing their usual heavenly backup vocals, Lynn warms herself at the fire of her past in a tune that feels more bluegrass than Nashville. She tells us of how "Mommy scrubbed our clothes on a washboard every day" till her fingers bled, of shoeless summers, of how her daddy worked so hard just to "make a poor man's dollar," of how she's still "proud to be a coal miner's daughter." (Ma used a washboard, too, when I was little, and she skun her knuckles up something wicked.)

Toward the end of the song, in one of the great understatements in country music, Lynn sings, "Well, a lot of things have changed since way back then." And when it comes to that little cabin on a hill in Butcher Holler, all that's left is the floor and, more important, "the memories of a coal miner's daughter."

Home is the spitting snow ticking at the windows and sighing onto the pines . . . The frog pond's seductive rind of black ice . . . Red birdberries blistered and burst after the blizzard.

In "Talk About the Good Times" (1970), Jerry Reed treats memory as if it were a gospel revival. He kicks off his hymn to the good old days with rambunctious Pentecostal guitar—say, son, did ya remember to bring along that sack a snakes like I done asked ya?—and calls out to his listeners, "Let's talk about the good times!"

Reed, who's best known for his funky Cajun stomp "Amos Moses," craves the days when "if you ever needed help, a friend was there," when community was stronger, folks knew what being a neighbor meant, and friendship was genuine. Even in 1970, Reed saw people slipping into comas of solipsism, of lives centered on the TV and the telephone rather than the front porch and church. There was a time when lending a hand meant bowing your back and pushing, not absentmindedly writing a check then vanishing back inside to watch the latest episode of *Gunsmoke* (or *The Sopranos*).

When, on the instrumental break, he tells his guitar, "Preach it, son," Reed's trying to use those ringing electric notes to wake his listeners, to snap them out of their self-inflicted catatonia and epidemic selfishness.

The whole situation disgusted and ticked off my old man. He just couldn't understand how, when he was a kid and nobody had *nothing*, people found a way to give of themselves. But as he got older and folks had a little folding money, people found a way to make themselves scarce.

What frustrates my father is that he *didn't* leave the homeplace. It left *him*. He's spent his whole adult life watching it vanish before his eyes. That's why, I think, the old man still sings his favorite old songs when he's out working in the dooryard: "Party Doll" by Buddy Knox, "From a Jack to a King" by Ned Miller, "Hello Walls" by Faron Young. Kingston may have changed, but he hasn't—and neither have the songs. When he starts singing "Come along and be my party doll," it's 1957 again, and though times are hard, all's right in his small world.

In "Talk About the Good Times," Reed's granddaddy agrees with my old man. He's so fed up, in fact, that he's ready to go "rest on the other side," so that down by the river Jordan he can "see all the friends I knew in the good old days."

So, yes, Reed is saying, there were good times in the past, but, too, there'll be even better times in the time to come.

Home is the bees grazing in the eaves and chickens pecking at the dirt . . . The slap of beaver tail on the pond . . . Bats darting and spiraling at dusk, marking double helixes—*italics with wings*.

Like Bill Monroe and Bobby Bare, the main character in Merle Haggard's "Sing Me Back Home" (1967) aches to go back to the old home. But in Haggard's song, written for a San Quentin buddy of his who was executed, it's just about too late.

The man, the killer, is being led to the gas chamber—unlikely material for a No. 1 hit—when he makes his last request: he wants his guitar-picking pal to play him a song. "Let him sing me back home," he asks the warden, "with a song I used to hear." He understands at this midnight moment in his life that the right song can ferry him back home, back to the Eden of childhood, when he was pure, before he bore the mark of Cain. A man who has spent his life steeped in sin knows that his friend's art can somehow redeem him. The state will claim his lifeless body . . . but not his soul.

Most of us don't do time in prison, but we all end up building metaphorical prisons of compromise that cut us off from the essence of childhood, of the homeplace. We move to cities where we can no longer see the stars prick the night sky. We take jobs that promise a good living, but not a good life. We chase the hollow winds of honor, power, riches, and fame. Then we spend the rest of our lives trying to get back home.

We all want to be sung back home before we die.

We don't know, in real life, whether Haggard sang his friend home. But we do know that Haggard redeemed himself through his magic—resisted the insistent demons that could've hounded him back to San Quentin—and that his songs gave solace to countless others, including all those poor country boys, black and white, dying in the jungles of Vietnam in the late 1960s.

Merle Ronald Haggard, who was born in 1937 in Bakersfield, California, was able to sing himself back home.


Home is the screen door whanging shut . . . whanging shut . . . *whanging shut.*

# Folsom Prison Blues

The prison lament is one of country's defining genres, bursting with songs like "Mama Tried" and "The Fugitive" by Merle Haggard, "San Quentin" and "Folsom Prison Blues" by Johnny Cash, "In the Jailhouse Now" by Jimmie Rodgers (and, later, Webb Pierce, among many others), "I'm Just Here to Get My Baby Out of Jail" by the Blue Sky Boys, and "Green, Green Grass of Home" by Porter Wagoner. Ain't it funny how music made by the poor and the dispossessed produces so many powerful prison songs? The cabaret and light opera just haven't done a good job of mining the genre.

And, country or city, North or South, black or white, it's almost always the poor who fill our prisons. They were mostly small-timers where I grew up—drug dealers and recreational break-in artists— country boys and country men who weren't anywhere near's clever as they thought they were. They all knew how to use their fists. But their wits? Well, that's why they got sent up to the state prison in Concord, or, if they were lucky, only over to the County Farm in Brentwood.

Some of them *were* scary bastards, because they didn't just step over the line, they obliterated it—or didn't even know it was there in the first place. Those who came back from prison, though, owned an odd glamour. They'd made a mistake or two, gone inside, and returned having learned lessons that the rest of us could never understand.

Still, they were just ordinary country boys. Most country singers knew that with one hideous roll of the dice they could've found themselves behind state-sanctioned bars the same way their peers Merle Haggard and Johnny Paycheck did. The singers knew, too, all the other kinds of prisons that could lead a poor boy astray, leave him shackled in the jail of his soul: the prisons of shame and ignorance, of being so inarticulate that you only know how to speak with your fists. I can't count the times I heard it said of someone: "He don't know no better." We understood that, somehow, we were all prisoners, some healing our wounds in actual jail cells, others in shacks, those drafty prisons of the poor. So many of my kinfolk were like mad, scored dogs chained to a stake in a dooryard with no shade. And they were crazy: *crazy* with booze and lust, *crazy* with hate and envy—all the usual prisons.

And sometimes they needed a good, sad prison song to make them feel better about their own lives.

A fell darkness seized America in 1968, an almost biblical darkness, and in that darkness Johnny Cash's Man in Black persona became fully formed. Cash embraced his own dark side—and those of two thousand inmates at Folsom State Prison in Represa, California—and, in turn, America embraced him.

Cash's flagging career was at a crossroads as 1968 opened. He hadn't had a real hit since "Understand Your Man" in 1964, his addiction to amphetamines had turned him mean, mercurial, and unreliable in the studio and on the road, and his self-destructive streak had become legendary: no other star of country music had ever seen fit to stomp the footlights at the *Grand Ole Opry*, not that the *Opry*'s management didn't have it coming, the smug bastards. To some, his insistence on recording a live album at Folsom Prison seemed to be just another nail driven into the coffin of his career.

He recorded *Johnny Cash at Folsom Prison* on January 13, 1968. Photographs from that day show a man who was thirty-five, but looked at least ten years older, a man dressed in black who looked like an undertaker, or a preacher, or maybe an over-the-hill gunslinger.

Cash did not sugarcoat his show that day. He met the prisoners' darkness with his own. He opened with his "Folsom Prison Blues," then followed it with songs like "Busted," "Cocaine Blues," "Dark as a Dungeon," and the gallows humor (literally) of "25 Minutes to Go."

The raucous prisoners loved him, and Cash loved them right back. There was no mediation here, no worries about offending somebody. It was just Cash and his music, and the sorry men who needed it. But as Cash and his troupe, which included June Carter, whom he'd marry on March 1, and the rockabilly stalwart Carl Perkins, boarded their bus afterward, all they understood was that they had done a right and Christian deed that day. They didn't realize that they'd revived Johnny Cash's career, and then some.

Come summer, *At Folsom Prison* was one of the hottest-selling albums in the nation, and the live version of "Folsom Prison Blues" was No. 1 Country and a Top 40 hit, proving that there were a lot of legs left in shooting a man in Reno "just to watch him die." And somewhere along the line during that impossible summer, Cash ceased being a mere country singer and became an abyss-voiced prophet bringing back the hard, dark news from the inside. Most Americans don't know someone who's done time. But when they looked at Cash in 1968, listened to his album, they saw a man who, like Jesus, had rubbed shoulders with hardened criminals, saw a man who could at least stand in for the convict that they suddenly felt they needed to know, needed to invite to dinner. *At Folsom Prison* was Grammy Jennings's favorite album that year. As she listened, sometimes with her eyes closed, you could see her remembering her men who had gone to prison and jail, see her wondering who, among her sons and grandsons, might yet end up there.

By 1969, Cash had the No. 1 album on the Billboard chart—the utterly calculated *Johnny Cash at San Quentin*—and his own TV variety show on ABC. Cash's darkness, though *At Folsom Prison* had come from the heart and *At San Quentin* from marketing, had become America's darkness.

In the liner notes to *At Folsom Prison*, Cash wrote: "Listen closely to this album and you hear in the background the clanging of the doors, the shrill of the whistle, the shout of the men—even laughter from men who had forgotten how to laugh."

To the men of Folsom Prison, America's darkness couldn't hold an unlit candle to their own inner darkness. But when Johnny Cash came among them, humbled himself before them, they gave back as good as they received.

"Them poor babies were listening to John so hard you could feel it," June Carter said later.

And once that song, once that album, came out, the rest of America listened that hard, too.

Billy George—that lying, sneak-thieving mama's boy—is a drunken rat who gnaws at the ragged edges of our frayed lives. If you saw him at the town dump tilling the swill, you might be tempted to shoot him—then say you mistook him for a varmint. Venom seethes in his veins. His hair, no-haircut long, is a thick, dirty pelt. Great-Uncle

Billy is a wife beater and a child beater, and the family whisper with their eyes averted that he once raped his estranged wife. He's managed to spend a few nights in jail, too. Uncle Billy's proudly disorderly when he's drunk.

His nose, broke and rebroke like a mediocre boxer's, is mashed on his face. He scuttles, shack to shack, with a sideways limp. His favorite saying: "It's not who you know, it's who you blow."

One spring day toward supper, Billy, who's my mother's uncle, is hauling his sorry self up the hill from his shack to Nanna George's house, probably to mooch a meal. My old man's changing a tire on the car . . . I'm watching the bats waltz the twilight eaves of Nanna's place.

"There's Uncle Billy," I say.

Dad looks, stands up, cleans his hands on his dungarees. Billy's been at our house again, when Dad's at work, weasel-wording my mother, telling her that she ought to leave the old man, who he says is less than good for nothin'.

"Billy!" Dad shouts, my uncle stopping, squinting. "If I ever catch you talking to my wife like that again, you'll wish you never got born."

Now, he could've bowed his head and gone on to his free supper. Instead . . . "Kiss my ass!" Billy yells.

The old man grabs the tire iron and bears down on Billy, who's stumping toward his mother's house fast as he can. He just makes it, but my old man stands there, at the bottom of the steps, gripping that tire iron, till Nanna George, much more of a man than her son will ever be, shoos him away.

My old man, talking about Billy:

"One time, I had a tire blow out and I accidentally run over some of his corn. So I went and told him about it, and that sonuvabitch told me I had to pay for the corn. So I get back in my car and I flatten all his fuckin' corn. And I didn't pay for none of it, neither."

Some men create their own solitary confinement. They shun their family, lose their friends, and like it that way. Uncle Billy haunts the back roads of Rockingham County in a pickup that limps just like him (it ain't registered, of course) that his father (Grandpa Ora) sold him, a cheap beer lounging between his legs, looking for *God-knows-what*. We were lucky, I suspect, that he never quite found it.

Uncle Billy's driving a brand-new Chevy pickup truck.

He pissed some guy off down to Haverhill, Massachusetts, got flung down a flight of stairs, and broke his hip. The cops found him unconscious on an icy sidewalk, and Billy threatened to sue the city for negligence. He turned the out-of-court settlement into that new Chevy.

"That conniving cocksucker," my old man says.

Uncle Billy's no longer driving a brand-new Chevy pickup truck.

Drunk one night on New Boston Road, he stopped his truck to take a leak by the side of the road . . . right when a cop came by. Goodbye, driver's license.

"The ass," my old man says.

Johnny Cash sang in prisons long before his Folsom and San Quentin albums transformed him into a star to the working class (and to those who like to sniff the sweat of the working class). When he performed at San Quentin on New Year's Day 1958, it seemed to one young hellion doing time there that Cash spoke directly to him.

Merle Haggard, imprisoned for robbery, resolved then and there that he would try to nurture his gift for music, understood that Cash, without knowing it, was showing him a way to be in the world, a way to live without stripes on his shoulders and steel bars before his face.

Haggard got out of prison in 1960, and by 1968, on the strength of songs like "I Threw Away the Rose," "The Fugitive," and "The Bottle Let Me Down," he had become one of the biggest stars in country music—backed by his loyal band, the Strangers. He'd also learned that country fans were hypnotized by his life as an ex-con, and that led him to write and sing tunes like "Branded Man," "Sing Me Back Home," and "Mama Tried."

"I turned twenty-one in prison, doing life without parole," Haggard explains in "Mama Tried," a No. 1 Country hit for him in 1968, a few weeks after Cash's live version of "Folsom Prison Blues" claimed the top spot—each song for four weeks. But where Cash broke into the pop Top 40 with "Folsom Prison," Haggard didn't even enter the Hot 100: Cash had a fan base outside country, including people like Dylan, but Hag's songs rarely went pop. Even "Okie from Muskogee" only went to No. 41. Middle-class Americans loved it that Johnny Cash sang to prisoners. But they still weren't quite ready for an ex-con who sang.

There were plenty of prisons to go around for young men in 1968, and not just state penitentiaries. There were the prisons of the Vietnam War, of drug addiction, and of the false hopes promised by over-the-top militancy (on both the right and the left). The usual personal prisons were with us, too, the jail cells that beckon when the Ten Commandments are shattered again and again. And all those prisoners—and potential prisoners—responded to Cash's and Hag's songs by buying the records. You could now own a true scrap of prison darkness, and store it in the record case right next to Aretha and the Beatles.

Haggard is blunt about his particular prison. He sings of Mama, "She tried to raise me right, but I refused."

"Mama Tried" opens with a swirling guitar figure that conjures the sifting and drifting sands of time, and Hag sings the song without self-pity, at a remove that suggests the narrator has been granted understanding. Of a lifetime squandered in prison, he sings there's "only me to blame."

Simply put, the old man and his buddies broke the law.

They speeded beyond reason (sometimes even racketing their stock car—that black 1937 Pontiac coupe—up and down Route 125), they hunted and fished out of season and without the required licenses, they drove unregistered vehicles and made their own license plates. And they stole: chickens and watermelons, goats and corn. They siphoned gasoline from center-of-town cars and plucked radiators out of junkyards. But they were never armed— save for their fists—and they never broke-and-entered. They were poor country boys just trying to get along . . . lucky they never got caught. And the old man will admit, after he's had a couple beers, that when he was a kid he was "a little hood."

But Dad and his buddies were just having clean, small-town fun compared with some of the men I knew growing up: the robbers and the baby beaters, the rapists and the drug dealers.

And, to be honest, when it comes to my own extended family— the Jenningses and the Georges—none of the Ten Commandments were safe. Ours was a family of mangy foxes, a sly, shifty, and shiftless lot, who, when faced with authority, licked its shiny boots. We had adulterers, drunks, and glue sniffers (ah, Testors!); wife beaters, husband beaters, and child abusers; pyros, nymphos, and card cheats; smugglers and folks who were always sticking their cold, bony hands where they didn't belong.

Whether through luck or guile, most those people never paid the debt they owed society.

The prisoner's debt is never paid.

He is obliged to spend the rest of his life rolling his unforgiving boulder up the Sisyphean hills. "I paid the debt I owed 'em," Merle Haggard sings in "Branded Man" (1967), "but they're still not satisfied."

He's right. You can shake an ex-con's hand, bust your ass next to him at Kingston Steel Drum, and drink a beer with him. But you can't ever forget that he's been to prison. In the back of your mind you believe that a once-mad dog never bites just one time.

"I'd like to hold my head up," Haggard laments, then adds later, "but they won't let my secret go untold."

Hag got lucky, though. He turned his unpaid debt, his secret, into art. Most men can only turn it on themselves.

We knew a couple guys pretty well who did time for armed robbery. They were young and stupid and thought that maybe the world owed them a few sweat-free bucks. I'm not going to name them. I refuse to rekindle their shame on the prison of the printed page.

They both blinked back into the sunlight chiseled and tattooed, roosters wearing too-tight T-shirts to show off muscles earned the hard way. And they were quick to flash the rolls of bills they kept wadded in the pockets of their snug Levi's. But the swagger and the crisp twenties didn't fool nobody. Still, there *was* a mystery to them—even if they weren't aware of it—because they'd gone to the other side and been swaddled in a darkness we couldn't know. Yes, they were assholes for stealing (and, in our eyes, more so for getting caught), but we respected them.

The old man and his pals welcomed them back, still bummed smokes off each other, still shared Schlitzes on a hot summer's day, still barrelhoused down the power-line road. The men would shrug, say it was just one of those things, going to prison. In a sense, the guys who got sent away were their scapegoats, had done time for all their sins—real and imagined. The men understood that all of them were just one god-awful miscalculation from being sent away. So they weren't quick to pass judgment. Poor boys had to hang together. Because when you're poor, in exile from the community, you're always a suspect.

Dad still tells the story of how him and a couple of the guys got pulled over by the Newton cops. Someone had broken into a summer cottage, and when the cops saw the poor boys drive by in their broke-down car, they decided to search it. They rifled through the glove compartment, tore out the backseat, and dumped all the tools and tires from the trunk by the side of the road. The men didn't say nothin'. Just watched. And when the cops drove off, leaving them to put the car back together, they knew they were going to be suspects for a long, long time, whether they deserved it or not.

With "In the Jailhouse Now" (1955), Webb Pierce is the happiest jailbird you ever did hear. Maybe it's because "Jailhouse" spent twenty-one weeks at No. 1—now, that's some *serious* time—and thirty-seven weeks on the country chart altogether. Sounding downright giddy, Pierce sings about his pal Rambling Bob, who likes "to steal, gamble, and rob," in the what-me-worry spirit of Jimmie Rodgers, who wrote the song in 1928—or, to be more accurate, who cobbled "Jailhouse" together from his bottomless knap-sack of free-floating blues and string-band verses.

Pierce is just one in a long line of country singers—including Gene Autry, Ernest Tubb, Hank Snow, Lefty Frizzell, and Merle Haggard—who are musical bastards of Mr. Rodgers.

Backed by the Wilburn Brothers, Pierce's "Jailhouse" is such an upbeat romp that you could jitterbug to it. When Pierce belts out, "He's in the jailhouse now," it's almost as if he's singing, "We're in the money." This version of "Jailhouse" is definitely the spiritual pappy of Elvis's hell-raising "Jailhouse Rock" from 1957.

Pierce fully understands that sometimes to have a good time you need to take "in every honky-tonk in town." And that sometimes the price you pay is a charge of drunk and disorderly and a night spent in the local jail.

Just ask my uncles Lloyd and Billy . . . or Johnny Cash.


Frank Nay, who, you may recall, used to beat Grammy Jennings, liked to winter at the County Farm in Brentwood. So he'd willfully do something right after Thanksgiving to provoke the authorities: get in a fistfight at a bar, speed on Route 125 with his suspended li-cense, take a drunken leak in public, and then curse off the munici-pal court judge. Frank liked the County Farm: it was warm, he got three square meals a day, and it dried him out.

One day, when me and Sis were little, he took us to the County Farm, which was an actual working farm. He knew everyone, the guards and the prisoners, said hello and shook their hands. He showed us off to his friends, then he showed us the cornfields and the tomato patches, kicked at the chickens, and scratched the pigs' ears. He even knew the names of the cows, whose milk we watched sizzle into tin pails from their pink udders.

Frank acted as if he owned the joint. But it's only now, decades later, that I realize the county jail owned Frank Nay.

When it comes to prison, there are the ones who are marked for it from birth, the ones whose demons caper in their DNA. Then there are the unlucky ones: the drunk driver who doesn't see the kid on the bicycle; the barroom brawler who doesn't know his own strength; the guy away on business who comes home a day early to surprise his wife.

"The Cold Hard Facts of Life" (1967) by Porter Wagoner, like the best horror fiction, has a terrible inevitability to it. We know, even before the narrator himself knows, what the deal is and what he'll be forced to do. Even so, we can't tear our ears away.

The 1960s were a decade of cold, hard facts. We learned, among other things, that we couldn't keep our leaders alive, that the government lied to us and lied to us again, that being black—despite what the government preached—always made you a suspect, and that Father, after all, didn't know best. (We in Kingston knew that already.)

The situation in Bill Anderson's song, though, is simpler, just tawdry: a husband comes back to town early from a business trip and discovers that his wife is having an affair.

Unsurprising and, perhaps, unpromising material, but the tale is all in the telling, and Wagoner is a master storyteller who made his name with songs like "Green, Green Grass of Home," "Satisfied Mind," and "Carroll County Accident." His big blond hair—the kind a Texas cheerleader would lust after—didn't hurt, either. He was so country that Waylon Jennings once said of him: "He couldn't go pop with a mouthful of firecrackers."

Wagoner, born in the Missouri Ozarks in 1927 and educated in a one-room schoolhouse, doesn't rush his story, but savors it like the hell-haunted hard-shell preacher he looks like. Finally, the singer confronts his wife and her lover, a knife in his hand. They beg for a mercy that he's not capable of.

After he kills them, he asks the listener: "Who taught who the cold hard facts of life?"

# Amos Moses

Country celebrates hard, lonely men. They're one of the music's archetypes: truckers and convicts, cowboys and miners. Then there are the men who need to live down a long dirt road, men who lived off the grid before there was even a grid to live off of. In Kingston, those men lived out to Cedar Swamp, or up to Rockrimmon, or deep *somewhere* in the piney woods.

George Kelly . . . Dirty Willy . . . Charlie Kelly, who died of a heart attack hanging curtains, of all things, in his shack.

Men so deep that if they look too close into themselves, they'll drown. They understand that if you're going to get along in this world, you need to get along by yourself. Rural nihilists choosing rural solitary, whose granite faces say, "I'd just as soon slit your throat as look at ya." They never start fights . . . they only finish 'em.

Pop . . . Chief . . . Leo DesMarais, who loved his chain saw more than he loved any of his wives.

Monday through noon Saturday, work's their middle name. Weekends, it's whiskey or beer. Leathery country sonstabitches, skin cured by wind and sun, wood-smoke voices thick with Dickel's and Luckys, sledgehammer hands, kerosene breath. Bumming smokes, using cupped, stony hands as ashtrays; bareheaded crags who, come winter, smoke something fierce to spite the snow, the bitter cold. A brick of butts just as good as a mackinaw. Hunters and trappers . . . loggers and roofers . . . scavengers and junkyard dogs, cussing and talking pussy, intimate with dirt-floor houses, the screak of outdoor water pumps, the wick-hiss of kerosene lamps, living where the rent never comes due. Reeking nineteenth-century men dragged into the twentieth by the scruffs of their filthy necks.

Harry Cain . . . Frank Nay . . . Jake Marble, our outhouse impresario.

They savor their scars, those train tracks of ghosts that criss-cross gristly flesh, rub them for good luck like a rabbit's foot. Those men, they fret calluses on phantom fingers, and their knees and hands don't thaw come morning till after that first shot . . . sometimes the second. Men who piss beer, blood, and oil, who know that nothing good ever walked through the front door. Whose women and children, to prove their love, *flinch*.

Leathery country sonstabitches (dungarees *just* clutching hip knobs) stealing one last hit on a Camel . . . *making damn sure there's no cancer left in that bastard* . . . and heeling it into the gravel.

"Amos Moses" (1970) by Jerry Reed is 100 percent pure country-boy swamp funk. This song brings funk so fierce that James Brown—who, believe it or not, once appeared on the *Opry*—could've covered it without shame. Telling the tale of a hard-ass alligator hunter, Reed gleefully sings in the voice of an unreconstructed hick, which maybe explains why the song only hit No. 16 Country but reached No. 8 Pop—most nobody in Nashville was sounding this hillbilly in 1970, they would've been embarrassed to do so.

But it wasn't unusual for country-style tunes to sidle onto the pop charts disguised as novelties—though, like many of Roger Miller's songs, "Amos Moses" is much more than a comic diversion. Bumpkin novelties included Sheb Wooley's "Purple People Eater" and Homer and Jethro's "Battle of Kookamonga," a spoof of Johnny Horton's "Battle of New Orleans"; Ray Stevens's "Ahab the Arab" and "Gitarzan"; Little Jimmy Dickens's "May the Bird of Paradise Fly Up Your Nose"; and Johnny Cash's "A Boy Named Sue," in which, metaphorically, the Man in Black became for one song the Man in Plaid. To the middle classes, country singers were always good for a dose of down-home humor. For all the dark power of many of Cash's songs, "Sue" was his highest-charting pop song, sitting at No. 2 for three weeks, though he did manage to get the angry prison anthem "San Quentin" onto the single's flip side. But it was the same people who watched *The Beverly Hillbillies*, *Green Acres*, and *Petticoat Junction* on TV who made "Sue" a hit, and who planted "Amos Moses" in the pop Top 10.

Lynn Anderson's slick and catchy "Rose Garden" was the prototypical country hit in 1970, and she might not've been promising anyone a rose garden, but, then again, neither was ol' Amos Moses.

From its opening "bawk-bawk-bawk" funky-chicken guitar, you just know that this song's going to take you places you ain't never been. Reed, who wrote the song, plops us smack-dab in the middle of Amos Moses's Louisiana bayou, where "he lived by hisself" and where his daddy once used him for alligator bait. He's the meanest sonuvabitch in the swamp, even if his left arm is just a stump where a gator bit it "clean up to the elbow."

Reed was born Jerry Reed Hubbard in Atlanta in 1937 and had a varied career that included work as a session guitarist (influenced, like most Nashville pickers, by Merle Travis and Chet Atkins), a songwriter, and an actor on TV and in movies like *W.W. and the Dixie Dancekings* and *Smokey and the Bandit*. And, like so many other country singers from his era, he did time in an orphanage as a kid.

Reed had bigger country hits than "Amos Moses," like "When You're Hot, You're Hot" and "She Got the Goldmine (I Got the Shaft)," but none of them were as fully realized. In "Amos Moses," Reed creates a Twain-like (that's Mark, not Shania) tall tale that we can't help but vanish into—the same way Amos makes a certain Louisiana sheriff vanish.

Where the Kershaw brothers' "Louisiana Man" breaks your heart, "Amos Moses" busts your gut, from laughing so hard.


Way up north, my bloody-handed fathers scrawled the word "ax," scragged the blunting *e*. Frank Nay scants talk, but Frank can make a mute ax—its blade seasoned by sap and gore, sweat and Old Crow—*speak* in a riven tongue that makes my blood run cold. He's Grammy Jennings's rugged lover, her nightmare, her grudge: all dark squints, grained skin, and skun knuckles. The dead weight of a steel plate, won at that county fair they called World War II, seams the skull of sledge-boned Frank.

He was a prick, but he took care of the old man, Lloyd, and Junior after Grammy broke down and got sent away to dry out.

He was a prick, but he went and found Dad up in the granite-scar fissures of Devil's Den after Gram had chased after him with a butcher knife.

Frank Nay was too ugly to thumb with. Frank Nay was a dry barn burning after midnight. Frank Nay'd give you the shirt off his back—when he was sober—and the back of his hand when he wasn't.

Drunk at dusk, *again*—the bats basking in the owl-light—Frank growls, all ratgut reek, and starts knocking Grammy around, *again*, until my old man ups and rimrocks him.

But when I think of Frank Nay, I can't ever forget that blood bucket next to his cot, the cancer bucket—Gram cuffing the snuffing mutts away—and Frank's ironwood arms buckled and withered to gray deadwood.

And when Frank Nay, that granite sonuvabitch, finally went, my old man sat down hard and wept—*wild, wild* masculine rain that I had never, ever seen.

"The Fields Have Turned Brown" (1949) . . . "Man of Constant Sorrow" (1950) . . . "Rank Stranger" (1960): three lamentations that paint the Stanley Brothers' triptych of despair. These three plaints sounded as if they were weird breezes from another century, even when they were recorded, sounded as if they were sung by Appalachian ghosts, rather than Ralph and Carter Stanley.

All three tunes ken what sends a man to the deep woods, understand the bleaks that badger a man into turning his back on his family, his community, and God.

The Stanley Brothers were born in the Clinch Mountain region of southwestern Virginia, Carter in 1925 and Ralph in 1927. Along with Bill Monroe and Flatt and Scruggs, they laid the foundations for what came to be known as bluegrass music. As young men, they were marked by the Primitive Baptist Church, and their church learning suffuses many of their songs, including these three.

"The Fields Have Turned Brown," written by Carter, is a simple tale: A man who's spent his days rambling the country finds out by letter that his parents have been dead for four years, learns that there's no one left waiting for him back home. The news chills him. Reinforced by Les Woodie's forlorn fiddle—almost acting as a sorrowing Appalachian chorus—the narrator recalls, "Son, don't go astray, was what they both told me, remember that love for God can be found."

But for now, God is out of his reach. The fields back home have turned brown, the fields of his heart are withered.

"Man of Constant Sorrow," made popular in the Coen Brothers film *O Brother, Where Art Thou?*, is a deathbed confession. The narrator's lover is gone, and he has no friends except death and grief. "I've seen trouble all my days," Carter pines and groans. "No pleasure here on earth I find." He swears, "I'll meet you on God's golden shore," but doesn't sound too persuasive. The tune also resonates with premonition: Carter died just sixteen years later, done in by hard living and liver disease.

After "Fields" and "Sorrow," it made perfect sense for the Stanleys to record "Rank Stranger," written by the gospel giant Albert E. Brumley. The brothers are right at home with the hymn's alienation and yearning toward heaven. The narrator wanders back home, to where he grew up, and everybody he meets seems "to be a rank stranger"—"they knew not my name, and I knew not their faces."

In that moment, the whiskey bottle whispers . . . the dark groves of oaks call. Deep country soul, spooky mountain keening, gets no better than this.

Pop and Chief, who were both Indians, could've been characters in one of Johnny Cash's stinging songs about Native Americans. In old age, they'd each managed to secure their shred of the American Dream—a swatch of land to grow their vegetables on complemented by a tidy woodstove shack. But even a lone wolf, especially one whose hair has gone white, can be ambushed.

Chief lived up on the granite-knobbed washboard of Rockrimmon Road, and Pop lived near us on New Boston Road. Both men were given to suspenders, flannel shirts, and pipes. They'd sputter into town in their 1940s sedans for a haircut and to stop at Bakie's Market to buy a loaf of Sunbeam bread, a pound of bologna, and a tin of tobacco. They didn't trust words, but they'd always wave when they saw you.

My old man basked in their company: the sweet stink of pipe to-bacco, a cheap beer, and, mostly, silence. They were men who un-derstood that a grunt or a sigh was an essential part of speech. They were lonely old men in search of sons, and Dad needed his stand-in fathers.

Still, like dogs who've been beaten, they kept their distance, sought to fence their lives in a barbwire of wariness. So, yes, they were wary, but not wary enough.

Chief was robbed, and beaten so badly that he vanished into the county nursing home.

And Pop, trying to help a nephew, went against his nature and signed a piece of paper that granted the boy his land—with the un-derstanding that Pop could live on it until he died. A house trailer arrived on Pop's property one weekend soon after, and we never saw him again.

Spend too long living alone in the woods and the swamp and, no matter how often you tramp into town, you start to become more animal than man. Some men go snake, sneaking the shadows and sunning on granite boulders like so many copperheads. Others stalk the crepuscular forests like wildcats, snarling at anyone who comes near. And some go bear—or even bare—like the fella in Johnny Horton's "Ole Slew Foot" (1960).

Quickened by hillbilly harmonica and bear-trackin' banjo, "Slew Foot," written by Howard Hausey and James C. Webb, takes us on a rollicking bear hunt. It's as if Twain rewrote *The Bear* by Faulkner.

Giddily drunk on the bloodlust of the hunt, Horton sings of

"bear tracks, bear tracks looking back at me" and of a beast "ain't never been caught, he ain't never been treed." Then comes the surprise refrain as Horton confides: "Some folks say he looks a lot like me."

Our man has gone bear-native, gone Sasquatch. As long as Ole Slew Foot never gets caught, neither will the singer.

Dirty Willy works the cover blaster at Kingston Steel Drum—slipping filthy covers in, plucking clean ones out—wallowing in the cloud of steel-shot dust that billows about him. From the top of his bald head to the tips of his steel-toe boots, he's smudged in black dust—a real Man in Black.

When he shows up to work, he's just as dirty as he was when he knocked off the night before. There *is* one difference in the morning: he has reverse raccoon eyes from rubbing them. But within an hour of his turning on the cover blaster, his eyes are blacked up again. In his loose black pants and a floppy black sweatshirt, Dirty Willy looks like an industrial wraith, or a forgotten character from Dickens who somehow survived into the second half of the twentieth century.

Dirty Willy spends the workday lost in the rickety shack of his mind. If he can tolerate you, he ignores you. If you piss him off, he'll chase you with his shovel, snapping and snarling, murder in his eyes. Whenever our foreman walks by, about thirty seconds later Willy mutters, "F-f-f-fuckin' cock-knocka," then laughs . . . the call of a loon. He sits alone at lunch, his lips worming.

He lives in a rust-rabid house trailer on the Newton Junction Road, ramshackle chicken coops behind it. Besides working at the drum factory, Willy runs an egg route—I always imagine his hens being blacker than ravens—and seems to do all right. When, one sunny summer's day, he plunged his truck into the creek by Tricklin' Falls and stove his vehicle all to hell, he went out and bought a new one the next week: *cash*.

And when Dirty Willy smiles, showing the ragged stumps of his teeth, he looks like a child who's just gotten an A on a spelling test.

Jimmy Dean is best known these days for his pork sausages. But Dean, named Seth Ward when he was born in Plainview, Texas, in 1928, was a full-on TV star who had shows on CBS and ABC and was a country singer who spun out a handful of Top 10 hits. His signature tune, "Big Bad John," went No. 1 Country *and* Pop in 1961, and helped Dean, who also wrote the song, to become country music's sausage king.

Big John, who stands six-six and weighs 245 pounds (that's a lot of sausage and beans, boys), is a throwback to the days when a real man earned his muscles the hard way, through ball-busting work, not in the mirrored vanity of some gym.

In Dean's recitation, Big John is a hulking mystery, a laconic loner who steals into town one day and goes to work in the mine. No one knows where he lives, and some folks whisper he's on the run from a New Orleans murder. But everyone knows you don't "give no lip to Big John." And the ubiquitous Jordanaires, singing backup, deepen the big man's secrets with their spectral choruses of "Big John, Big John, ooo-ooh, ooo-ooh."

Where I come from, the big men never said much: Great-Grandpa Ora, who was six-four and had arms like tire irons, or Lurch at Kingston Steel Drum, who like Big John stood six-six, but weighed a fair bit more than 245. It was the banty-rooster bastards who never shut their traps, who'd puff their chests and brag about how they'd been in the Marines or played semipro football. The actions of men like Ora and Lurch always spoke louder than their words. Same with Big John.

There's an accident in the mine, but John props up a sagging timber and twenty men scramble to safety—all of them except Big John.

Throughout "Big Bad John," Floyd Cramer, one of Nashville's best piano players, clanks a chunk of steel with a hammer, setting the song's rhythmic foundation and suggesting a pickax working a vein of coal. But as Dean intones "At the bottom of this mine lies one hell of a man," we know what Cramer's really been doing throughout the tune: driving spikes into Big John's metaphorical coffin.

Grammy Jennings hungered after men whose hands were horned gardens of calluses, whose skin was dark as fried bacon, whose arms were thick with work—hard bastards who liked to drink and fuck. But that was okay, because she liked to drink and fuck, too. Men like my grandfather Bub and Frank Nay, Reggie Goodwin and Harry Cain.

Gram, who gave as good as she got, could not face this world without a man. When thunder shuddered the windows and lightning scarred the sky, she needed a good, strong man in bed beside her. If she was home alone, she'd crawl under the bed—still just a little orphan girl after all—and wait out the storm.

Most of her men were like crowbars. And even when they knocked her down and kicked her, the way Frank Nay did, she couldn't give them up. Her eyes blacked and her face purpled, she'd still cry when the cops would haul Frank off to jail. Gram would sacrifice her tears to Frank Nay, but she was never one to hold a child's hand. I suppose that would be a line in the country song of her life.

Oh, she *was* a woman, though. Woman enough to lure men out the swamps and off the dirt roads, men steeped in whiskey and Hank, men so lonesome they were beyond crying.

Reggie Goodwin, who lived in a half trailer up a gutted dirt road, used to bray like a jackass to make Gram laugh and pick out "Sugarfoot Rag" on his guitar to make her smile. He had fleas in his beard . . . adders under his steps.

Harry Cain, who always made it clear right away that he could fight like a hurricane, was one rawboned Indian sonuvabitch who always had a Pabst Blue Ribbon at hand. Sometimes he'd break out his collection of 78 rpm dirty blues records; he'd be cackling before the needle crackled onto the disc. He died working at a salvage yard when a piece of wild steel sheared and pierced his skull.

Grammy Jennings, for some of these men, was the last stop before the deepest piney woods. She was all that stood between them—in her slip, a whiskey sour in her hand—and damnation.

Way down Cedar Swamp, where the last of the last of the wildcats roamed, where there were snapping turtles bigger than a washtub, the Boston & Maine freights were your only friend. After a supper of B&M baked beans and sweet brown bread, men like Jake Marble and George Kelly would stretch out in the shack shadows and listen for the train's whine and groan.

Bill Monroe's funereal version of "In the Pines" (1952), with him and Jimmy Martin singing, conjures those men and their shacks for me: "In the pines, in the pines, where the sun never shines." The tune stops time in an ancient train-haunted world that's vanished. When the narrator asks his captain for the time, "he said he throwed his watch away."

Which is kind of what Bill Monroe did—stop time—as he refined his music. As always, country was evolving in the 1940s. The so-

phisticated western swing of Bob Wills, the electric honky-tonk of
Ernest Tubb, and the sleek vocal stylings of Eddy Arnold and Red
Foley had supplanted country's string-band roots.

But Monroe, defying convention, looked to the past and the
present, and helped influence the future. He breathed new life into
the string band—fiddle, banjo, mandolin, stand-up bass, and guitar—added a touch of the blues and jazz's syncopation, then speeded
it up. (It's no shock that the second song Elvis recorded for Sun
Records was Monroe's "Blue Moon of Kentucky.") All the while,
Monroe suffused his bluegrass with loss, melancholy, and a yearning for the homeplace. It was that yearning and Monroe's insistence
on that acoustic string-band sound that made his music an atavistic
pleasure, even in the 1940s and '50s.

Bill Monroe was the master of the mournful cry, and he came by
it as a birthright. He was born on a farm near Rosine in Ohio
County, Kentucky, in 1911, the youngest of eight children. A loner
by nature, he was orphaned at sixteen and taken in by his uncle
Pendleton Vandiver, a local fiddler of some renown—and a leathery
sonuvabitch who inspired Monroe's standard "Uncle Pen"—who
started him on the path toward becoming a professional musician.
Which brings us back to "In the Pines."

(It's worth noting here that "In the Pines"—one of those songs
that were in the air—was recorded in 1927 by the Tenneva Ramblers
in Bristol, Tennessee, during the sessions in which Jimmie Rodgers
and the Carter Family were discovered. Rodgers—the future Father
of Country Music—and the Ramblers had arrived in Bristol together, but broke up before recording over matters of billing. It's as
if, after the Beatles fired Pete Best and replaced him with Ringo
Starr, Best went on to lead the British Invasion, and not the Fab
Four.)

Anyway, "The longest train I ever saw went down that Georgia
line," Monroe's version opens. The engine passes at six, and the ca-

boose at nine. Then again, a death train has no need to travel fast. And the singer knows "I'm on my way back home."

For the leathery sonstabitches of my boyhood, the deep woods were the last way station before death. They single-mindedly put themselves out of reach—even of God—made their lives into half-lives, ghosted through a world of shades and beasts where the wind howled through the trees and rocked their shacks. And on one certain night, men like Jake and George'd hear the Boston & Maine pine through the brakes, groves, and thickets . . . and suddenly know it was time to go.

# King of the Road

Country music has always been a haven for men—and it's most always men—on the move. Drifters, hustlers, killers, some of them suffused with the sureness of Manifest Destiny, others mere wraiths marking time till Judgment Day. It's one of the great American narratives, isn't it—just ask Melville, Twain, or Kerouac—that ability to yank up stakes and head west or south or north? *Anywhere but here*. Or, more insidious, the ability to live in the seams, almost anonymous, ghosting through town after town, never to be seen again. American tales . . . country tales.

The two world wars and the Great Depression unmoored America. Some people simply shrugged, let themselves be carried by the tides of history, and tried to make a living wherever they washed ashore, while others hunkered down even harder and tried to stay put. Those were lean years, when husbands from all walks of life left their families "to look for work" and never came back. Years when children were told that their parents had died young, but had actually gone rambling, faded into the wind. When you've got to keep moving, kids'll just slow you down.

By the time the 1950s were firmly in place, a certain segment of the population was permanently infected with what Grammy Britton used to call "the wandering evils." It was a kind of attention deficit disorder of place, an inability to see the gifts you already had in hand. They were men who couldn't sit still for long in one small town, with one woman, one life. So they'd throw their old life away—heeling it out like a cigarette butt—and ramble: to Florida and Colorado, Texas and California. Some drove off in their own vehicles, others jumped southbound freights, and yet others stood out to Route 125—the main road through Kingston—thumbs out, praying for a trailer truck that had Georgia plates.

A lot of them came back, leathered up by outdoor work, skinnier, Yankee accents diluted by the road, drinking a bit more than they used to. They'd shake your hand, tell you that you've just got to see the Grand Canyon before you die, and then, when you blinked, they'd be off again.

More than any other country singer (and maybe more than any other singer, period), Hank Williams perfected the art of personal apocalypse. In his bleakest songs, like "Lost Highway" (1949) and "Ramblin' Man" (1951), he projects an abject end-of-the-world loneliness, where it's too late to pray.

Kerouac and the Beats gloried in the open road, but all Hank sees is the Lost Highway. Where Kerouac's road is full of hipster saints, Hank's is full of country sinners. "I'm a rolling stone, all alone and lost," Hank pines in the opening line of "Lost Highway." His heart has been seared as he travels a sere landscape; it's as if he's trapped in a Hiroshima of the soul. After World War II, this country was full of people who felt that way but who couldn't articulate that feeling.

The singer has been cut loose from God and community—

seduced by a deck of cards, a jug of wine, and a woman's lies—and now he's sorrow bound on a "road of sin." The song is suffused with the violent postwar anomie of those populist noirists James Cain and Jim Thompson. And there's a sense, once the song ends, that the singer is ready to do something that he'll regret for the rest of his life.

Hank aches through "Lost Highway," written by Leon Payne, with hymnlike fervor. But in this hymn, God is dead.

In "Ramblin' Man," a kind of sequel to "Lost Highway," Hank reaches the end of the road.

This song, written by Hank, is all about the music as Hank's Drifting Cowboys bear him to the graveyard: Harold Bradley's lurching rhythm guitar sets us out on this death march, Jerry Rivers cries the funeral blues on fiddle, and Don Helms's eerie, out-of-tune steel completes the minor-key deathbed for Hank's spectral voice.

It's clear that the singer's rambling days are over, but it's also clear that he's still being called by the open road that's killing him. When Hank moans, "When the Lord made me, he made a ramblin' man," it sounds as if he's confessing to every sin in God's creation.

"Lost Highway" creaks open the singer's coffin. "Ramblin' Man" nails it shut.

As I've said, the old man got Ma knocked up with me when they were just seventeen. They had their eighth-grade educations, each other, and not much else. Dad says he thought about running, about riding Route 125 right out of town and leaving Ma and me behind for good, to take his chances on Hank's Lost Highway.

But he also thought about his father, Bub—a trucker and a rounder—who walked out on the family and left Dad to raise himself. He knew, even at seventeen, that no boy ought to have to raise himself. And he stayed, though staying is much harder than going.

More than fifty years later, Ma and the old man are still married.

Where Hank Williams's rambling songs wallow in gloom, Hank Snow's "I'm Movin' On" (1950) revels in utter freedom.

"I'm Movin' On," a fiddle-powered freight if ever there was one, pulls out of the station at speed, and it's clear from the opening notes onward that the song's "true-lovin' daddy ain't comin' back." Snow blames a woman—"I ain't got time for a triflin' woman on my main line"—for his departure, but that's just a lame-ass excuse.

This is a man who believes that you've got to move if you want to stay alive, a song so rowdy and randy that Snow's hero, Jimmie Rodgers, could've sung it. And an awful lot of people must've dreamed of flagging that fireballing freight, because the song—written by Snow—spent forty-four weeks on the country charts, including twenty-one at No. 1. You sure could see a lot of the country in forty-four weeks.

Snow knew what he was writing about. Born in Brooklyn, Nova Scotia, in 1914 and essentially orphaned, he spent his life on the move, starting when he went to sea as a cabin boy. Known as the Singing Ranger, he crisscrossed Canada, then made his way to the United States. He did time in Wheeling, West Virginia, and Hollywood, Dallas, and Nashville, where he finally settled down as a member of the *Grand Ole Opry*. He was an expert trick rider and, for a time, was managed by Colonel Tom Parker, that expert trickster who became Elvis Presley's lifelong Geppetto.

"I'm Movin' On" was Snow's first No. 1, but twelve years later he was on the road again with another No. 1 hit, "I've Been Everywhere":

*Monterey, Ferriday, Santa Fe, Tallapoosa*
*Glen Rock, Black Rock, Little Rock, Oskaloosa.*

Movin' on, indeed.

Me and the old man are train-haunted men, and the Boston &
Maine Railroad ghosted through both our childhoods. We grew up
in a place and time where wild, wild kids raced the night freights.
We are connoisseurs of railroad deadfalls and trestle whistles and
broke-down trains, of abandoned spur lines and locomotive boneyards, of railroad rain-crows and the low moan that tells us we ain't
going nowhere—again. And when a freight crosses our path, after all
these years, we still can't help but count the cars and grin as the ca-
boose rattles toward the vanishing point—as if we're little boys
mesmerized down to Newton Junction, where the trains don't stop
no more.

There was no rambling in the mid-twentieth century without trains
and trucks, and trains and trucks bellow and roar throughout country music. At the most basic level, they mean jobs and freedom. But
trains and trucks themselves are also a kind of country music: the
groan of the Boston & Maine . . . the reassuring thrum of freight car
kissing steel track . . . the blat and grumble of an 18-wheeler grudg-
ing up Malloy's Hill. But, finally, the most important train is that
glory-bound train, and the most important truck is the one carrying
you home to your woman after "six days on the road," as Dave Dudley sang in 1963.

Jimmie Rodgers and Roy Acuff partly made their careers by
climbing aboard train songs: Rodgers bluesing on "Waiting for a

Train" and "Hobo Bill's Last Ride," and Acuff keening on "Fireball Mail," "Wabash Cannonball," and "Night Train to Memphis."

There was no shortage of train songs after them, either: the Delmore Brothers' "Freight Train Boogie," Hank Snow's "Golden Rocket," which was a sequel to "I'm Movin' On," and "Orange Blossom Special" by just about anybody who knew how to cradle a fiddle, to name a few.

Merle Haggard starts "Mama Tried" with "The first thing I remember knowing was a lonesome whistle blowing." True and resonant words for many a country boy and girl. And train songs, like songs of the Old West, do seem to bring out the boy in country singers. When Johnny Cash tears through "Rock Island Line" (1957), he sounds like an Arkansas Huck Finn who likes nothing better than to smoke corn silk, go fishing, and savor a freight train blowing by.

When his version of "Rock Island Line," a folk song popularized by Leadbelly, gets up to speed, it's classic Cash and the Tennessee Two, all boom-chicka, boom-chicka, boom-chicka, a runaway freight of a song—both literally and figuratively. Though the song ends with one hellacious crash—"northbound train on a southbound track, he's all right a-leavin', but he won't be back"—Cash belts out the tune with joy and bounce. You can hear the grin in his voice.

"Rock Island Line" opens Cash's first album, *Johnny Cash with His Hot and Blue Guitar*, and is followed by three more train songs: "(I Heard That) Lonesome Whistle," "Wreck of the Old 97," and "Folsom Prison Blues."

Those were all my first lullabies, almost as good as falling asleep to the Boston & Maine itself shushing through Cedar Swamp.

My grandfather Bub Jennings spent his life driving truck: oil trucks and propane trucks, snow trucks and chicken trucks, beer trucks and sawmill trucks. He drank like a trucker, fucked like a trucker, and owned thick trucker arms. My old man drove truck for a while, too, and my youngest brother, Mike, drives truck today.

I didn't meet Bub till I was nine, ten years old. Though we didn't know, he'd found out where we lived on New Boston Road, and at least a couple times a month he'd drive his green Apple Yards Oil truck slow past our house.

He finally stopped one day, a gray Saturday afternoon. Dad had set an old overstuffed couch that smelled like nine dead cats out by the side of the road and stuck a "For Sale" sign on it. I was inside, but I heard the oil truck creak to a stop out front the house and start idling. When I got outside, I saw this guy I didn't know give Dad ten bucks for that couch.

"I'll come by for it later," he said, walking to his truck.

When he saw me, he nodded in my direction, got back in the truck, and rolled off.

"Who was that, Daddy?"

"Oh, him? That was your fuckin' grandfather."

Trucks were never as romantic as trains, were more about hard work (and hemorrhoids) than freedom. Still, 18-wheelers are an important part of the economy of rambling. The trucker, though he has to go back home eventually, has a few hours or days of open road ahead in which he can be a desperado on wheels. And the tramps, hobos, and down-and-outers can always stick out a grimy thumb and flag down a truck instead of hopping a freight.

(Lest anyone forget, Elvis drove truck for Crown Electric back in Memphis.)

In the 1960s, truck songs became a staple of country radio—as country radio became a staple in truckers' cabs—with songs like "Six Days on the Road" by Dave Dudley, "Giddy-Up-Go" by Red Sovine, "Little Pink Mack" by Kay Adams, and "A Tombstone Every Mile" by Dick Curless.

Jimmy Martin's "Widow Maker" (1964), written by Penny Jay and Buddy Wilson, is one of the best of the lot. It's a straight-ahead bluegrass tragedy sung in a raw Tennessee voice a good fifteen years out of date but that still took a surprising bite out of the country chart at a time when the Nashville Sound ruled.

Martin, a former Blue Grass Boy and the self-styled King of Bluegrass, who was born in little Sneedville, Tennessee, in 1927, tells the tale of the brave Billy Mack who leaves his purty Wanda Ann behind only to die in the mountains, buried beneath twenty tons of steel. As "he fought the wheel," he flung his diesel rig off the highway to keep from killing some kids stalled on the road in a pickup.

It's a good old-fashioned story of self-sacrifice. And back in 1964, a young man like Billy Mack, he would've been proud and glad to serve in Vietnam.

Every morning, George Kelly rose up out of Cedar Swamp, where he lived with "that, that *colored* woman," as my great-aunts used to say (when they were feeling kind), and ghosted through Kingston, a khaki shadow stuffing his tote sack with pinecones and cans, roadkill and tonic bottles. There was never a cigarette butt or a cigar stub that George Kelly wasn't grateful for.

One hot August afternoon, one of those red-faced and breathless afternoons when it seems summer's never going to end, my sister sees George Kelly scuffing down our back road, a cloud of dust boiling behind him.

"George Kelly's comin'! George Kelly's comin'!"

Sis and I run into the barn and hide in the dark cool.

An oak tree stands across the road from our place, one of those great-great-grandfather oaks that draw lightning, stray cats, and drunk drivers. When George Kelly gets to that tree, he stops. He looks up the road . . . he looks down the road, his head swiveling like an owl's.

Satisfied that no one's around, George Kelly pulls down his pants, slaps his hands onto his knobby hips, arches his back, and, ballicky bareass, proceeds to piss on our tree.

Roger Miller was one of country's most improbable stars. His intensely personal mix of talking blues, nursery rhymes, and stand-up comedy spawned off-kilter hits like "Dang Me," "Do-Wacka-Do," and "You Can't Roller Skate in a Buffalo Herd"—hits that sounded as if they'd been recorded in the Twilight Zone. But he ended up winning eleven Grammys, got a Tony for his score to the Huck Finn–inspired Broadway musical *Big River* (1985), and even had a short-lived TV show in 1966.

On the other hand, he was orphaned soon after he was born in 1936, and raised in poverty by an uncle in Erick, Oklahoma. He quit school in eighth grade, and spent time in the military. As an adult he was intimate with the world of flops, run-down houses, single-wide trailers, and even half-long trailers.

All those strands twine together in Miller's greatest hit, "King of the Road" (1965), which soared to No. 1 Country and No. 4 Pop as the Beatles and Motown were slugging it out over pop supremacy.

"King of the Road" is absolute Miller: hipster finger snaps, jazzy phrasing, and exhilarating wordplay. When he sings lines like "I'm a man of means by no means" and "Ah, but two hours of pushing broom buys a eight-by-twelve four-bit room," he puts them across with such relish that you'd think he was devouring a particularly fine cut of steak. The tune's tone is so insouciant that it should be about a Park Avenue swell played by Cary Grant, not some rambling bum who hoboes from town to town.

Before he imploded on uppers—"speckled birds," he called them—Miller, that Oklahoma orphan, proved the worth of just being himself, of not trying to conform to conservative Nashville's norms.

Miller brags about not paying union dues in "King of the Road," but there were plenty of other dues to pay, bills that came due and finally killed him when he was just fifty-six years old.

"He was too fast for the world," Waylon Jennings told the writer Lyle Style. "He was just too fast."

Miller once wrote a song called "The Last Word in Lonesome Is Me." That's a sentiment that any Rambling Man can understand.

# Long Black Veil

*Ghosts, Murder, Orphans, and Worse*

The kingdom of country is sometimes otherworldly, nightmarish: Orphans freeze to death, crazed men kill their lovers and each other, unquiet ghosts roam the hills. It seems as if the sun is eternally blood red and going down, seems as if the land is swathed in a long black veil. In country music, if you can't make peace with the preternatural darkness, you will have no peace at all.

My kin were cloaked in country darkness, a darkness that comes of want and rage, a darkness articulated in alcohol-fueled rural violence. Now, this wasn't the stylish blood-poems of Sam Peckinpah's Westerns or Arthur Penn's *Bonnie and Clyde*. It lurched, stumbled, and bellowed: fistfights and car crashes, men crushed and maimed working the woods, women and children abused and abandoned. And sometimes there was murder. Small-town killings tend to happen over the same grievances as big-city murders: sex, money, drugs.

But, to us, killing was still personal. Growing up, I never heard of one local murder where the killer and the victim didn't know each other. My aunt Shirley knew the arsonist who killed her and her children.

Me and Sis were told not to talk to strangers, but we already understood that the most dangerous people are the ones you know. No one has ever hit me harder than my old man hit me. That's not a complaint, just the way it was.

Sure, we grew up in the specter of mutually assured atomic destruction, but me and Sis had local monsters to consider. Grammy Jennings's boyfriend Frank Nay and our uncle Billy George scared the hell out of us. Then there were the snakes, some of them thick as a man's wrist, that whisked through the sandpit down back, and snapping turtles in the cattail marsh, and rats, *big rats*: shit-house rats, junkyard rats, rats, man, that were big enough to drive Grandpa Ora's pickup truck. It makes perfect sense to me that Stephen King grew up in small-town Maine. The sticks are always where true horror, true mystery, skulks and lurks.

Country music gets at that. Songs like the Louvin Brothers' "Knoxville Girl," Lefty Frizzell's "Long Black Veil," and Bobbie Gentry's "Ode to Billie Joe" are steeped in blood and mystery, know that noir and manure go together.

One of the rough cultural truths that country music acknowledges is that, for most men, most women are prey or, at best, chattels. "So round, so firm, so fully packed," as Merle Travis sang, they're honky-tonk angels and cowboys' sweethearts meant to be fully possessed. But sometimes a woman is stolen. When that happens, a man just might have to kill her to prove the purity of his love. Back at the dawn of recorded country music, Jimmie Rodgers sang about shooting poor Thelma just to see her "jump and fall."

The Louvin Brothers' "Knoxville Girl" (1956) and Johnny Paycheck's "(Pardon Me) I've Got Someone to Kill" (1966) are two such songs drenched in blood, sex, and obsession.

Based on a traditional Anglo-Celtic ballad, "Knoxville Girl" is one of the most chilling songs in the country catalog. Sung from the killer's point of view, it tells how "Willie dear" takes his sweetheart for a walk one evening, then takes her life. He clubs her to death so the ground flows with her blood, then throws her in the river—"Go down, go down, you Knoxville Girl."

With no explanation.

That's the terrifying hole at the heart of this song. The Knoxville Girl is killed in cold blood, and we don't know why. Trilling in their usual unearthly harmony, the Louvins tell the tale straight, matter-of-factly. Even at the end, when they sing, "Because I murdered that Knoxville Girl, the girl I loved so well."

The Louvins came by their Southern Gothic chops naturally, born and raised on isolated Sand Mountain in northeastern Alabama—Ira in 1924 and Charlie in 1927. They also represent the last gasp of country's classic brother harmony acts, bridging the gap from the Delmore Brothers (also from Sand Mountain) to the coun-trified rock (or was it rock-ified country?) of the Everly Brothers.

Though the Louvins only had a handful of hits, their harmonies, repertory of hymns, and songs like "I Don't Believe You've Met My Baby" and "You're Running Wild" had a profound impact on blue-grass and later on artists like Emmylou Harris and Alison Krauss.

The Louvins originally recorded "Knoxville Girl" in 1956 for their album *Tragic Songs of Life* because, as Charlie told the country music historian Charles K. Wolfe, "it was the most requested song we ever sang, maybe almost the first song we ever sang." They even persuaded Capitol to release a single of it in 1959, and it sneaked to No. 19 Country.

How odd is that? A song like "Knoxville Girl," drawn from some ancient well and sung like a 1930s brother duet, holding its own against songs like George Jones's "White Lightning" and Marty Robbins's "El Paso"—as satellites spun through space and Americans fell more deeply into their television addiction.

But, as in all great works of art, there's a strangeness and mystery to the Louvins' "Knoxville Girl" that rewards a constant returning to the song.

Where "Knoxville Girl" is all restrained mystery, Paycheck's "(Pardon Me) I've Got Someone to Kill" is hard-boiled honky-tonk from the hell-raiser who gave us songs like "If I'm Gonna Sink (I Might as Well Go to the Bottom)" and "He's in a Hurry (to Get Home to My Wife)."

There are no unanswered questions in "Pardon Me," which was written by Paycheck and Aubrey Mayhew and is told in the first person. Our man's woman has been stolen from him—even though he warned the guy not to do it—and he's packing the gun that he plans to use to earn back his pride. "I've got a promise to fulfill," he tells the bartender, and as he excuses himself, he says, with the grim inevitability of a loser in a Jim Thompson crime novel: "Pardon me, I've got someone to kill."

Paycheck once worked in George Jones's band, and "Pardon Me" echoes the deliberate pace and phrasing of Jones's classic cheating song, "Window Up Above." In fact, "Pardon Me" could be its sequel. When the cuckolded Paycheck vows, "So tonight when they get home, I'll be waiting," you can hear a hint of Jones in there, too.

Paycheck was born Donald Lytle in Greenfield, Ohio, in 1938, and, like Merle Haggard, he tried to use his call to music to save himself from himself. He did land as a songwriter in Nashville, worked in the bands of Jones, Ray Price, Faron Young, and Porter Wagoner, and in the early 1960s embarked on a solo career as

Donny Young. But Paycheck had the unfortunate talent of being his own worst enemy. He spent two years in a Navy prison in Portsmouth, New Hampshire, for slugging an officer, and he spent another two years in prison thirty years later for shooting a man (who didn't die). By the end of the 1960s—and before "Take This Job and Shove It" (1977) made him a country star—Paycheck had indeed sunk all the way to the bottom, picking and grinning for cheap beer on Skid Row in Los Angeles.

Paycheck's 1960s work can be an acquired taste. For some reason, most folks don't cotton to tunes about a premeditated murder-suicide ("Pardon Me") or honky-tonk Armageddon of the nuclear variety ("The Cave"). But once you get used to Paycheck's hard stuff, the same way you get used to the taste of stout or Kentucky bourbon, you don't want to go back to that watered-down Nashville Sound.

The Louvin Brothers weren't interested in the Nashville Sound, either. But where their "Knoxville Girl" sounds like news ferried from the seventeenth century, Paycheck's "Pardon Me" is as fresh and lurid as an episode of *Cops*.


The word "orphan" sounds quaint nowadays, a throwback to the nineteenth century, to Dickens at his bleakest (and Huck Finn at his wildest). But orphans weren't just a storybook conceit to country singers of the 1950s and '60s, many of whom had been raised by the Great Depression. There's no shortage of country singers who were left behind as children by their parents—either by death or by disposition: Bill Monroe and Willie Nelson, Roger Miller and Jerry Reed, to name a few.

Just kids, and abandoned like a truck that won't start no more.

Grammy Jennings grew up in an orphanage (when she wasn't running away from it), and her first husband, Bub, was passed among his uncles as a boy. Then there were all the country kids who, on mighty flimsy paper, had at least one parent, but who were really left to raise themselves—like the old man and Ma.

In 1945, when Mom was five years old, her mother, Lilla Britton, farmed her only child out to do "light housekeeping" so that she could go and work at her cop boyfriend's hamburger joint in Salisbury Beach, Massachusetts. Why not just lead her into the deep woods and leave her there?

The older boys in the house where Mom worked teased her, burned her fingers on the stove. When her auntie Lee—Lilla's twin sister—noticed her niece's red and blistered fingers one weekend, she refused to send her back to "her job," deciding right then and there that little Flossie would be raised by her, her sister Helen, and their mother, Nanna George. Lilla be damned.

My mother . . . a real rural Cinderella.

To be honest, whenever I wrestle with this family story, I can't keep the tears at bay—five years old and farmed out . . . five years old and farmed out—and I retreat to a kind of fairy tale I've made up to try to see more clearly my five-year-old mother and her lost childhood:

The slave girl, that forsaken hank of hair—the one daughter whom the Queen's woodsman refused to slaughter—withers behind a scrim of tears, a would-be sacrifice sent away to sleep in thorn and burdock. Her low November sky boils with ash and snow. She feasts on gravel stew, on her skinny wrists, licks gravestone moss.

She's our skittish kitchen mouse, scrubbing, sweeping, scouring, sleeking the beds, lugging logs from the shed as cold-blooded mothers and uncles, cutthroats shawled in barbwire, count and connive, caulking their souls with cash.

Childhood deposed—proud braids beheaded, her dolls, those prim co-conspirators, are kindled in the grim woodstove: white silks sizzle then whisper, varnish vanishes, oak cheeks crack as burled skulls burst. Her two kittens, who purred sedition, are cursed to prison—the womb of the swamp . . . where little sisters already steep.

In "Jimmie Brown, the Newsboy" (1951), Flatt and Scruggs paint a musical picture of a day in the life of an orphan—think chiaroscuro Rockwell. Jimmie wanders the town from "daybreak to when," selling his newspapers, his clothes thin, his gut rumbling with hunger. Of course, if folks would only look close, they'd realize that *he's* the news, with no hat upon his head or shoes upon his feet.

But even though he's a kid who's been thrown back on himself, he doesn't want sympathy—"don't look at me and frown"—or a handout. He just wants you to do your bit to sustain the town's economic ecosystem by buying a newspaper. He knows his place in God's scheme of things, and he expects the same of you.

Lester Flatt sings with the expert fatalism of the Carter Family, sad (but not too sad) and gentle, while Earl Scruggs sets down his banjo to play guitar in the style of Mother Maybelle Carter. (The song itself is a nineteenth-century parlor tune rearranged in 1929 by A. P. Carter, who founded the Carter Family.)

Flatt and Scruggs, who in the 1940s helped Bill Monroe fully realize the sound of bluegrass music, by the 1960s had become the public face of bluegrass. They appeared at Carnegie Hall; were regulars on the *Beverly Hillbillies* TV show, taking its theme, "The Ballad of Jed Clampett," to No. 1 Country in 1962; and their "Foggy Mountain Breakdown," powered by the *Sturm und Twang* of Scruggs's three-finger banjo style, energized the film *Bonnie and Clyde* (1967).

"Jimmie Brown" is unusual for the band in that Scruggs, born in 1924 in Flint Hill, North Carolina, doesn't get to set loose the hounds with his banjo, but the tune suits Flatt, born in 1914 in

Duncan's Chapel, Tennessee, just fine. His mellow, sipping-whiskey voice assures us that hard living on your own is better than a life squandered in an orphanage. And when Jimmie tells us, "I'll get a place in heaven, sir, to sell the Gospel News," it breaks your heart.

Weren't nobody happy when Ma got pregnant with me in 1957, what with her being barely seventeen and all and the father being my old man, who wasn't nobody's idea of a young go-getter. Me? I can't complain—I got borned, didn't I?—but the Georges sure bitched. Lilla wouldn't sign the paper for Ma and the old man to get married till eight days before I was born; she remembered that her sister Helen had had a miscarriage *after* Nanna made her marry Allen West. And Uncle Billy would ease on up to Mom and hiss his poison, saying she'd be better off shed of that Jennings boy . . . and certainly better off without me.

Now you can begin to understand what killed so many young women back in those old-time ballads, maybe even that poor little Knoxville Girl.

In 1957, my fetal being, the divine spark glowing in my mother's belly, found itself in a kind of internal exile: My kinfolks, cursing . . . coaxing, all ache, all hunger to coat-hanger me, to banish blood, tissue, soul. They want to sack my amniotic Eden.

*But my mother whispers, "No."*

A feral clan of backwoods Grendels—their razor tongues veiled in lies—they lust after savaged fetal ruins, bloody burlap bags of fragile angel bone buried bog deep in Cedar Swamp. Placenta bestowed on the hog.

*But my mother whispers, "No."*

Their knotted leather talons drown kittens like washing the dishes. They favor December baptisms, fierce abortions in Kingston Lake; they savor a sharp shove down dark attic steps; then there's Nanna's ancient venoms hidden *deep* in her dirt-cellar keep.

*But my mother whispers, "No."*

Years later, when I come up a man and stand six feet tall, Uncle Bill still snarls when he sees me, still sharpens his lips as he whittles at his thumbnail with a jackknife.

*"No!"*

"Long Black Veil," first recorded in 1959 by Lefty Frizzell, pulls off a neat trick. Its primary author, Danny Dill, wanted to write what he called "an instant folksong"—this was at the height of the folk revival and its left-wing pretensions—just add guitar and soul and, voilà, old-time credibility. Well, he and Marijohn Wilkin succeeded. They wrote a song that sounded as if it were written the same week as "Knoxville Girl," but was so resonant and timeless that it's been covered by hundreds of acts, including Johnny Cash, Joan Baez (talk about the Folkie Good Songwriting Seal of Approval), the Band, the Grateful Dead, the Dave Matthews Band, and Nick Cave and the Bad Seeds. All that, and Frizzell had a hit with it, too.

"Long Black Veil" is the triple threat of country noir: part ghost story, part murder ballad, and part cheating song—goth country.

The tale is told from beyond the grave by a man hanged for a murder he didn't commit. He declines to give the judge his alibi, for, as he sings, "I had been in the arms of my best friend's wife." His lover doesn't come forward, either—a scarlet letter apparently being a fate worse than the death of her man—but does penance by walking "these hills in a long black veil" and crying o'er his bones.

Born in Corsicana, Texas, in 1928, Lefty Frizzell was a boozer and a brawler who sang like an angel. Influenced by Jimmie

Rodgers, he caressed vowels as if they were lovers, never hurrying along his songs like "If You've Got the Money, I've Got the Time," "Always Late (with Your Kisses)," and "I Love You a Thousand Ways." His approach to a song is heard in singers as diverse as Merle Haggard, Roy Orbison, and George Jones, and, later, George Strait, Keith Whitley, and Randy Travis.

"When I sing, to me every word has a feeling about it," Frizzell told the journalist John Pugh. "I had to linger, had to hold it, I didn't want to let go of it."

Making him perfect for "Long Black Veil," which is all about lingering: a lingering death, the woman who lingers at his grave, a lingering love. A bride of darkness, she wears her long black veil and is still cheating on her husband—but now with a ghost.

In the country, certain times of year are ripe with blood and shadows—late August, when the night air carries the faintest trace of the autumn to come, when sundown wakes the shades of widows and orphans; and October, when skeletons of cornstalk and oak snick and bicker—when, as Lefty sang, she walks these hills in a long black veil.

There's a wilderness in the blood that lusts after twilit mystery, lonely barrens that are often bared in the tunes of Bill Monroe and the Stanley Brothers. The deep feeling stirs as sunlight thickens, beckons the dark Karo syrup of August dusk. Out back the barn, a quarry-black Buick eats its own guts in the puckabrush. But even as the spooks pool in the half-light, life never stops. We are lured by the whisper of noir. But the divine spark won't be denied.

Out to our snake-crooked back road, a devout crow is bowed to his holy task (black cowl and bleak vows), redeeming a dead squirrel's past. The bloodiest guts are sneaked first, then tongue, eyes, gristle, and cracked bone as the crow harrows what crows must . . .

sucks marrow. And one fussy bite at a time is still supper, is still piecework, this cradling the dead, this lusting after the heart on a dusk-licked back road.

And it don't get dark till late . . . it don't get dark till late.


"It was the third of June, another sleepy, dusty Delta day."

That's how Bobbie Gentry, her voice as dusty as the day she's singing about, opens "Ode to Billie Joe" (1967). A day like any other out in the boonies, which means it's pretty much like the day before, and tomorrow don't promise to be too much different, neither. There's cotton to chop, hay to bale, acres to plow—and please, Mama begs, y'all don't forget to wipe your feet.

But we know something's wrong right away, that this isn't just another day in the endless freight train of days. Gentry's scratchy guitar work is hypnotic—like the relentless whine of high summer—but she worries the strings, plays as if it's almost too painful to make the chords, tipping us off right away that something ain't quite right.

And soon enough we find out that the singer's secret beau has committed suicide, learn that just that morning "Billie Joe MacAllister jumped off the Tallahatchie Bridge." From that moment on, "Billie Joe" blossoms into exquisite Southern Gothic mystery:

Why did that fool boy jump? How come the girl doesn't know why? How come she didn't tell nobody about her and Billie Joe? What was it that she and Billie Joe had thrown off that bridge just the day before? How can someone you love be here one eyeblink, then gone the next?

And how can Mama, Daddy, and Big Brother not see that their darling girl loved Billie Joe? She sits at the dinner table pale, silent, not eating, flinching at each and every mention of her boy's name. And they can't see. They pass each other the black-eyed peas, talk about Billie Joe's death as though it were just a particularly nasty storm that'd blown through and that they'll soon forget.

Born in Chickasaw County, Mississippi, in 1944 and raised on her grandparents' dirt farm till she was six, Bobbie Gentry—née Roberta Lee Streeter—started life suffused by those sleepy, dusty Delta days. And in late summer 1967, the pretty twenty-three-year-old who sounded world-weary beyond her years would take that bone-deep knowledge and strike a collective nerve. "Ode to Billie Joe" went No. 1 Pop, chased by, of all things, the Beatles and "All You Need Is Love."

The United States was being led straight to hell by its leaders that summer, and most folks didn't know why—but they had their theories. Billie Joe MacAllister jumped off the Tallahatchie Bridge that summer, and most folks didn't know why—but they had their theories.

Despite her youth, Gentry sounded as if she just might know the answers to both those questions. Folks listened to "Ode" over and over, spellbound, straining to find the deep hidden meaning.

But sometimes all you're left with is the mystery. Just ask that poor Knoxville Girl.

# I'm So Lonesome I Could Cry

You just need to wallow sometimes.

Your man or your woman's gone, the whiskey don't work no more, you're aching for the homeplace—and God ain't listenin'. You just need to sink into the dark, scratch your mutt's ears, and baptize yourself in the river of self-pity as you listen to the wild and blue moans of Hank Williams, the bleak deeps of Johnny Cash, or the lonesome smolder of Patsy Cline. Anyone, rich or poor, town or country, still today, can't help but be moved by the pure heartache and desolation that pulses in those singers' most mournful work.

You listen to those songs and tunes like Faron Young's "Hello Walls," Roy Orbison's "Crying," and Connie Smith's "Once a Day" because they understand that—like the first tablets that Moses flung away in anger—we are broken, know that our souls are tossed by November gales.

My people drank deep from the wells of loneliness. They were men and women of constant sorrow, and melancholy was their natural state. Why else would you sometimes call your only child "Tomorrow," as Lilla Britton did my mother? Why else would you permanently pull down the shades—creating eternal twilight in your shack—then watch television for more than fifty years, as my auntie Helen did?

*Lonely and melancholy . . . Lonely and melancholy.*

Willfully cut off from community, family, God, their own souls, they tried to vanish into booze, lust, and sheer meanness. And as they aged, they found out that gray hair without wisdom is its own kind of despair. Never mind Charlie Rich's "Lonely Weekends," try, *oh*, those lonely decades.

In the end, what's more lonesome than peering in the mirror and not recognizing yourself?

You tumble so far down the rabbit hole of sorrow sometimes that the only buddies you have left are four walls.

That's what happens in Faron Young's "Hello Walls" (1961) as the singer, jilted by his woman, confesses his pain. "Hello, walls," Young sings, "how things go for you today?" Pretty sad and creepy, but what's even more unsettling is that the walls—in the ghostly voices of the backup singers—answer back: "Hello, hello."

It's easy to imagine our man: He's just gotten off work from the hardware store or the barber shop, and he's driven home nudged by the hope that maybe, *just maybe*, his true love has returned. But she hasn't—and she won't—and he pours a tumbler of whiskey and asks the window, "Aren't you lonely?" and "Is that a teardrop in the corner of your pane?" He refuses to believe that it's only rain.

"Walls" was Willie Nelson's first smash hit as a songwriter—significant success as a performer didn't arrive until the 1970s, and his role as sagebrush sage came even later—and the biggest hit of Young's long career, spending nine weeks at No. 1 Country and even going to No. 12 Pop. In his autobiography, Nelson wrote, "When I got my first royalty check of $3,000 from 'Hello Walls,' I ran to

Tootsie's and found Faron sitting drinking at a table and kissed him flush on the mouth I was so excited." Well, hello, Willie!

"Walls" was a change of pace for Young, who made his reputation in the 1950s with cocky honky-tonkers like "Live Fast, Love Hard, Die Young" and "If You Ain't Lovin' (You Ain't Livin')." And while lots of country acts wilted before the first onslaught of rock 'n' roll, Young weathered it and even thrived. His combination of good looks, Elvis attitude, and hard country kept him on the charts well into the 1970s. Young, born in Shreveport, Louisiana, in 1932, also diversified by acting in Western movies like *Hidden Guns* and *Raiders of Old California*.

Those horse operas rode into the sunset years ago—six-gun fetishists aside—but "Hello Walls" lives on, through Willie's fine writing and Young's controlled delivery. Toward the end of the song, by the time he's talking to the walls, windows, and ceiling, we already know that his mind has made it out the back door, is headed down the road, and won't be back for a good long while.

This is what I remember of fourth grade: My mother sits at the kitchen table sipping Lipton tea sweetened with Pet condensed milk. She stares out the window—crying, as far as I can tell, for no good reason.

I missed 73 out of 180 school days that year. I can still see the notes Ma wrote to my teacher, Miss Gove, in her cramped and tortured hand: "I kept Andy home from school to help me out around the house because I didn't feel good." Miss Gove, my mother's age, drove a lipstick-red Corvette convertible.

Ma broke down that year, wore the caul of depression. At twenty-seven years old, she'd already been married ten years. Money was tight. The old man worked too much and drank too much. She spent her days in rural solitary, doing the wash, cooking, caring for three children. She needed me there to keep her company.

We didn't talk much. We didn't touch; people in my family never touched back then—unless it was to hit. Mornings we sat together and watched the game show *Concentration* and reruns of *The Beverly Hillbillies*. After a lunch of Campbell's tomato soup and a tuna sandwich, we'd listen to Patsy Cline on the record player or old Elvis 45s: "Love Me Tender," "Return to Sender," "Are You Lonesome Tonight?" I was there just in case, a safety net. I guided Ma through the silence of her days, the spontaneous tears and sighs. And I watched the old man, inarticulate and afraid, smolder, wonder whether he was somehow losing the love of his life. My parents needed me that year. I was a bridge, no matter how narrow and rickety, a son and a suture.

And not one word from school. I was the phantom of the fourth grade, and no one had a word to say. Dirt's invisible, too.

Miss Gove wrote one comment on my report card the entire school year: "Dana has missed a great deal of math instruction and this is reflected in his work."

Like "Hello Walls," Connie Smith's "Once a Day" (1964) ponders the forsaken back road that leads from sadness to madness. In "Walls," Faron Young is reduced to chatting up windows and ceilings; Smith, though, is down to crying just "once a day, every day, all day long."

"Once a Day" is a catchy true-confessions tear-fest with Smith tear-ing through the song and Weldon Myrick's steel guitar acting as the sob sister that bawls right back at her. (There'd be no tears in country music without the pedal steel and the fiddle.) Misery indeed loves company, especially when it's as exquisite as Myrick's touch on the steel.

And when Smith sings about a girl who "sat around and cried her life away" until she lost her mind, we know that she's looking into the mirror of the tears pooled at her feet.

With "Once a Day," which spent twenty-eight weeks on the country chart and eight of them at No. 1, Smith fulfilled another Nashville fairy tale. The year before, in 1963, she had been just another unremarkable Ohio girl tamed by motherhood and marriage who liked to sing at local Grange meetings and square dances.

One year later, after being discovered by the country star and songwriter Bill Anderson, she was singing on Jimmy Dean's and Lawrence Welk's network TV shows and had been anointed "The Sweetheart of the *Grand Ole Opry*" by the venerable Roy Acuff. As with any fairy tale worth its salt, she became an *Opry* princess only after starting out in life with next to nothing.

Constance June Meador, born in 1941 in Elkhart, Indiana, was one of fourteen children in a family of migrant farmworkers. She and her brothers and sisters were beaten by their alcoholic father. To escape his fists, she'd shinny up a tree and sing her blues away for hours—maybe even once a day, every day, all day long.

I grew up in a kingdom of deep, deep sighs. Oh, how the women did *sigh*—all of 'em. Sighs like Psalms . . . sighs that lasted a week . . . sighs you could drown in. Fissures of breath that seemed to bear all the grief this world has ever known.

*Sighs*.

Auntie Fat Dot and Auntie Irene sitting in dark shack kitchens, Red Rose tea steeping or instant coffee cooling, sorrowing and sighing as if they could sigh away the useless men they'd married.

Grammy Britton, mistress of sigh and scowl, and Grammy Jennings, who at least sighed before cracking open another beer.

Ma's sighs suffused our house. They were sighs of longing and sorrow, of feelings she couldn't voice. They were her prayer—deep calling unto deep—the holy breath she summoned to keep her demons at bay.

The men didn't sigh. They hit.


Harry Choates's "Jole Blon" (1946) has to be one of the most improbable country hits (and eventual standards) ever recorded.

A fiddler by trade, Choates covered one of Cajun music's earliest recordings—"Ma Blonde Est Partie" (1928) by Amedee Breaux and Cleoma Breaux Falcon—then keened through French lyrics that were as unintelligible (save for the occasional "jole blon" or "jolie fille") as a rawboned farmhand on a Saturday night drunk in Lafayette.

But Choates's squeaky fiddle and singular Cajun moan tap hundreds of years of Acadian exile. This is music that can speak to the diaspora of your choice. While most folks couldn't understand what Choates was singing, they responded to the emotion in his musical cry. This was 1946 and 1947, and many rural dwellers, whether they could articulate it or not, knew that their world was about to change, that dislocation, both physical and psychological, was inevitable. World War II was over—and how were you going to keep those boys down on the farm after they'd kept the world safe for democracy?— and the industrial engine fired by the war was now ready to be set loose on America itself, creating the consumer society that defined (and defiled) the second half of the twentieth century. It was time to bend over and kiss your cow goodbye.

On the surface, "Jole Blon" is just another song about love gone wrong, but, really, it's a timeless waltz of exile that harks back to

1755, when the British drove the French-speaking Acadians from Nova Scotia, New Brunswick, and Prince Edward Island. Many of those refugees by 1764 had resettled in the backwoods and bayous of Louisiana. Country music fans reacted viscerally to the tune's timeless anguish, pushing it to No. 4 Country. Then it was covered right away by artists as diverse as Moon Mullican, Red Foley, and Roy Acuff. In a sense, Hank's Cajun romp from 1952, "Jambalaya," is a cover in spirit and a tribute to "Jole Blon."

Choates, born in 1922 in Vermilion Parish, Louisiana, never really capitalized on his hit. A rough and rowdy alcoholic, he died in an Austin, Texas, jail cell in 1951. The official report states that he died from causes related to his alcoholism. But a bitter myth has persisted that he was beaten to death in jail—no one wants a hero to die of cirrhosis of the liver. Whenever Choates's name comes up, bayou old-timers will still debate how po' ol' Harry Choates died.

But "Jole Blon" lives on. Cajuns—whether it's events from more than 50 years ago or 250 years ago—never forget the tears in things.

My great-uncle Henry George knew that there ain't nothing lonelier than the ass-end of a Boston & Maine freight train. Uncle Henry knew that there ain't nothing more sorrowful than to look into the face of your children and wonder why they don't look like you. And he knew that you didn't have to go far to spend your life in exile. When the time came to leave the house of his father, Ora, he shuffled down the hill from his old man's place and with his own two hands built the shack where he would live for some seventy years till he died. To the east lay the seductive shadows of Cedar Swamp, to the south a sandpit, to the north a shady grove of pines and then the power-line road, and to the west, just a few hundred yards up the hill, was Route 125.

With his purposeful exile, Henry was typical in my family. His exile was defined by what his life lacked: education (he couldn't read or write), ease with other people, money. The Land of Poverty is also the Land of Exile. His hawky Indian face bore a look of constant mourning, and he wore his cloak of unspoken loneliness without complaint until he died in his nineties.

He burned days on end out to Cedar Swamp, hunting, trapping, and fishing. Going into town meant picking the dump. If you needed help putting in your corn or if you'd buried your car up to the doors in a sandbank in the gravel pit, he'd get his rusted tractor sputtering and harrow your plot or tug you out the sand, then go back to puttering his day away.

I can't recall a single word that Great-Uncle Henry ever spoke to me beyond "Hi, Andy." But when he said it, he meant it, and I can still see him: flannel shirts and overalls, his oil-stained billed cap pulled low so that all you saw were his nose and his high, hard cheekbones.

He expected nothing from this world—as far as he was concerned, the president could've been Castro instead of Kennedy—and, in turn, the world expected nothing from him.

Roy Orbison was no one's vision of a rock star.

With his mole eyes and double chin, his high school classmates should've voted him most likely to manage the butcher counter at the local A&P. But when Orbison, born in 1936, opened his mouth, that was another matter. Even when he was young, they all knew that the Orbison kid could *sing*.

At sixteen, he had his own band, the Wink Westerners, named for the West Texas town where he grew up. By age twenty, he was cutting eccentric but effective rockabilly for Sun Records like "Ooby Dooby," "Devil Doll," and "Rock House." And at age twenty-four in 1960, he had the No. 2 Pop song in the nation, "Only the Lonely."

Along the way, he wrote "Claudette," named for his future wife and a modest hit for the Everly Brothers.

Which brings us to "Crying" (1961), a kind of sequel to "Only the Lonely." By 1961 Orbison had perfected the pop formula that would produce hits like "Blue Angel," "It's Over," "Running Scared," and "Crying." Backed by Nashville A-teamers, Orbison's producer, Fred Foster, couched his boy's delicate, multi-octave voice amid lush strings and choruses the way a jeweler sets a diamond against plush velvet to show off its facets. (Even on songs that don't use strings, like "Dream Baby" and "Oh, Pretty Woman," you swear that you can hear them.) The result is over-the-top orchestral pop, opera satisfyingly reimagined by a bunch of hillbillies—the son of Okie refugees from the Great Depression creating a new kind of pop music that didn't forsake Lefty Frizzell and Jimmie Rodgers.

In "Crying," written by Orbison and Joe Melson, the singer dissolves before our very ears—*"I've been cry-y-y-ing over you"*—as the song builds and builds and *builds* to an orgasm of tears. Tears, really, of transfiguration: thick, scalding, purifying.

You could argue, even, that Orbison, who hid himself in black suits and behind hipster shades, was making proto-emo, was expressing vulnerability when boys were told to take it like a man . . . when presidents would risk blowing up the world rather than being perceived as weak.


The past wells within us like tears (wells within us, too, like a good country song):

I see Mom walking out the doctor's office—wobbly, as if she's wearing heels, but she isn't. Her cheeks are red. She's sobbing. Me and Sis stare at her, at each other. Ma's crying in public. We all know we ain't supposed to cry, ain't supposed to make a fuss, ain't supposed to let on that we hurt—inside or outside. Like Pharaoh, we're supposed to harden our hearts, bite back the tears until our goddamn lips bleed. But here's Ma, crying out in the open for all the world to see. We don't understand . . . and we feel our own tears burn.

Mom's pregnant again.

Well, friends and neighbors, it's time to turn on the oven, break out the razor blades, and load the shotgun.

"I'm So Lonesome I Could Cry" just might be the saddest country song ever written. Hank, who wrote this song, spent his career dallying with the blues in tunes like "Long Gone Lonesome Blues" and "Moanin' the Blues." But the stakes in "I'm So Lonesome I Could Cry" are mortal . . . and more.

Robins weep as leaves die. Whip-poor-wills are too blue to take wing. The moon hides its face behind a cloud and cries. All this as the midnight train whines low. The song's original title, in case you don't get the point, was "I'm So Lonesome I Could Die."

"Lonesome" is as stately as a funeral procession—Jerry Byrd's steel and Tommy Jackson's fiddle bear the body very well—and as terse as a haiku. But as suffused with sorrow as the song is, it's also cause to hope. In writing "Lonesome," Hank—at least temporarily—refused to give in to the burden of his worldly grief. Instead, he plucked out the glowing coal of pain from his soul and wrote what many people feel is the best country song ever made, maybe even the best song—period.

With "I'm So Lonesome I Could Cry," Hank Williams is both lonely and holy. He is like the supplicant in Psalm 30: "Though one goes to bed weeping, one awakens in song."

# I'll Never Get Out of This World Alive

Death at least winks, and sometimes downright leers, from between the notes of songs about prison and poverty, cheatin' and drinkin', murder and melancholy. And on occasion, Old Man Death himself takes center stage, bows his head, and preaches to the converted in songs like Roy Acuff's "Wreck on the Highway," Bill Monroe's "The Little Girl and the Dreadful Snake," and Porter Wagoner's "Green, Green Grass of Home."

How could country music not echo the endless death march that was the twentieth century: two world wars, the Great Depression, the atomic desolation of Hiroshima and Nagasaki, the Cold, Korean, and Vietnam wars, the Holocaust and other multi-continent genocides, the shadow of nuclear suicide? Even God was dead, some philosophers said, but most country folk wrote that off as just city-slicker bullshit. Still, there was no denying the cult of death the century nurtured. In rock 'n' roll, we're all going to live forever, and in pop, death is an inconvenient rumor. But country (and R&B), in its earthy and forthright way, understands that there's music to be found in the sound of dirt cascading onto a coffin. And art that's willing to grapple with death is art that lasts.

But in the end, death, like politics, is local. When I was growing up, the Vietnam War was a grainy black-and-white abstraction until two of Kingston's own, David Bunker and John Steer, were killed in 1967.

But beyond morally bankrupt wars that Washington could never explain to us properly—funny how some things never goddamn change—the cities might've been dens of sin and iniquity, but living in the country was still hard and dangerous. Infant and child mortality rates were higher than in the cities, and even today farming and mining—country work—are still two of the most dangerous jobs in America. There are lots of ways to die or get maimed and crippled way out in the country, too many: a car crash on a winding, rain-slick back road; your mind wandering down to the sawmill; drinking; loneliness; neglect; hunting accidents; drowning . . .

Death's bony finger is always crooked, always beckoning. But most the men—cloaked in their vices, ripping seat belts out their cars and trucks, half-assed when it came to safety on the job—flipped Death the bird, were strangely smug in their fatalism.

They were just waiting for their number to come up. Along with Hank Williams, they reminded us that none of us get out of this world alive.

Roy Acuff's "Wreck on the Highway" (1942), on the surface, is a simple, heartfelt song about unfortunate death and destruction. But dig a bit deeper, and it's really about the tension between the old ways and modern technology—and, more important, God's place in this new world.

As speeds soared on the not-so-open roads, the car wreck gave the twentieth century a new Bosch-like spectacle and nightmare:

warped and jagged steel, glass starring the blacktop, whiskey and blood and gasoline flowing together, and bodies burst through windshields. But as Acuff sings—seconded by Bashful Brother Oswald Kirby's mournful Dobro—"I heard the crash on the highway, but I didn't hear nobody pray."

Dorsey Dixon wrote "Wreck on the Highway," and his son Dorsey junior told Dorothy Horstman: "My father wrote this song in 1936 when the '36 Fords came out with a V-8 engine and began to kill people all over the nation." In other words, if you give people more speed and more power, they're going to use it, even if they don't know how to handle it.

Though the song was as modern as that shiny new Ford, its tune sounded as if it'd been lifted from some gloomy nineteenth-century hymn that takes at least an eternity to sing. That made Acuff, with his preacherly, from-the-heart vocals, the right man for the job.

Acuff, the son of a farmer who was also a Baptist preacher, was born in Maynardville, Tennessee, in 1903. He joined the *Grand Ole Opry* in 1937 and became one of its biggest stars, known for chestnuts like "Wabash Cannonball" and "Great Speckled Bird." More important, he laid one of the cornerstones to Nashville becoming Music City U.S.A. when he and the songwriter Fred Rose established Acuff-Rose Publications in 1942. Among other things, Acuff-Rose encouraged and developed the career of a young singer-songwriter named Hank Williams, who certainly learned a thing or two about selling a song to an audience from Acuff's gut-wrenching delivery on "Wreck on the Highway."

The song became a country standard and found its way into the repertory of most every act that had to make peace with the highway. The road is never kind to musicians—country or not—who, in the old days, were forced to make long-distance jumps by sedan, station wagon, or bus to make a living. Country musicians made a habit of laughing about the wrecks they walked away from, but the road killed some of them, too.

Johnny Horton died in a car crash, as did Ira Louvin. And Jack Anglin, of the duo Johnnie and Jack, died in a car wreck in 1963. He was on his way to funeral services for Patsy Cline, Cowboy Copas, Hawkshaw Hawkins, and Randy Hughes, who had all died together in a plane crash.

Speed is a temptation that is not discussed in the Bible. That temptation to slam the gas pedal flush to the floor and bury that red needle past 120 miles an hour. The temptation to zip from one part of the county to another faster than God, or physics, intended. To beat that onrushing line of cars through the intersection.

We moved into a rented house at the corner of New Boston Road and a new, soon-to-be-open stretch of Route 125 in January 1964. The road opened that spring, routing people away from the center of town, black asphalt gleaming, smooth, straight, and *fast*. (This is the same piece of road that claimed my great-grandfather's house and the first house I ever lived in.)

Within a month, as we ate supper one night, we heard brakes shriek, steel crumple, and glass shatter. Someone had tried to dart across Route 125 but hadn't made it. The lights of police cars, fire trucks, and ambulances flickered in the living-room windows. You could smell burnt rubber and gasoline, just like at Pines Speedway.

But that crash was just the overture to the aria of anarchy to come. *Shriek* . . . crumple . . . shatter. *Shriek* . . . crumple . . . shatter. More terrifying was when there was no squeal of brakes at all, just the thunderclap of a car getting T-boned at speed. There were severe injuries and death; in those days, the impact aside, real steel and real glass were unforgiving in a car wreck. Some accident victims said they hadn't seen the stop signs posted on New Boston Road, so the state installed a blinking red (along with a blinking amber for Route 125). The crashes slowed, but still continued.

The true problem was impatience. Some folks couldn't abide waiting for the long line of cars, couldn't stand getting stuck behind a car going the speed limit. Sooner or later, they'd say, "Aw, fuck it," and just go—then see what happened.

The death of a child rends the soul, shreds the very fabric of the universe. Popular culture flinches at such death. It's a rare novel, movie, or TV show that dares kill a child. They will place that child in peril, but death? When in doubt, put your money on that plucky kid with leukemia pulling through.

Then there's the world according to Bill Monroe.

In two classic songs that he wrote—"I Hear a Sweet Voice Calling" (1947) and "The Little Girl and the Dreadful Snake" (1952)—Monroe imagines the deaths of two children and, like Hemingway, refuses to look away.

Monroe, that melancholy Kentuckian, knew the desolation of childhood, knew what it was like to live alone and lonely way back in the country with no mother or dad. He survived his childhood, but also arrived at a dark yet practical common sense. You can pray every morning, noon, and night and try to lead your life the best you can as a sturdy, upright Christian man. But sometimes, like Job, you will be afflicted for no better reason than a wager between God and Satan.

Your child will tumble down an abandoned well or get bitten by a poisonous snake, or simply take ill and fail. That's what happens in "I Hear a Sweet Voice Calling." One moment the little girl is walking home from school, and the next she's blissing in her deathbed.

Monroe is powerless before the girl's dying. All he can manage is his bluest moans as the girl says, "I hear a sweet voice calling, way up in heaven on high."

The only promise that parents and child can cling to is that they'll meet again on that bright and peaceful shore.

"The Little Girl and the Dreadful Snake," part two of Monroe's doleful double feature, is even more harrowing. The little girl in question loses her way in a dark wood and her parents can't find her. Then, from far away, they hear her scream, "Hurry, Daddy, there's an awful, dreadful snake." The father only gathers up his daughter after she's been bitten by a poisonous snake, and it's clear that she's going to die.

"I Hear a Sweet Voice Calling" is leavened by the sure promise of heaven, but "Dreadful Snake" has the German woodcut quality of a dark parable. The parents can only *hope* to be reunited with their darling in heaven. In the five years between the two songs—five years in which the dreadful snake of nuclear war shook its death rattle louder and louder, five years in which many Americans wondered whether their children would even see the age of twenty-one—doubt has even insinuated itself into the heart of a stout Christian man like Bill Monroe.

Children are vulnerable. Children die.

They get hit by cars . . . they die by fire . . . they wander off into the woods . . . they die for no good reason in the crib . . . they fall through false ice and drown.

I had a friend named Lisa when I was seven, eight years old. We weren't best friends, but close enough. We sledded together, built sand castles at the beach. She was one of those skinny little girls who could laugh and run from sunup till sundown. She was there one season—I blinked—and the next she was gone.

A brain tumor killed her. I remember being sad, but fascinated, too: so children really do die. When I think about her now, some forty years later, I see us skipping stones on a frog pond. They skip and skip and skip, the water puckering at their passing until, finally, they sink and the pond goes glass as if they were never even there.

But, Lisa Martin, you still skip and ripple in my memory.


The Stanley Brothers' version of the traditional "Angel Band" (1955) is a pure slice of heaven. "My latest sun is sinking fast," Carter Stanley opens the song, "my race is nearly run."

But this is no prelude to woe-is-me whining. This song is sung in the attitude of Ecclesiastes, sung with the wisdom of a man who knows there is nothing new under the sun, a man ready to greet Death's crazy arms.

Supported by Curly Lambert's supernal mandolin and the whole group joining in on vocals, Carter pleads: "Oh, come, Angel Band, come and around me stand. Oh, bear me away on your snow-white wings to my immortal home."

Of course, in the singing of this hymn, Carter, Ralph, and the Clinch Mountain Boys sound as if they're about to cross over Jordan themselves, sound as if they've traded in mere flesh and blood for the robes and wings of angels.

This is how a rugged, old-fashioned Christian faces death— flagging the angels as if he's flagging a ride out to Route 125.


Grammy Jennings, who was just four-foot-ten and who, by her own count, had had at least ten miscarriages, always had her eye out for the runt of the litter, the kitten or puppy least likely to make it. She'd feed it milk and sugar water through an eyedropper, smear it with Vicks VapoRub so it could breathe better, pet it so that it knew it had someone in this cold world to care for it, and nest it next to the stove so it wouldn't shiver. She constantly fussed over those cats and dogs like the lonely little orphan girl she had once been . . . and still was.

Porter Wagoner's "Green, Green Grass of Home" (1965) is a song where home, prison, and heaven converge. In other words, it's a song about death. In his warm baritone, Wagoner tells us that the old hometown looks pretty much the same, though he's been away for years. He already sees his folks and his beloved Mary, who has "hair of gold and lips like cherries." You can almost hear Wagoner sigh in doglike satisfaction as he sings, "It's good to touch the green, green grass of home."

(Of course, with this song coming out in the mid-1960s, I heard more than a couple people sing about "smoking the green, green grass of home.")

Then Curly Putman, who wrote the tune, stings us with his O. Henry twist: Our man isn't home at all, but in prison, where he'll be executed at daybreak. He was only dreaming about the green, green grass of home. Sure, it's a hackneyed device, but Wagoner makes the turn work because he believes in the song, inhabits it as he sings it.

That's one of the essences in the best country, that singers can sell the song because they become the song. Hank had it, George Jones has it still, Roy Acuff sometimes sacrificed true tears as he sang. Pop singers could always give you a pleasant and catchy "reading" on a tune, but country singers offered up their hearts and guts.

That's why we're moved, as the angelic Anita Kerr Singers bear our man away, when Wagoner makes it clear that he will only make it home to be laid beneath its green, green grass.

I grew up among men and women who worked themselves to death before they were sixty, and who, when in doubt about something, took a goddamn hammer to it.

They were people who insisted on chain saws that had no safety catch . . . who kept the shotgun loaded and leaning next to the front door . . . who drove drunk, too fast, and would only pass on a double yellow.

*Aw, fuck it.*

They were people who smoked filterless Camels and Lucky Strikes, drank rubbing-alcohol cocktails, and raced their motorcycles up and down Route 125 without a helmet . . . who jumped off Tricklin' Falls in the dark . . . who had sex without birth control, even though they already had six kids they could barely feed.

*Aw, fuck it.*

They were people who put their canoe into Pow-Wow River even as the thunderheads bulked and boiled . . . who hunted without a license, drove without a license, and, yes, got married without a license . . . who let the brakes on their trucks get as mushy as their brains.

*Aw, fuck it.*

The subtitle to Hank Williams's "I'll Never Get Out of This World Alive" could've been: "But I'll Get Another No. 1 Hit." The song, written by Hank and his mentor, Fred Rose, came out on December 20, 1952, just days before Hank died in the backseat of a chauffeured Cadillac on his way to a January 1 show.

"I'll Never Get Out of This World Alive" soon became the first of Hank's four posthumous No. 1 hits. The others were "Kaw-Liga," which spent thirteen weeks at No. 1, "Your Cheatin' Heart," and

"Take These Chains from My Heart." Easily the best chart run ever pulled off by a dead guy.

Hank would've laughed at the black humor in that, because that's what "World Alive" is all about—grinning through the pain. "I had lots of luck, but it's all been bad," Hank explains, telling us that his woman's run off, his creek's full of sand, his fishing pole's broke, and the soles of his shoes are so thin (probably from chasing after his fickle woman) he bets that he could tell whether a worn-out dime is heads or tails.

"No matter how I struggle and strive," he moans, "I'll never get out of this world alive."

Hank dresses his song up in grins and giggles, but that's still pretty bleak hick wisdom for a guy who isn't even thirty yet.

Country music has always loved tribute songs, from Jimmie Rodgers to Elvis, and there were plenty recorded after Hank died. But Hank did Rodgers and Elvis one better. In a sense, with "I'll Never Get Out of This World Alive," he got to write his very own—and best—tribute.

# I Saw the Light

God was not much present in our lives when I was a kid. Or, if he was among us, no one went out of the way to acknowledge it—on either side of the holy ledger. God was a rumor, a Sunday morning accessory for the fine, upstanding middle-class folks who strolled to the white wood-frame church in the center of town. One of our cherished cultural clichés is of the poor and pious. The penniless souls have holes in their shoes, holes in their pockets, and holes in their bellies, but at least they have the Father, the Son, and the Holy Ghost to fill up on.

I didn't grow up among the poor and pious, though . . . I grew up among the poor and pissed off.

Most those men had more use for a spent shotgun shell than they did for God. All that "holy bullshit" was for the women. My uncle Billy George used to call prayer "kissing God's ass," which, at the very least, indicated that he believed there was some divine ass to kiss. Those leathery sonstabitches like Billy (smoking Camels was as close as most of 'em ever got to the Holy Land) were good for the occasional *"Jay-sus Sufferin' Christ*," but that was about it.

Those men, nursing their Wild Turkey like a grudge, died too soon to reconsider their relationship with the Lord. When one of my old man's friends, Al Smart, died, he was buried with a case of Bud, not a Bible—the King of Beers, not King James. In memory, it is almost as if Al Smart's coffin was carried to the cemetery, borne heavenward, by a team of Clydesdales.

And the women? Well, some the women were as hard as the men. Their gray lives crucified on the unforgiving cross of the Great Depression, they believed that hell was this life on earth. So why not embrace the thick smoke, dim lights, and loud, loud music? Why not embrace that tall, dark stranger whose lust scars his face?

But others of those women were so God-fearing that the mere thought of walking to church made them *tremble*. Yet others were Bible-nippers, sipping from the Good Book when their men weren't around—reading the Bible being both an act of defiance and a rebuke—the way other women took a medicinal shot of heat from the old man's whiskey bottle.

It was not a Rockwellian world of prayer, hymns, and ham-and-bean suppers. Just as those men and women scrabbled in the margins, God, if he moved at all in their lives, existed solely as a tangent to that marginality.

Country singers understood all that; this is the world they had fled. And, as flawed as they were, those singers were willing to bow their heads and round their shoulders to act as the Good Lord's intermediaries, able to articulate a relationship with the holy for their listeners. The hellions knew and loved all the old hymns—maybe especially the hellions. Even rogues like Johnny Paycheck and George Jones recorded gospel, and independent spirits like Willie Nelson and Merle Haggard, even that smoldering ladies' man Conway Twitty. (After all, gospel numbers are the ultimate love songs, right?)

Hank Williams and Johnny Cash fancied themselves latter-day

prophets, though certainly not saints. Hank recited Christian cautionary tales as Luke the Drifter—then promptly went out and did what his alter ego Luke told folks not to do—while Cash cultivated the uncompromising persona of country's wrathful Everyman, the Man in Black, and insisted on recording hymns throughout his career.

They all believed that the right singer with the right song at the right time could create a moment of holiness for himself and for the listener—no matter how far down the path of sin either of them had staggered. The best hymn singers, like Hank and Cash and Bill Monroe, never sing by rote. They feel each word, each note, each time out. They test the song, even as the song tests them.

Ira Louvin was surely tested.

Like Cash and Hank, Louvin embodied that tension between the life lived and the life sung. He spent his career hymning about salvation and the wages of sin with the Pentecostal certainty that he'd learned as a boy on Sand Mountain, Alabama, but he spent his days raging, boozing, and chasing women. It's as if he could only be the man he truly wanted to be when he immersed himself in the healing waters of his music.

But even on the cover of the Louvin Brothers' best-known gospel album, *Satan Is Real* (1960), where Charlie looks nearly saintly, Ira looks downright demonic, leering among burning stones as a twelve-foot-tall Satan (Ira built it from plywood) looms in the background. The brothers are dressed in white linen suits of baptismal purity, and Charlie appears ready to be God-dunked in the river Jordan. Ira appears ready to be (gladly) baptized by fire.

The twelve-track album features six compositions by the Louvins, including "There's a Higher Power," "Are You Afraid to Die," and "The Christian Life." With their usual saintly harmonies and with Ira's mandolin sounding like an angel's lyre, the brothers tell sacred tales of old country preachers, old country churches, and Satan's jeweled crown. They want you to ease into the cool waters of their music and be made whole.

The album's highlight is "The Christian Life," which quickly became a country-gospel standard and was even covered by Gram Parsons and the Byrds on *Sweetheart of the Rodeo* (1968). "My buddies shun me since I turned to Jesus," Ira sings. But even so, the brothers emphatically and beatifically affirm, "I like the Christian life."

Throughout *Satan Is Real*, Ira Louvin sounds like a man who was called to preach. But he didn't. And maybe, in the end, that's what destroyed him.

Johnny Cash had always wanted to sing gospel. Cash and the Tennessee Two first approached Sam Phillips at Sun Records as a gospel act. But Phillips, who was intrigued by their spare sound, told them to either get secular or get lost. They got secular fast. But it still stuck in Cash's craw that Phillips wouldn't let him go gospel. That's one of the reasons Cash cited for leaving Sun for Columbia in 1958: Columbia promised to let him make gospel albums. As Cash said, he wanted to be able "to tithe" his music.

That "tithing" even paid off with a No. 1 hit hymn in 1969, "Daddy Sang Bass" (written by Carl "Blue Suede Shoes" Perkins). It was sandwiched between two other No. 1 hits for Cash, "Folsom Prison Blues" and "A Boy Named Sue," written by Shel Silverstein, the *Playboy* humorist and children's book writer. Now, that's range, going from prison to the sublime to the just plain goofy. Even at the very end, Cash, who died in 2003, was consumed by matters of ultimate concern. The title song on the last album released before he died, *The Man Comes Around* (2002), was written by him and bristles with imagery from the book of Revelation.

Sam Phillips at Sun did toss Cash one holy bone before they

parted, though, letting him record "I Was There When It Happened" on his first album, *Johnny Cash with His Hot and Blue Guitar.* Written by Fern Jones, an itinerant Pentecostal shouter, and popularized by acts like the Blackwood Brothers and Jimmie Davis, former governor of Louisiana *and* member of the Country Music Hall of Fame (*only* in Louisiana, man), "I Was There When It Happened" was one of the first songs that Cash, Luther Perkins, and Marshall Grant learned together.

Cash sings the song with his trademark stark conviction. We believe him when he tells us that he knows when Jesus saved him, that he knows salvation is real. And we nod in agreement as he intones, "Well, I was there when it happened, and so I guess I ought to know."

But, as with most country singers, there's a chasm between the faith sung and proclaimed and the life as it's lived. Still, it meant a lot to country fans that Johnny Cash was a man of faith. Here was a hard-living hellion, usually high on women and pills, who could be as mean as a stepped-on snake, a man's man who swaddled himself in black to tip his hat to the darkness in this world (and within himself), but who bowed his head before the holy breath that sustains the universe. The women will moan and swoon over a square-jawed man of God. The men might not be convinced, but they will at least stop and consider the holy.

Every kid, until the inevitable taint sets in, understands that there is something greater than he is, something greater than his parents, than his town. *Something.* Dust motes waltzing in a shaft of sunlight confirm that, or one long look at the unfathomable night sky. But my people were so beaten down they couldn't even raise their heads to see that sky, to really *see* it. It was much easier to stare at the bottom of an empty bottle.

Most my relations were too invested in their lusts and grievances to taste the holy. They were slaves in exile, and poverty kept
them from God, made them so hungry and feral and mean that God
didn't cross their minds—the way God doesn't cross the mind of a
fox or a possum or a fisher cat.

They could not draw God into their lives, because you cannot
draw water from a dry well.

Hymns are often concerned with "crossing over," fording that wide
Jordan River and entering the promised land that, for Christians, is
heaven. Ferlin Husky's "Wings of a Dove" (1960) doesn't have
crossing over on its mind explicitly, but the song itself did manage
to cross over and become that rare thing: a Top 40 gospel hit.

"Wings of a Dove," written by Bob Ferguson, not only spent
thirty-six weeks on the country chart (ten of them at No. 1), but it
soared as high as No. 12 Pop. Some of its unlikely peers on the pop
chart in 1960 included teenage dramas like "Cathy's Clown" by the
Everly Brothers and "Teen Angel" by Mark Dinning, dance-floor
favorites like "The Twist" by Chubby Checker and "Save the Last
Dance for Me" by the Drifters, and that uncategorizable chunk of
bubblegum, "Itsy Bitsy Teenie Weenie Yellow Polka Dot Bikini" by
Brian Hyland.

Pretty strange company for the song's revival hand claps, Salvation Army drums and tambourines, and Husky's vocals that strike
just the right balance between earnest and ecstatic: "On the wings of
a snow-white dove, he sends his pure sweet love." And once the
song revs up, Husky and the band sound as if they could keep on
going till kingdom come, sustained by the manna of what they're
singing.

"Wings of a Dove" was the most enduring hit for Husky, who was
born in Flat River, Missouri, in 1927, and it became a country-gospel

standard. Husky, who began his career as Terry Preston because he thought his real name sounded as fake as a pro wrestler's, came out of the same Bakersfield scene that gave us Buck Owens, Merle Haggard, and Wynn Stewart. Though he was still charting in the mid-1970s, Husky recorded his best-known songs, like "A Dear John Letter" and "Gone," between 1953 and 1960. But two or three hits could keep a man on the road for decades; country fans are loyal.

"Wings of a Dove" arrived as the Eisenhower years wound down and the 1960s loomed—Husky and the charts offering listeners "a sign from above, on the wings of a dove."

What a blessing, a dove of peace to usher in the new decade. Wasn't it pretty to think so?

Though she could not articulate her belief—she endured the opposite of speaking in tongues—Ma believed in God. She could not persuade the old man to go to church with her—so she stayed home, too—yet her belief was deep . . . if silent. Ma eventually hung up a picture of the doe-eyed Jesus in the living room. You know, the surfer dude with the perfect blond hair who could catch a wave, then turn it into wine afterward. And she bought an oversize, gilt-edged Bible that she dropped on the kitchen table every Sunday morning and made me and Sis read from.

The old man, a child abandoned to indifference, violence, and rage, had no relationship with God that I could discern, no use for religion. Church was beyond his upbringing. He found solace in raising Cain with his buddies, in swilling beer, and in sports—those traditional religions of the workingman.

Bluegrass gospel, which often cuts closer to the Holy Spirit than its country cousin, conjures a lost world of wood-frame churches, prayer-skun knees, and plank tables laden with dinner. The music, at least metaphorically, keeps alive the tradition of "singing all day and dinner on the ground" that Jimmy Martin refused to forget.

As Bill Monroe worked out bluegrass music in the 1940s, he made sure that gospel was a crucial part of it. He understood that his audience didn't think a show was complete if it didn't include at least a couple sacred numbers. Monroe and his band members might succumb to the temptations of the road, but at least once a day they took off their hats, bowed their heads, and sang hymns like "Wicked Path of Sin," "Little Community Church," and "Walking in Jerusalem." They were giving their listeners a taste of the divine and, at the same time, self-administering a little holy inoculation.

Most of the early bluegrass bands had repertories that were more than one-quarter gospel. The music tended to be Southern, rural, and Protestant, and besides raiding old hymnals, it drew on the catalogs of performers like the Carter Family, the Monroe Brothers, and the Blue Sky Boys.

In bluegrass's earliest days, you'd hear the Stanley Brothers hymning away on "Gathering Flowers for the Master's Bouquet," "Just a Little Talk with Jesus," and "Cry from the Cross." And you'd hear Flatt and Scruggs on "Back to the Cross," "I'm Working on a Road," and "Brother, I'm Getting Ready to Go."

In fact, after they left Monroe's Blue Grass Boys, the first two songs that Lester Flatt and Earl Scruggs recorded—in the fall of 1948 at the WROL radio studio in Knoxville, Tennessee—were "God Loves His Children" and "I'm Going to Make Heaven My Home." A far cry from the 1960s and headlining at Carnegie Hall and making guest appearances on *The Beverly Hillbillies*, but the boys wanted to get their new career off on the right foot. They knew their gospel records weren't going to be bestsellers. But they also knew that gospel fans were loyal fans, and would get themselves to Flatt and Scruggs's local schoolhouse shows when they could and would write letters to the radio stations on which they played.

More important, they understood that out in the country it was hard to get to a satisfactory church sometimes. So, of a Sunday morning, or afternoon, you could read a little Scripture, then, if you were so blessed, you could crank up the Victrola and bask in the holy words of Brother Flatt and Brother Scruggs in a song like "Preachin', Prayin', Singin' " (1950).

Even in 1950, "Preachin'," written by E. C. McCarty, seemed more like wishful thinking, a harking back to the old, old days, than reality. (Why is it that the good old days always seem more holy?) But "Preachin' " is entrenched in the bluegrass canon, and it's easy to understand why: it paints a vivid picture of a bygone world in which "all of God's children seem to gather there, preachin', prayin', singin' down on the public square."

A stranger stumbles upon this prayer meeting, and right away is asked to stick around and join in. It's as if he's lucked upon heaven—and, who knows, maybe he has—found a place where he can rest his weary bones and lay his heavy burdens down.

Grammy Jennings didn't allow card playing or cursing in her house on Sundays. Which really wasn't too much of a problem given that her sons, their pals, and her current man were usually passed out till well past noon. Besides, in those days you couldn't buy beer in New Hampshire before noon on Sundays, anyways. Gram *did* allow drinking in her house on Sundays—"her boys" should be granted the privilege of taking off the edge from the night before—but only beer, because the Devil hides in whiskey. It was the Sabbath after all.

When the Bailes Brothers used to sing their popular hymn "Dust on the Bible" (1946), the story goes, their mother, Nannie Ellen, a widow who raised her four boys all by herself, would sob. And not just because she was so moved by their elegant harmonies; mainly because she knew that her sons were singing a lie.

As soon as her boys—Kyle, Johnnie, Walter, and Homer Jr.—arrived in Nashville and became stars on the *Grand Ole Opry*, they were known for their singing, their drinking, and their whoring. Their mother, a domestic, had raised them in poverty in a neighborhood called Dogtown on the outskirts of Charleston, West Virginia, and they couldn't handle the transition from having next to nothing to, what seemed like, having everything. The doors in postwar America were being flung open wide, and the Bailes Brothers wanted to taste it all. There's a line in "Dust on the Bible" that goes, "Get that dust off the Bible and redeem your poor soul." Problem is, the boys probably didn't own one Bible between 'em, and they couldn't get that damn dust off their souls. Not that you could tell from their song.

With smooth, heartfelt harmonies, they tell us that "dust on the Bible will doom your soul." The brothers and their songs are one of the bridges that lead from the Delmores to the Louvins and, eventually, the Everlys. And parts of their repertory were later gratefully absorbed by bluegrass music. Kitty Wells, the Queen of Country Music, even covered "Dust on the Bible" and made it the title track to her first gospel album.

While men like Hank Williams, Lefty Frizzell, and Johnny Cash somehow transcended their rough ways to reach the pinnacle of country music, the Bailes Brothers, as talented as they were, didn't come close. After their peak years of 1944 to 1949, they became the kind of act of whom people would ask: "Whatever happened to those

Bailes Brothers?" Walter, who wrote "Dust on the Bible," and Homer became ministers like their late carpenter father; Kyle ministered to air conditioners in Alabama; and Johnnie, the wildest of a wild bunch, ended up in federal prison for a while, having violated the Mann Act, which forbids the interstate transport of women or girls for immoral purposes.

The brothers continued to dabble in music as the years passed. But in the end, they faded from most memories—dust gathering on their once-promising careers—just leaving us with this lasting hymn.

I grew up in an unforgiving land of demons.

Our lives were circumscribed by Route 125 and Cedar Swamp. Tamped in between, we lived on rock and stump, swamp and gravel, on a swatch of land infested with snakes, spiders, and tar-paper shacks. There was no joy, little laughter, no God—God cannot dwell long where there is no laughter.

Plenty of demons, though: poverty and alcoholism, envy and fury, thieving and adultery, and on and on and *on. Demons.* Demons, wherever you looked, and no talk of God, no nod toward the holy.

For a child, it paid to be cautious, paid to be watchful, paid to be quiet—so no one would notice you. There was always the sense that if you made one wrong step, you could be devoured . . . by *something.* That you could vanish off the face of this earth, and no one would notice.

No one.

O my people. So wretched, so bitter, so godless. There wasn't a commandment that they didn't gladly bushwhack as they drank and fucked and brawled—sucking the blood from your skun-up knuckles was way better for you than any Sunday morning Communion wine. As far as my people were concerned, they scrabbled by in a God-free zone. Any thought of a life of the spirit had been boiled out of them by circumstance, World War II, and the Great Depression.

In the end, some of them seemed more creature than man, somehow less than human—or maybe too human for me to bear as a kid.

Demons.

Brother Claude Ely surely understood those demons that afflicted my people and the poor like them (he understood the serpents, too). Ely spent a good part of his life as a traveling Holiness evangelist, testifying and healing, prophesying and speaking in tongues, trying to purify whatever flocks he could gather round him in the fires of the Pentecost.

Born in 1922 in Pucketts Creek, some five miles out of Pennington Gap in Lee County, Virginia, Ely sang and preached in a big voice as bold as his one gold tooth. The reason we know this is from recordings he made for King Records in 1953 during a Holiness revival meeting at the Free Pentecostal Church of God in Cumberland, Kentucky.

And those recordings are, indeed, a revelation.

Preaching hymns like "I'm Crying Holy Unto the Lord," "There's a Leak in This Old Building," and "There Ain't No Grave Gonna Hold My Body Down," Brother Claude Ely, spurred by a freight-train, proto–rock 'n' roll guitar, gets out of his body and lays down a hoarse holy groove of unmediated spirit.

This is religion better than bonded whiskey. This is preachin', prayin', and singin' to send all demons within a ten-mile radius packin', their pointy tails tucked between their spindly legs. This is a revival that could sustain a man or woman for weeks, if not months. This is salvation—almost a kind of punk-gospel music that has no truck with chord changes—that could've slapped my people in the face and woke them up.

It's sanctified singing like Ely's that we hear echoes of in Elvis and Little Richard, in James Brown and especially Jerry Lee Lewis. But not a one of them ever burned on record, not even Jerry Lee Lewis, the way Ely burns on these recordings.

The main difference is this: Most musicians were merely called by fame, by the *Opry*. Brother Claude Ely had been called by God.

Sometimes, though, it seemed as if Hank Williams had been called by God, too.

Certainly when he wrapped himself in the prophetic cloak of his alter ego, Luke the Drifter, and recorded didactic recitations like "Too Many Parties and Too Many Pals," "I Dreamed About Mama Last Night," and "Be Careful of Stones That You Throw." And certainly when he wrote and sang "I Saw the Light" (1947), one of country's most popular sacred numbers.

Hank's longtime fiddler, Jerry Rivers, told the writer Colin Escott that Williams "liked the old, shoutin' country-type gospel music," and "I Saw the Light" fulfills that style. For all his woes, for all his sins, Hank sounds transfigured as he belts out: "I saw the light, I saw the light, no more darkness, no more night" and *"Praise the Lord!* I saw the light."

There are no theological subtleties here—"straight is the gate and narra's the way"—and Tommy Jackson on fiddle acts as a one-man amen corner, propelling the song along to its rousing finish. It was covered right away by Clyde Grubb and Roy Acuff, even beating Hank's version to market, and was later reprised by Acuff, backed by the Nitty Gritty Dirt Band, in 1971. And it's become a staple of bluegrass jam sessions.

Not bad for a tune that came to a half-drunk Hank on his way back from a show in Fort Deposit, Alabama. He was inspired by the beacon at Dannelly Field Airport in Montgomery. God *does* work in mysterious ways.

(For a long time, I've considered the Louvin Brothers' "Great Atomic Power" of 1952 as a kind of apocalyptic companion to "I Saw the Light." Where Hank dwells on the light of the Lord—that primordial light that extends from one end of the universe to the other—the Louvins extol the light of Revelation and end-time: "Will you rise and meet your Saviour in the air?" As fire rains from on high, never mind using your Bible as a road map, buddy, it's time to use Jesus Christ as your fallout shelter.)

It's hard to tell whether ol' Hank ever got that intimate with the Father, the Son, and the Holy Ghost. He saw the light, he sang the light, but toward the end of his short, incandescent life he'd sometimes refuse to sing "I Saw the Light," because he was lost in the darkness that you can touch and he could no longer see any light at all.

All we know for certain is that we were left an enduring hymn forged by an enduring hell-rake.

Amen, brother.

# Lovesick Blues

*The Past, Present, and Future
of Country Music*

The classic country music of 1950 to 1970 starts with Hank
Williams's nearly stillborn version of "Lovesick Blues," which was
recorded in December 1948 and released in 1949. Until then, Hank
had had three modest hits—"Move It on Over," "Honky Tonkin',"
and "I'm a Long Gone Daddy"—and nobody but Hank was expecting
much from "Lovesick Blues," a 1920s Broadway show tune that he'd
probably learned off of records by the blackface minstrel Emmett
Miller and the country singer Rex Griffin.

Fred Rose, who was guiding Hank's career, didn't want to record the song and only grudgingly released it. He said it was an
absolute mess, and just about everyone involved with it agreed
that "Lovesick Blues" was a goddamn sorry excuse for a song. All
Hank knew was that whenever he sang it on the *Louisiana Hayride*
in Shreveport, the crowd jumped to their feet and roared themselves hoarse calling for encores. Hank told folks that the song was

so hot he could walk offstage, toss his hat out, and *the hat* would get an encore.

Hank was right. "Lovesick Blues" shot to No. 1 on the country chart and stayed there for sixteen weeks, tarried for forty-two weeks on the chart altogether, and even hit No. 24 Pop; Fred Rose was beginning to wonder whether he knew what a hit was anymore. It wasn't long before the *Grand Ole Opry*, which had been leery of Hank's alcoholic antics, came calling and made him a member of the show. He was just twenty-five years old, and his career was made. He'd be dead before he turned thirty.

What makes "Lovesick Blues" pivotal is that it just doesn't sound like any other country record of its time. Williams spurned the pitchfork croon of stars like Eddy Arnold and Red Foley, and sang like the unreconstructed hick that he was, gave rise to the cry of a poor boy raised in the deepest South, but—and this is crucial—without the clichés of hayseed buffoonery. Along the way, he stole the bluesy yodels of Emmett Miller and Jimmie Rodgers, swiped a pinch of Pentecostal gospel, adopted the black man's blues that he'd learned as a street kid from Rufus "Tee-Tot" Payne, and stirred it all into the country music that he'd grown up on. No wonder "Lovesick Blues" sounded like a mess—it was—the same kind of mess that would give rise to rock 'n' roll a few years later.

The song opens with a slightly distorted electric guitar—almost as if it were yodeling, too—then Hank lights into the tune: "I've got a feeling called the blue-ue-ues, oh Lord, since my baby said good-bye." As he tells us that he's "lo-oo-oo-onesome" and "nobody's sugar daddy now," Hank's voice fractures and slides, moans and soars, winks, slinks, and thrusts its hips. In a live recording made at the *Opry* on June 18, 1949, just one week after he was hired, the crowd cheers and claps five separate times during the course of the song. You might say it was a hit.

Yeah, "Lovesick Blues" was a mess all right—a mess that changed the course of country music, which is to say, American music. Williams directly influenced future country stars like Webb Pierce and Faron Young, and George Jones and Ray Price, and caught the ears of future rockabillies like Elvis, Carl Perkins, and Jerry Lee Lewis.

But the hits, the love of his fans, and his deep influence still couldn't keep Hank from getting fired from the *Opry* for being a drunken screwup. And that's part of his legacy, too, the dark myth that Nashville savored in the 1950s and '60s: the cautionary tale of guitar-poet country boys who thumb into town with empty stomachs and outsize dreams and who consume themselves in flames of self-destruction.

But Nashville doesn't allow "messes" like "Lovesick Blues" no more, and poverty-bred messes like my extended family rarely exist anymore, either: all that drinking and whoring, all that lying and cheating, all that *venom*, all that furiously clinging to *next to nothing*. I know now that not only did I grow up listening to country music, I grew up entangled in a particularly harsh country song, like something by Haggard or early Paycheck, a song that would never make the charts nowadays.

But it's all gone now: the shacks and those tumble-down husks that we pretended were houses, the ant-infested cords of wood and the rust-riven well pails, the chickens and the hogs, the briars and the prickaburrs, the shitbox cars that seemed to burn more oil than gasoline.

My little northern Appalachian holler—*gone*, all gone.

Most the people are gone, too. Raging, kerosene-soaked torches always burn out before quiet candles do.

For the first time as an adult, I recently visited the ghost of my old homeplace, more than forty years after the state decided that our invisible lives were less important than a wider highway. As Fiddlin' John Carson knew, as Bill Monroe knew, as even Joni Mitchell knew, our Edens get torn down, get paved over.

The only thing left standing was Great-Uncle Henry's red-shingle shack, some hundred yards off the road, buckled yet defiant, serving as a kind of perverse historic marker for those who knew what to look for. The land has backslided to puckabrush and sumac—"shoe-mack," the old folks say—and the northbound lane of Route 125 runs right through what had once been our dooryard, the primal playground of my childhood.

We moved from that house in August 1963—"the house *they* tore down," me and Sis came to call it—and, as always, there were country songs in the air: "Act Naturally" by Buck Owens, "Ring of Fire" by Johnny Cash, "Sweet Dreams (of You)" by Patsy Cline, "Lonesome 7-7203" by Hawkshaw Hawkins, who had died the previous March in the same plane crash that killed Cline.

So, yeah, most the shacks and most the people are long gone. And, eventually, I was long gone, too. But the music, the songs, live on.

But what about country music today? What about Nashville?

We listen nowadays in the era of Corporate Country—and have been for a long time—in which image trumps everything else.

We have cheesecake for the men: Carrie Underwood, Miranda Lambert, Sara Evans, Gretchen "Redneck Woman" Wilson (who's marketed as trashy but very available), and Shania Twain, who has always been more about looks than memorable songs.

And we have beefcake for the women, men whose jaws are as square as SUVs: Jason Aldean, Kenny Chesney (who seems to refuse to wear a shirt in any of his videos), Tim McGraw, Joe Nichols, and

Trace Adkins. (Thank God for Toby Keith; he actually looks like the slobby guy next door.)

We even have country music "boy bands" like Rascal Flatts and Emerson Drive. Then there's that Australian pretty boy Keith Urban. (Urban? To balance the pop-culture ledger shouldn't there be a hip-hop star named MC Shit-Kicker?) All of them are featured in music videos that hang just enough denim shreds on the women to still be considered God-fearing family entertainment. Think of it as soft-core porn that *twangs*—with the occasional sacred number tucked in between.

Poor ol' Ernest Tubb would be too ugly, too human, to be a country star today, and Little Jimmy Dickens would need to take steroids and/or human growth hormone, or join the circus. And I'm afraid that Kitty Wells and Loretta Lynn, in their gingham dresses and with all those inconvenient real-life children, just wouldn't be *hot* enough to make a career of it. (Patsy Cline, on the other hand, would do just fine.) Never mind that Lynn put out one of the best country albums of the last twenty-five years in 2004, *Van Lear Rose*, shaming so-called stars who could be her great-grandchildren.

The music itself today is always competent (if tame), always professional—sometimes, it's even good. But what's marketed as country these days is an amalgam of Southern rock (thank you, Allman Brothers), country rock (thank you, Eagles), the phony Caribbean strains of Jimmy Buffett (no thanks, mon), pop, and even a taste of hip-hop. Oh, and there's some country influence, too.

This is the real problem, and it's not one we can blame on Nashville and Corporate Country: the times and circumstances that produced classic country music between 1950 and 1970 mercifully no longer exist. The poverty and hardship that suffused the lives of Hank and Cash, of Monroe and the Louvins, of Cline and Wynette, are mostly a thing of the past—just as living way out in the sticks is generally a thing of the past. As Lynn told the writer Michael Streissguth: "They don't have no country music now."

There are still a few old-timers, as I write this in 2007, who soldier on: Willie Nelson and Merle Haggard, George Jones and Ralph Stanley, Kitty Wells and Lynn herself. But they'll be gone soon enough . . . taking country music with them. Or, at least, the country music that gave my relations sustenance and solace, the wise, old country music that still lives on in the cultural imagination.

But that's what happens in popular music. Musical styles are an expression of a time and a place: the blues, bebop, rockabilly, soul, Bronx-style hip-hop, swing (western and otherwise), and, yes, country. They have life spans. They flourish, decline, wither, and leave us their residue of excellence. Ultimately, the revivalists, the preservationists, and the collectors arrive and proclaim the patient good as new—if not quite alive.

What's marketed as country music today is actually *country-style* music or, to be postmodern, country music about country music. It can be entertaining, but the difference between today's country and the summits of the 1950s and '60s is the difference between the lightning and the lightning bug.

Country music has lapsed into being just another brand in the cultural bazaar—one that's still profitable—and all the bands today are just tribute bands on an assembly line that spews out pop music that (sometimes) *twangs*. It's certainly not music you can live your life by, not wisdom backed by a fiddle and a steel guitar.

Most of the men trade on the minstrelsy of cowboy hats and gaudy brass belt buckles—perfect for selling pickup trucks—and many of the women still trade on racy *Tobacco Road* stereotypes that seem to never go out of style as cleavage trumps grit.

Country music didn't devour Nashville after all, as the city's snob elite worried in the 1960s and '70s. Nashville devoured country music.

It was a gift and a blessing to escape Kingston. But it has been an even greater gift to have come where I come from and to be able to write about the music and the people who raised my country soul . . . to get sung back home.

A few years after I left home, in 1984, I spent six weeks in Mount Sinai Hospital in Manhattan, struck down by a radical case of ulcerative colitis. My brother Tim, still back home in New Hampshire, mailed me a tape cassette: on one side was *Rock 'n' Rollin' with Fats*, on the other was *Johnny Cash with His Hot and Blue Guitar*.

So, for the first time in years, I gratefully listened to those old record-player-on-the-porch songs: "Cry, Cry, Cry," "Folsom Prison Blues," "So Doggone Lonesome." And what that tape reminded me in those vulnerable weeks—when *nothing* was certain . . . *nothing*—was that even though I worked for *The Wall Street Journal*, had married an upper-middle-class Jew from North Jersey, and had lived in Paris for a year, I was a hick.

*I was still a goddamn hornpout-eatin', rat-shootin', stock car lovin' hick.* And I'd better stop speaking in the subjunctive voice and get used to that homely and stubborn fact.

Slowly, at first, I started weaving country music back into my life—Hank and Hag, Monroe and Lynn—trying to make amends for exiling them from my life in exile. I was the prodigal son, not quite returning home but returning to the land of country music. Gradually . . . the music became an obsession and, finally, a quest whose ultimate destination was always the songs themselves.

This has been an inverted quest, though. Usually, we return home to tell those left behind wondrous tales of the broader world. Here, I'm telling the broader world about the classic country songs and tales of home that made up my vanished world. I wriggled free, and in that freedom I chose to go back and examine the scar tissue of the past. And I've tried to honor two things here: the true stories I was born to tell . . . and the even truer stories that the best country music tells.

In this spirit-numbing information age, we gorge on the Web and on CNN, we cannot free our hands of our BlackBerrys and laptops and cellphones, but, in the end, we know less and less . . . of each other . . . of our hearts . . . of our souls. But Johnny Cash singing "I Walk the Line" or Hank sorrowing through "I'm So Lonesome I Could Cry" still gives us more insight in three minutes, tells us more about what matters most in our lives, than we get in an entire twenty-four-hour news cycle.

The old hard stuff still resonates today—and well beyond its original ghetto of *twang*—because it once proudly displayed its thick coat of sweat, cow shit, and whiskey. Hank Williams and his "Lovesick Blues" endure—even if their intended audience is as long gone and lonesome blue as Hank—because they are honest, human, and from the heart. (What did you say that Garth fella's last name was?)

After all these decades, twin fiddles still kill me, still kill Ma and the old man. But, too, they're killing people who might not know Webb Pierce from Franklin Pierce. People who came to the music through the alternative country of Uncle Tupelo and the Jayhawks, through the hip-hop producer Rick Rubin coaxing a shocking burst of creativity out of Johnny Cash in the twilight of his career, and through the White Stripes' Jack White helping Loretta Lynn make her best music in decades.

Twin fiddles saw open my chest and show me my hick heart, red, raw, and bitter. Between the silvered notes a mournful tale still lives and breathes. When twin fiddles kick off a country song—no big bang here, but a grief-stricken whisper—creation is made new. The world is conjured once again as every goddamn sad story you've ever heard is told once more, as every bit of melancholy you've inherited is invited to come ghosting back from the past and two-step into your heart.

In the end, I still can't shake the image of Grammy Jennings—orphan, alcoholic, the *other woman*—up at four in the morning, *again*, sitting at the kitchen table in the dark, *again*. Tim McGraw and Faith Hill, I'm afraid, ain't powerful enough to ease the very real pain anchored in her soul.

But, like Hank, Gram knows that the good sleep she aches for won't ever come, knows that her cheatin' heart won't ever stop whispering hot and humid in her ear.

All she can do is cling to the songs she loves . . . and try to ride out the night, try to ride out the storm that is her life.

> *Your cheatin' heart will make you weep*
> *You'll cry and cry and try to sleep*

**Discography**
**Bibliography**
**Acknowledgments**
**Index**

# Discography

I know, I know, in this age of the digital download and the iPod, the idea of a compact-disc-based discography seems hopelessly quaint, like cranking up the Victrola to listen to your lacquer-heavy 78s or holding your best girl's hand at the Fourth of July carnival. If you've gotten this far in *Sing Me Back Home*, you've probably already swiped at least a couple songs off the Internet or, the record companies hope and pray, forked over your metaphorically sweaty ninety-nine cents to iTunes.

But I'm old-fashioned. I still believe in the sanctity of the object and can't be satisfied by conjuring songs from the digitized ether. I was shaped by a world that revolved around a stack of 45s and the thrill of owning the occasional album. So, in writing this book, I didn't resort to the Web, but took pleasure and solace in being surrounded by minarets of CDs and bricks of boxed sets.

When it comes to country music boxed sets (and other genres, too) there are none consistently better than those made by Bear Family Records of Germany (www.bear-family.de). Coming from a time and place in which, if an artist truly killed you, you might own one album and a handful of singles, owning a Bear Family set seems somehow decadent— maybe, even, a defiant act of getting above your raisin'. Take, for example, the Carter Family's *In the Shadow of Clinch Mountain*. It contains *every* studio recording made by the original Carters *and* a hardcover book by the late country music historian Charles K. Wolfe. It's not just a CD set, but a time capsule, an object of artistic adoration. A good boxed set is the anti-iPod.

What follows is an attempt to distill my country music heart to twenty-five CD collections—boxed sets and single discs. But first I want to give a plug for *Infamous Angel*, by Iris DeMent (Rounder, 1992), the only modern CD included on my extended discography, which follows these notes. DeMent is the perfect example of a musician who absorbed the sounds and lessons of the entire history of country music, ran them through her soul, and made a classic album. Her song "Mama's Opry" should've been a No. 1 Country hit in 1992.

Anyway, this is how my country heart beats and twangs.

### "WILDWOOD FLOWER": BEDROCK

The history of recorded country music flows from two mighty rivers: Jimmie Rodgers and the Carter Family. And each was discovered at the same legendary recording sessions at Bristol, Tennessee, in 1927—you might call it the Big Bang of country music. Bear Family has two boxed sets—*The Singing Brakeman* and *In the Shadow of Clinch Mountain*—that hold all the studio recordings made by Rodgers and the Carters. Owning these two sets feels like owning Mount Rushmore or the Lincoln Memorial.

Jimmie Rodgers, the Singing Brakeman and America's Blue Yodeler, was country's original rough and rowdy rounder. While the Carters gently tended toward God, hearth, and home in their music, Rodgers, his hat cocked and with a leer and a grin, tended toward trains, bars, and bedrooms (where he didn't quite belong). The list of those he directly influenced is long and impressive, and includes Gene Autry, Bill Monroe, Hank Snow, Ernest Tubb, Lefty Frizzell, and Merle Haggard. Rodgers could be parlor sentimental, but his best work, like his blues-suffused "Blue Yodels," "In the Jailhouse Now," "Waiting for a Train," and "Mule Skinner Blues," was the pure work of a hick Dionysius.

Jimmie Rodgers was loved and emulated, but the Carter Family was absorbed into the bloodstream of anybody who cared about country music. A.P., Sara, and Maybelle Carter established a repertory steeped in Appalachian reticence that has sustained country music, especially bluegrass, to this day. Their songs like "Wildwood Flower," "Keep on the Sunny

Side," and "Will the Circle Be Unbroken" are taken out like treasured family heirlooms whenever country pickers gather. Charles K. Wolfe, who wrote the biography that accompanies this twelve-disc set, wrote: "These recordings are as elemental as the wind or the water." In this set, there are 287 different reasons to believe him.

### "BLUEGRASS BREAKDOWN": BLUEGRASS

In the big, rambling farmhouse of country music, bluegrass is the back porch, the most congenial spot for pickin', grinnin', and sneakin' a sip of whiskey. But that porch ain't real big, and that creates a peculiar problem for modern bluegrass musicians: in a day when you can still listen to Bill Monroe, who created the music, and Flatt and Scruggs and the Stanley Brothers, who polished it, who has the time (or inclination) to listen to the new guys?

Bluegrass is a limited template: it's acoustic string-band music with a freight-train thrust and deep roots in Jimmie Rodgers and the Carters, garnished by jazz and the blues. But step even just a bit outside the template, and the music becomes something else, stops being bluegrass.

The music sounded old-fashioned even when Monroe was tinkering with it in his bluegrass garage in the 1940s. Even as country changed, bluegrass kept alive older virtues—instrumental virtuosity, harmony singing, and gospel—while reminding listeners of God, mother, and home. And where else could you hear the finer examples of orphan song?

For today's listeners, it's a place to stumble upon pre-twentieth-century repertory and to get a *sense* of what country music and America was like before World War II. The Coen Brothers—not a bluegrass band—understood this when they laced the soundtrack of *O Brother, Where Art Thou?* (2000) with bluegrass by Alison Krauss, the Cox Family, the Stanley Brothers, and others. The music has also become a haven for country stars like Dolly Parton and Ricky Skaggs who find that it's a comforting counterpoint to Corporate Country.

And remember, the drive of bluegrass was one of the things that first got Elvis's leg to shakin'—Monroe's "Blue Moon of Kentucky" sat on the flip side of Elvis's first single back in 1954.

Speaking of which, Monroe's *Blue Moon of Kentucky: 1936–1949*, another Bear Family set, gathers all of his work from those years, starting with the duets with his brother Charlie—"My Long Journey Home," "What

Would You Give in Exchange?"—to the crystallization of the true bluegrass sound. The highlight of the set is the primal twang made by Monroe's first great band: Monroe on lead and tenor vocal and mandolin, Lester Flatt on lead vocal and guitar, Earl Scruggs on banjo, Chubby Wise on fiddle, and Cedric Rainwater (Howard Watts) on bass. And the bluegrass standards are endless here: "Heavy Traffic Ahead," "Kentucky Waltz," and "Blue Grass Breakdown," to name a few.

The folks at County Sales in Floyd, Virginia—a mail-order outfit that specializes in bluegrass and old-time music—say that *Flatt & Scruggs: 1948–1959* is their most popular boxed set. And it's easy to hear why. Lester Flatt and Earl Scruggs broke Bill Monroe's heart—and ticked him off, too—when they left his band to strike out on their own. But they blossomed into the central bluegrass band of the 1950s. This set features their definitive takes on songs like "Old Salty Dog Blues," "Roll in My Sweet Baby's Arms," and "Dim Lights, Thick Smoke (and Loud, Loud Music)," and also highlights the fast and furious banjo picking of Scruggs—Jimi Hendrix was the Earl Scruggs of the electric guitar—on moonshine runs like "Foggy Mountain Breakdown," "Earl's Breakdown," and "Flint Hill Special." In the 1950s, this was music played at schoolhouses and town halls and was meant to stave off rock 'n' roll and the too-sweet strings that were starting to strangle country.

The Stanley Brothers' first recordings for Columbia brought a more rugged, more mountain, sound to bluegrass. If Monroe and Flatt and Scruggs were raw lumber, Carter and Ralph Stanley were the trees themselves. *The Stanley Brothers & the Clinch Mountain Boys: 1949–1952* moans with such haunting bluegrass standards as "The Fields Have Turned Brown," "I'm a Man of Constant Sorrow," "Pretty Polly," and "The White Dove." (When you write about the Stanleys, it's impossible to strike the word "haunting" from your vocabulary.)

### "MOANIN' THE BLUES": HIS OWN MONUMENT, PART ONE

Hank Williams, more than fifty years after his death, is still the pivotal figure in the history of country music. With a Deep South yelp as country as cowshit on your workboots—even his twang twanged—Hank dragged country music into the post–World War II era. Along the way, he created archetypes that the music didn't really shake off till it went corporate and lost its soul:

He was the original God-haunted, doomed troubadour . . . He chased pussy and popped pills, washing it all down with whiskey . . . He set the template for killin' 'em at the *Louisiana Hayride*, getting hired by the *Opry*, then getting fired by the *Opry*. But all that is mere biography, the human trivia that surrounds the enduring music that Hank made.

Hank could boogie and rock: "Move It on Over" and "Hey Good Lookin' " . . . Hank could write genre-transcending standards: "Your Cheatin' Heart" and "Cold, Cold Heart" . . . Hank was a bluesman: "Long Gone Lonesome Blues" and "Ramblin' Man" . . . And Hank could take off his hat, press it to his heart—even when his knees wobbled and trembled—and sing gospel: "I Saw the Light" and "Calling You."

All that before he was thirty. All that (and more) in *The Complete Hank Williams*.

### "IF YOU'VE GOT THE MONEY I'VE GOT THE TIME": THE FIFTIES

Lefty Frizzell, Webb Pierce, and Faron Young are the defining honky-tonkers of the 1950s. They weren't quite young enough to be rockabillies, but were still raw, fierce, and rowdy in their own right. They embody the years when country music knew exactly what it was, and knew exactly who its audience was. Frizzell's *Look What Thoughts Will Do*, Pierce's *King of the Honky-Tonk*, and Young's *Live Fast, Love Hard* capture the three men at their creative peaks.

Frizzell's double-disc set includes "I Love You a Thousand Ways," "If You've Got the Money I've Got the Time," and "Always Late (With Your Kisses)." A sweeter voice never came from a tougher sonuvabitch.

Pierce was the biggest country star of the fifties, with twelve No. 1 hits and a mill-saw voice that could shred lumber. His disc includes "Back Street Affair," "There Stands the Glass," and "In the Jailhouse Now." Listening to it, you can imagine drowning in drafts on a slow Tuesday night at Bud's Café up in Eppin' back in 1955.

Just three years older than Elvis, Young was a transitional figure between honky-tonk and rockabilly, with his dark good looks and high-energy leers like "If You Ain't Lovin' (You Ain't Livin')," "I've Got Five Dollars and It's Saturday Night," and "Live Fast, Love Hard, Die Young"—all of which are on this disc.

While Frizzell, Pierce, and Young served up country's hard 1950s sound, the Louvin Brothers, harmonizing like Alabama angels, sound as if they are singing outside time. On songs like "When I Stop Dreaming," "You're Running Wild," and "Knoxville Girl," they sound as if they would've been right at home at a barn-raising in 1791 or at a county fair in 1883. And their hymns would've been welcome at the very first white, wood-frame church ever raised to the glory of God in America. *Close Harmony* from Bear Family collects all their studio recordings and rewards constant baptism in their Sand Mountain, Alabama, deeps.

### "THAT'S ALL RIGHT": ROCKABILLIES AND ROCKERS

In their rockist, blinkered enthusiasm, a lot of pop critics in the late sixties and early seventies acted as if the Byrds and Gram Parsons and, hell, even the Stones invented country rock. In their passion to anoint, they somehow forgot the original country rockers, the rockabillies—early Elvis, Carl Perkins, Jerry Lee Lewis, and all their bellerin' and hiccupin' buddies—and rock stars whose roots were hip deep in hick music, like Ike Everly's boys and Roy Orbison. Well, here are some real country rockers to thrill your collection.

All the Sun rockabilly essentials are here in *The Sun Records Collection*: Elvis, Lewis, Perkins, Billy Lee Riley, Warren Smith, Charlie Feathers, and Sonny Burgess. But, too, it includes early recordings by Johnny Cash, Orbison, and Charlie Rich, and a trove of blues and R&B by the likes of Howlin' Wolf, B. B. King, and Rufus Thomas. It's a one-stop seminar in mid-twentieth-century American roots music on three discs.

Listening to Elvis on *The Sun Sessions*, which includes outtakes and alternate takes, is like being allowed to be present at the Creation.

When your teenagers act as if their generation discovered sex—as all generations do—make 'em sit down and listen to ol' Uncle Jerry Lee yowl and pant his way through "Whole Lotta Shakin' Goin' On," "Great Balls of Fire," and "Breathless" on his *18 Original Sun Greatest Hits*. They just might faint.

Heirs to the Louvins' harmony tradition, the Everly Brothers combined Kentucky roots, boy-band good looks, and a Bo Diddley beat to create country rock for the teenage masses about, oh, fifteen years before the Eagles. Their *All-Time Original Hits* includes "Bye Bye Love," "Wake Up Little Susie," "Bird Dog," and "Cathy's Clown."

Roy Orbison made pop opera with a hick sensibility that has never been rivaled or, perhaps, even attempted. *The Essential Roy Orbison* collects his very best, including "Only the Lonely (Know the Way I Feel)," "Crying," "Dream Baby (How Long Must I Dream)," and "Oh, Pretty Woman." Some singers own a tear in their voice. Orbison's holds a monsoon of woe.

### "THERE AIN'T NO GRAVE GONNA HOLD MY BODY DOWN": SPEAKING IN TONGUES

Want to hear where the Pentecostal infernos that burned within Jerry Lee Lewis and Little Richard came from? Then listen to *Satan, Get Back!*, recordings made by the Holiness preacher Brother Claude Ely in the 1950s and 1960s. In hymns like "I'm Crying Holy Unto the Lord" and "There Ain't No Grave Gonna Hold My Body Down," Ely and his followers *lust* after God so hard that mere secular lust is just a faint throbbing of that verb. After listening to this CD, you might think that rockabilly was just Holiness hymns shorn of God. And, *yes*, my friends, those rattlesnakes over yonder *are* wearing blue suede shoes.

### "GUESS THINGS HAPPEN THAT WAY": HIS OWN MONUMENT, PART TWO

When it comes to Johnny Cash, it's important to remember that he originally came to us not from Nashville but from Sun Records in Memphis and Sam Phillips, who just might've had the best ear for raw talent in twentieth-century music. And, as with Elvis, if you truly want to *hear* Cash, hear him before all the myths and half-truths and half-lies, then you have to listen to his recordings on Sun. *The Original Sun Albums: The Complete Collection* brings together all seven of his Sun albums—complemented by a bounty of outtakes and alternate takes—and includes the primal *Johnny Cash with His Hot and Blue Guitar*.

*At Folsom Prison* picks up Cash in 1968 on the live album that would make him that unlikely creature: a country music superstar. But this album also started his gradual entombment in his own myths (and myths created by others), myths like fleas that he was never able to shake. The producer Rick Rubin revived Cash's career in the 1990s, but he never did manage to make him seem more human—which is probably how the Man in Black (and Rubin) preferred it.

## "CRAZY": THE SIXTIES

And you shall know them by their hits.

I'm a simple man who was raised up by simple people—and we wanted to hear the hits. That attitude, of course, is way too populist for music crit's earls of esoterica, who'd much rather ooze and aah over the ineffable virtues of an Aroostook County zither player who cut two and a half sides for Peckerwood Records in 1962. Well, screw that, and screw them. The essence of six essential country singers can be found in the following greatest hits collections:

*12 Greatest Hits* by Patsy Cline; *Vintage Collection* by Merle Haggard; *The Best of George Jones: 1955–1967; The Definitive Collection* by Loretta Lynn; *King of the Road* by Roger Miller; and *The Very Best of Buck Owens, Volume I.*

The exception that proves the aforementioned rule is Johnny Paycheck's *The Real Mr. Heartache: The Little Darlin' Years.* His voice is tough sixties honky-tonk, but, more important, these songs drip with his very own personal Satan. When you listen to Paycheck here, you know that he's the kind of guy you handle with special care at a bar. The kind of guy, after he staggers off from your house, that makes your wife say: "Don't you never, ever bring that sonuvabitch home again!"

Of the twenty-four songs on this CD, only one, "The Lovin' Machine," cracked country's Top 10; a few others nibbled at the charts, rabid mice skittering and scurrying in Nashville's kitchen after midnight. But on tunes like "(Pardon Me) I've Got Someone to Kill," "He's in a Hurry (To Get Home to My Wife)," and "Motel Time Again," Paycheck distilled whiskey-strong songs that completely understood the working-class darkness of the sixties. Sure, he craved hits as much as anyone in Nashville, but what Johnny Paycheck accomplished here is more important than what any evanescent No. 1 hit could ever be.

## TRADITIONAL DISCOGRAPHY

For those who need a more orderly—clip and save—approach to discography, here it is.

These CD boxed sets and regular issues were listened to in the writing of this book. When the liner notes are mentioned, that means they were consulted during my research.

### BOXED SETS

Carter Family. *In the Shadows of Clinch Mountain.* 12 discs. Bear Family, 2000. (Hardcover book by Charles K. Wolfe.)

Cash, Johnny. *Cash: The Legend.* 4 discs. Columbia/Legacy, 2005. (Liner notes by Patrick Carr.)

——. *The Original Sun Albums: The Complete Collection.* 7 discs, including the epochal *Johnny Cash with His Hot and Blue Guitar.* Varèse Sarabande, 2005.

Everly Brothers. *Classic Everly Brothers.* 3 discs. Bear Family, 1992. (Liner notes by Colin Escott and Richard Weize.)

Flatt and Scruggs. *Flatt & Scruggs, 1948–1959.* 4 discs. Bear Family, 1991. (Liner notes by Neil V. Rosenberg.)

Louvin Brothers. *Close Harmony.* 8 discs. Bear Family, 1992. (Liner notes by Charles K. Wolfe.)

Monroe, Bill. *Blue Moon of Kentucky, 1936–1949.* 6 discs. Bear Family, 2002. (Hardcover book by Charles K. Wolfe and Neil V. Rosenberg.)

——. *The Essential Bill Monroe and His Blue Grass Boys, 1945–1949.* 2 discs. Columbia/Legacy, 1992.

——. *The Music of Bill Monroe from 1936 to 1994.* 4 discs. MCA, 1994. (Liner notes by John W. Rumble.)

Pierce, Webb. *The Wondering Boy, 1951–1958.* 4 discs. Bear Family, 1990. (Liner notes by Otto Kitsinger.)

Robbins, Marty. *The Essential Marty Robbins, 1951–1982.* 2 discs. Columbia/Legacy, 1991.

Rodgers, Jimmie. *The Singing Brakeman.* 6 discs. Bear Family, 1992.

Various. *Classic Country.* 3 discs. Time Life Music, 1999.

Various. *The Sun Records Collection.* 3 discs. Rhino, 1994.

Wagoner, Porter. *The Thin Man from the West Plains: The RCA Sessions, 1952–1962.* 4 discs. Bear Family, 1993.

Williams, Hank. *The Complete Hank Williams.* 10 discs. Mercury, 1998. (Liner notes by Daniel Cooper, Colin Escott, and Bob Pinson.)

Young, Faron. *The Classic Years: 1952–1962.* 5 discs. Bear Family, 1992.

## REGULAR ISSUES

Acuff, Roy. *The Essential Roy Acuff, 1936–1949.* Columbia/Legacy, 1992.

Bailes Brothers. *Oh So Many Years.* Bear Family, 2002. (Liner notes by Eddie Stubbs and Richard Weize.)

Cash, Johnny. *Johnny Cash at Folsom Prison.* Columbia/Legacy, 1999. (Liner notes by Johnny Cash.)

———. *Johnny Cash at San Quentin.* Columbia/Legacy, 2000.

Charles, Ray. *Modern Sounds in Country and Western Music.* Rhino, 1988.

Choates, Harry. *Devil in the Bayou.* Bear Family, 2002. (Liner notes by Andrew Brown.)

Cline, Patsy. *12 Greatest Hits.* MCA, 1988.

DeMent, Iris. *Infamous Angel.* Rounder, 1992.

Ely, Claude. *Satan, Get Back!* Ace, 1993. (Liner notes by Tony Russell.)

Everly Brothers. *All-Time Original Hits.* Rhino, 1999. (Liner notes by Ken Barnes.)

Frizzell, Lefty. *Look What Thoughts Will Do.* Columbia/Legacy, 1997.

Gentry, Bobbie. *The Golden Classics of Bobbie Gentry.* Collectables, 1997.

Haggard, Merle. *Vintage Collections.* Capitol, 1995. (Liner notes by Rich Kienzle.)

Horton, Johnny. *Honky Tonk Man: The Essential Johnny Horton, 1956–1960.* Columbia/Legacy, 1996. (Liner notes by Colin Escott.)

Jones, George. *The Best of George Jones, 1955–1967.* Rhino, 1991. (Liner notes by Rich Kienzle.)

Lewis, Jerry Lee. *Another Place, Another Time/She Even Woke Me Up to Say Goodbye.* Raven, 2002.

———. *18 Original Sun Greatest Hits.* Rhino, 1984.

Lynn, Loretta. *The Definitive Collection.* MCA, 2005.

Martin, Jimmy. *20 Greatest Hits.* Highland Music, 1988.

Miller, Roger. *King of the Road.* Bear Family, 1990. (Liner notes by Otto Kitsinger.)

Orbison, Roy. *The Essential Roy Orbison.* Monument/Orbison Records/Legacy, 2006. (Liner notes by Chet Flippo.)

Owens, Buck. *The Very Best of Buck Owens.* 2 vols. Rhino, 1994.

Parton, Dolly. *Ultimate Dolly Parton.* BMG Heritage, 2003.

Paycheck, Johnny. *The Real Mr. Heartache: The Little Darlin' Years.* Country Music Foundation, 1996. (Liner notes by Daniel Cooper.)

Perkins, Carl. *Original Sun Greatest Hits.* Rhino, 1986.

Pierce, Webb. *King of the Honky-Tonk.* Country Music Foundation, 1994. (Linear notes by Ronnie Pugh.)

Presley, Elvis. *The Sun Sessions.* RCA, 1987. (Liner notes by Peter Guralnick.)

Reed, Jerry. *RCA Country Legends.* Buddha Records, 2001. (Liner notes by Rich Kienzle.)

Riley, Jeannie C. *The Very Best of Jeannie C. Riley: Harper Valley P.T.A.* Collectables, 1998.

Smith, Connie. *The Essential Connie Smith.* RCA, 1996.

Snow, Hank. *The Essential Hank Snow.* RCA, 1997.

Stanley Brothers. *1953–1958 & 1959.* Bear Family, 1993.

——. *1949–1952.* Bear Family, 1991.

Stewart, Wynn. *The Very Best of Wynn Stewart, 1958–1962.* Varèse Sarabande, 2001. (Liner notes by Colin Escott.)

Travis, Merle. *Hot Pickin'.* Proper, 2003.

Twitty, Conway. *25 Number Ones.* MCA, 2004.

Various. *The Greatest Country Hits of 1955.* Acrobat Music, 2006.

Various. *Perfect for Parties.* Bear Family, 2006.

Vincent, Gene. *The Capitol Collector's Series.* Capitol, 1990.

Wagoner, Porter. *RCA Country Legends.* BMG Heritage, 2002. (Liner notes by Rich Kienzle.)

Williams, Hank. *Live at the Grand Ole Opry.* Mercury, 1999. (Liner notes by Rick Bragg and Colin Escott.)

Wynette, Tammy. *Anniversary: Twenty Years of Hits.* Epic, 1987.

Young, Faron. *Live Fast, Love Hard.* Country Music Foundation, 1995. (Liner notes by Daniel Cooper.)

# Bibliography

A bibliography is like a large extended family. There are a few books that you love and that inspire you. Many of them are decent, and most are tolerable. And there are a few that you despise, and if you never see them again it'll be too soon.

So, here's the list of books I consulted during the writing of *Sing Me Back Home*. Some were indispensable (more on them below), and others helped form the bedrock of my knowledge. Some I wrestled with, and others I wish I'd never bought. And some I sipped from, the way a hummingbird sips nectar, grateful for the sweet information if not the literary style.

There were five books, though, that were essential: *Joel Whitburn's Top Country Singles: 1944–1988* (Menomonee Falls, Wis.: Record Research, 1989) and *The Encyclopedia of Country Music*, edited by Paul Kingsbury (New York: Oxford University Press, 1998); Dorothy Horstman's *Sing Your Heart Out, Country Boy* (Nashville: Country Music Foundation Press, 1996); and Dave Marsh's *The Heart of Rock & Soul: The 1001 Greatest Singles Ever Made* (New York: Da Capo Press, 1999); and David Cantwell and Bill Friskics-Warren's *Heartaches by the Number: Country Music's 500 Greatest Singles* (Nashville: Vanderbilt University Press and the Country Music Foundation Press, 2003).

Whitburn's sourcebook and the country encyclopedia are models of their genres, and music fans of all stripes could spend years geeking out on their factoids and facts, biographical sketches and ephemera. (This is as good a place as any to say that even though I consulted all these books and countless liner notes, any errors in *Sing Me Back Home* are totally and utterly my fault.)

Horstman's book is a bounty of lyrics to—and stories behind—hundreds of classic country songs, ranging from "Keep on the Sunny Side" by the Carter Family to "Back Street Affair" by Webb Pierce, from "Coal Miner's Daughter" by Loretta Lynn to "Honky Tonk Man" by Johnny Horton.

And in a genre of music writing that is often scarred by the monotone recitation of mere discographies and that too often dwells on the flaws, peccadilloes, and larger-than-life personalities of its singers while ignoring the actual music, both *Heartaches by the Number* and *The Heart of Rock & Soul* set bracing examples. They show how to write about music in a cultural context without fretting over the size of Dolly Parton's boobs, whether Bill Monroe sang so high and lonesome because his underwear was too tight, and just how many suits by Nudie Cohen did Hank actually own when he died.

Here are the rest.

## MUSIC HISTORY

Bronson, Fred. *The Billboard Book of Number One Hits.* New York: Billboard Publications, 1988.

Cantwell, David, and Bill Friskics-Warren. *Heartaches by the Number: Country Music's 500 Greatest Singles.* Nashville: Vanderbilt University Press and the Country Music Foundation Press, 2003.

Collins, Ace. *The Stories Behind Country Music's All-Time Greatest 100 Songs.* New York: Boulevard Books, 1996.

Country Music Foundation. *Country: The Music and the Musicians.* New York: Abbeville Press, 1988.

Dawson, Jim, and Steve Propes. *What Was the First Rock 'n' Roll Record?* Boston: Faber & Faber, 1992.

Escott, Colin. *Lost Highway: The True Story of Country Music.* Washington, D.C.: Smithsonian Books, 2003.

Horstman, Dorothy. *Sing Your Heart Out, Country Boy.* 3rd ed. Nashville: Country Music Foundation Press, 1996.

Kingsbury, Paul, ed. *The Encyclopedia of Country Music*. New York: Oxford University Press, 1998.

———. *The Grand Ole Opry History of Country Music*. New York: Villard Books, 1995.

———. *Vinyl Hayride: Country Music Album Covers, 1947–1989*. San Francisco: Chronicle Books, 2003.

Kingsbury, Paul, and Alanna Nash, eds. *Will the Circle Be Unbroken: Country Music in America*. New York: DK Publishing, 2006.

Malone, Bill C. *Country Music, U.S.A.* 2nd rev. ed. Austin: University of Texas Press, 2003.

Marsh, Dave. *The Heart of Rock & Soul: The 1001 Greatest Singles Ever Made*. New York: Da Capo Press, 1999.

Morthland, John. *The Best of Country Music*. Garden City, N.Y.: Doubleday Dolphin, 1984.

Whitburn, Joel. *Top Country Singles, 1944–1988*. Menomonee Falls, Wis.: Record Research, 1989.

———. *Top Pop Singles, 1955–2002*. Menomonee Falls, Wis.: Record Research, 2003.

## BIOGRAPHIES AND AUTOBIOGRAPHIES

Allen, Bob. *George Jones: The Saga of an American Singer*. Garden City, N.Y.: Doubleday Dolphin, 1984.

Amburn, Ellis. *Dark Star: The Roy Orbison Story*. New York: Lyle Stuart, 1990.

Burke, Ken, and Dan Griffin. *The Blue Moon Boys: The Story of Elvis Presley's Band*. Chicago: Chicago Review Press, 2006.

Cantor, Louis. *Dewey and Elvis: The Life and Times of a Rock 'n' Roll Deejay*. Urbana: University of Illinois Press, 2005.

Cash, Johnny. *Cash: The Autobiography*. With Patrick Carr. San Francisco: HarperSanFrancisco, 1997.

Cooper, Daniel. *Lefty Frizzell: The Honky-Tonk Life of Country Music's Greatest Singer*. Boston: Little, Brown, 1995.

Cross, Wilbur, and Michael Kosser. *The Conway Twitty Story*. Toronto: Paperjacks, 1987.

Dean, Jimmy, and Donna Meade Dean. *Thirty Years of Sausage, Fifty Years of Ham: Jimmy Dean's Own Story*. New York: Berkley Books, 2006.

Delmore, Alton. *Truth Is Stranger Than Publicity*. Nashville: Country Music Foundation Press, 1977.

Eng, Steve. *A Satisfied Mind: The Country Music Life of Porter Wagoner*. Nashville: Rutledge Hill Press, 1992.

Escott, Colin. *Hank Williams: The Biography*. With George Merritt and William MacEwan. Boston: Little, Brown, 1994.

Grant, Marshall. *I Was There When It Happened: My Life with Johnny Cash*. With Chris Zar. Nashville: Cumberland House, 2006.

Guralnick, Peter. *Last Train to Memphis: The Rise of Elvis Presley*. Boston: Back Bay Books, 1994.

Haggard, Merle. *Sing Me Back Home: My Story*. With Peggy Russell. New York: Pocket Books, 1981.

Hall, Tom T. *The Storyteller's Nashville*. Garden City, N.Y.: Doubleday, 1979.

Hemphill, Paul. *Lovesick Blues: The Life of Hank Williams*. New York: Viking, 2005.

Jennings, Waylon. *Waylon: An Autobiography*. With Lenny Kaye. New York: Warner Books, 1996.

Kershaw, Doug. *Lou'siana Man*. New York: Collier Books, 1971.

Lynn, Loretta. *Coal Miner's Daughter*. With George Vecsey. Chicago: Regnery, 1976.

Mason, Bobbie Ann. *Elvis Presley*. New York: Viking, 2003.

Nelson, Willie. *Willie: An Autobiography*. With Bud Shrake. New York: Simon & Schuster, 1988.

Palmer, Robert. *Jerry Lee Lewis Rocks*. New York: Delilah Books, 1981.

Piazza, Tom. *True Adventures with the King of Bluegrass*. Nashville: Vanderbilt University Press and Country Music Foundation Press, 1999.

Porterfield, Nolan. *Jimmie Rodgers*. Urbana: University of Illinois Press, 1992.

Riley, Jeannie C. *From Harper Valley to the Mountain Top*. With Jamie Buckingham. New York: Ballantine Books, 1981.

Rooney, James. *Bossmen: Bill Monroe and Muddy Waters*. New York: Da Capo Press, 1991.

Shaver, Billie Joe. *Honky Tonk Hero*. Austin: University of Texas Press, 2005.

Smith, Richard D. *Can't You Hear Me Callin': The Life of Bill Monroe*. Boston: Little, Brown, 2000.

Snow, Hank. *The Hank Snow Story*. With Jack Ownbey and Bob Burris. Urbana: University of Illinois Press, 1994.

Streissguth, Michael. *Johnny Cash at Folsom Prison: The Making of a Master-piece.* New York: Da Capo Press, 2004.

———. *Johnny Cash: The Biography.* New York: Da Capo Press, 2006.

Style, Lyle. *Ain't Got No Cigarettes: Memories of Music Legend Roger Miller.* Winnipeg: Great Plains Publications, 2005.

Tosches, Nick. *Hellfire.* New York: Grove, 1998.

Urbanski, Dave. *The Man Comes Around: The Spiritual Journey of Johnny Cash.* Lake Mary, Fla.: Relevant Books, 2003.

White, Roger. *The Everly Brothers: Walk Right Back.* London: Plexus, 1998.

Wolfe, Charles K. *In Close Harmony: The Story of the Louvin Brothers.* Jackson: University Press of Mississippi, 1996.

Wright, John. *Traveling the Highway Home: Ralph Stanley and the World of Traditional Bluegrass Music.* Urbana: University of Illinois Press, 1995.

Wynette, Tammy. *Stand by Your Man.* With Joan Dew. New York: Simon & Schuster, 1979.

Zwonitzer, Mark, and Charles Hirschberg. *Will You Miss Me When I'm Gone? The Carter Family and Their Legacy in American Music.* New York: Simon & Schuster, 2002.

## GENERAL

Bufwack, Mary A., and Robert K. Oermann. *Finding Her Voice: The Saga of Women in Country Music.* New York: Crown, 1993.

Burke, Ken. *Country Music Changed My Life.* Chicago: Chicago Review Press, 2004.

Dawidoff, Nicholas. *In the Country of Country.* New York: Pantheon, 1997.

Escott, Colin. *Good Rockin' Tonight: Sun Records and the Birth of Rock 'n' Roll.* New York: St. Martin's, 1991.

———. *Roadkill on the Three-Chord Highway.* New York: Routledge, 2002.

———. *Tattooed on Their Tongues: A Journey Through the Backrooms of American Music.* New York: Schirmer Books, 1996.

Goldsmith, Thomas, ed. *The Bluegrass Reader.* Urbana: University of Illinois Press, 2004.

Guralnick, Peter. *Feel Like Going Home: Portraits in Blues and Rock 'n' Roll.* New York: HarperPerennial, 1994.

———. *Lost Highways: Journeys and Arrivals of American Musicians.* New York: Harper & Row, 1989.

Haslam, Gerald W. *Workin' Man Blues: Country Music in California*. Berkeley: University of California Press, 1999.

Hemphill, Paul. *The Nashville Sound*. New York: Simon & Schuster, 1970.

Kingsbury, Paul, ed. *The Country Reader*. Nashville: Vanderbilt University Press and Country Music Foundation Press, 1996.

Kosser, Michael. *How Nashville Became Music City U.S.A*. Milwaukee: Hal Leonard, 2006.

Malone, Bill C., and Judith McCulloh, eds. *Stars of Country Music*. New York: Da Capo Press, 1991.

Marcus, Greil. *Mystery Train*. New York: Plume, 1997.

———. *The Old, Weird America*. New York: Picador, 2001.

Morrison, Craig. *Go, Cat, Go! Rockabilly Music and Its Makers*. Urbana: University of Illinois Press, 1996.

Nash, Alanna. *Behind Closed Doors: Talking with the Legends of Country Music*. New York: Knopf, 1988.

Rosenberg, Neil V. *Bluegrass: A History*. Urbana: University of Illinois Press, 1985.

Sample, Tex. *White Soul: Country Music, the Church, and Working Americans*. Nashville: Abingdon Press, 1996.

Savoy, Ann Allen. *Cajun Music: A Reflection of a People*. Eunice, La.: Bluebird, 1986.

Streissguth, Michael. *Voices of the Country*. New York: Routledge, 2004.

Tosches, Nick. *Country: The Twisted Roots of Rock 'n' Roll*. New York: Da Capo Press, 1996.

Wolfe, Charles K. *Classic Country: Legends of Country Music*. New York: Routledge, 2001.

Wolfe, Charles K., and Ted Olson, eds. *The Bristol Sessions: Writings About the Big Bang of Country Music*. Jefferson, N.C.: McFarland, 2005.

# Acknowledgments

I am grateful for the fierce love and determination of my parents, Florence May Jennings and Dana Floyd Jennings—for their enduring love for each other, for us kids, and for country music. As Lefty Frizzell sang and wrote in "Mom and Dad's Waltz": "I'd walk for miles, cry or smile, for my mama and daddy. I want them to know I love them so."

To my wife, Deb, I owe a thanks so deep that it's impossible to articulate—even though she still doesn't like to twang. Let's just say, for those of us who can go temporarily insane in the name of art, it's a blessing to have a spouse who can gently reel you back to reality.

Thanks to my sons, Drew and Owen, for always wanting to listen—to the family tales and to the music.

Thanks to my in-laws, Miriam and Evan Krieger, who have always believed in me—and never refuse my request for a boxed set from Bear Family Records.

Thanks to my sister and brothers, Sis, Tim, and Mike, for the sharing of childhood tales and of childhood music.

Thanks to those who supplied country conversation, country recommendations, and, sometimes, country CDs: Ted Anthony, Carol Beaugard at WFDU-FM in Teaneck, New Jersey, Todd Collins, Greta and Paul at Future Legend on Ninth Avenue in Manhattan, Kit Kiefer, Tammy La Gorce, Fran Liscio, Bob Mellman, Mark Rotella, Jeff Roth, Mark Satlof at Shore Fire Media in Brooklyn, Sam Starnes, and Andrew Steele. For those of you

I might've overlooked, just take me out behind the barn and give me a good switchin'—and a corn-silk cigarette.

Thanks to John, Cary, and the rest of the zany gang at the Montclair Book Center in New Jersey for special-ordering all those obscure hick books from dusty warehouses deep in the mystical heart of Tennessee.

And last, but certainly not least, special thanks to my agent, Paul Bresnick, and to my editor, Paul Elie, who both understood and supported this book from the very start.

# Index